# Investigating Language

𝔹

# THE LANGUAGE LIBRARY
### Edited by *David Crystal*

| | |
|---|---|
| The Articulate Computer | *Michael McTear* |
| The Artificial Language Movement | *J. A. Large* |
| Children's First School Books | *Carolyn D. Baker & Peter Freebody* |
| Children's Writing and Reading | *Katharine Perera* |
| A Child's Learning of English | *Paul Fletcher* |
| Clichés and Coinages | *Walter Redfern* |
| A Companion to Old and Middle English Studies | *A. C. Partridge* |
| A Dictionary of Literary Terms and Literary Theory (third edition) | *J. A. Cuddon* |
| A Dictionary of Linguistics and Phonetics (third edition) | *David Crystal* |
| The Foreign-Language Barrier | *J. A. Large* |
| How Conversation Works | *Ronald Wardhaugh* |
| An Informal History of the German Language | *W. B. Lockwood* |
| Investigating Language | *Ronald Wardhaugh* |
| Language and Class in Victorian England | *K. C. Phillips* |
| Language Crimes | *Roger W. Shuy* |
| The Language of *1984* | *W. F. Bolton* |
| Language, Society and Identity | *John Edwards* |
| Languages in Competition | *Ronald Wardhaugh* |
| Modern Englishes: Pidgins and Creoles | *Loreto Todd* |
| Non-Standard Language in English Literature | *N. F. Blake* |
| Oral Cultures Past and Present | *Viv Edwards and Thomas J. Sienkewicz* |
| Puns | *Walter Redfern* |
| Rhetoric: The Wit of Persuasion | *Walter Nash* |
| Seeing Through Language | *Ronald Carter and Walter Nash* |
| Sense and Sense Development (revised) | *R. A. Waldron* |
| Shakespeare's English | *W. F. Bolton* |
| The Study of Dialect | *K. M. Petyt* |
| Swearing | *Geoffrey Hughes* |
| Words in Time | *Geoffrey Hughes* |
| The Writing Systems of the World | *Florian Coulmas* |

# Investigating Language

## Central Problems in Linguistics

*Ronald Wardhaugh*

**BLACKWELL**
*Oxford UK & Cambridge USA*

First published 1993

Blackwell Publishers
108 Cowley Road
Oxford OX4 1JF
UK

238 Main Street, Suite 501
Cambridge, Massachusetts 02142
USA

*British Library Cataloguing in Publication Data*

A CIP catalogue record for this book is available from
the British Library.

*Library of Congress Cataloging-in-Publication Data*

Wardhaugh, Ronald.
Investigating language: central problems in linguistics /
Ronald Wardhaugh.
p.    cm. — (The Language library)
Includes bibliographical references and index.
ISBN 0–631–18753–7. — ISBN 0–631–18754–5 (pbk.)
1. Language and languages.   2. Linguistics.   I. Title.
II. Series.
P106.W315   1993
410—dc20                                92–38739
                                             CIP

Typeset in 11 on 12½pt Sabon
by Graphicraft Typesetters Ltd, Hong Kong
Printed in Great Britain by T.J. Press Ltd, Padstow, Cornwall

This book is printed on acid-free paper

# Contents

# Contents

# *Preface*

There currently exist several quite adequate introductory linguistics texts. These provide beginning students with a basic knowledge of many of the technical concepts of modern linguistics. However, they tend to say very little about how many of the issues with which they deal are problematic in some sense, i.e., why linguists actually have the concerns they do have. This book is an attempt to show some of these concerns by relating the kind of interests that linguists have to questions that we ask about language. The book, therefore, can serve as a kind of supplement to the aforementioned texts. Or it can stand entirely on its own for those who are familiar with basic linguistic concepts but seek to relate these to broader issues. For those who know little linguistics at all or who do not seek to learn much about the technical aspects of the discipline, the book can serve as some kind of guide to how linguists look at various interesting language issues.

I have tried to keep the writing simple and have sought to avoid jargon wherever possible in an attempt to be user-friendly. The text also uses quotes around words as an attention-getting device in order to make readers aware that I am using the words in the quotes in 'special' ways. I have also deliberately sought to cover linguistic thinking broadly rather than narrowly, in the belief that such a view best does justice to any really worthwhile attempt to consider how we might go about investigating language.

In the belief too that students and readers learn best by doing and thinking, I have concluded each section of the book with a number of suggestions for 'further investigation'. Necessarily these suggestions vary in purpose and scope. However, they should provide an instructor with material that is immediately usable as well as suggestions of kinds of activities that students might find to be interesting and profitable. The independent reader can use the same suggestions to find out more about particular issues and topics. A section at the back of the book (p. 273) indicates easily accessible books that are suitable for further reading on topics in the chapter. A glossary of language terms will also be found at the end of the book (p. 264). All users should find the *Cambridge Encyclopedia of Language* (Crystal, 1987) and the *International Encyclopedia of Linguistics* (Bright, 1992) to be extremely useful sources of further information about language in general, various languages in particular and linguistics as an intellectual discipline.

# 1

# *How might we talk about 'talk'?*

Language study can be a fascinating activity. We all learn how to use at least one language and, in that learning, often acquire a lot of information about it and about language in general. We find ourselves asking questions about language and we either work out the answers to these for ourselves or others give us various answers. We also hear other people ask questions that we would never think to ask, or answer the questions we ask in ways that may seem to be quite inappropriate. Nor can we always agree with others about what are the really interesting questions we should be asking, and, even on those occasions when we do manage to reach some consensus on this issue, we are still likely to come up with rather different answers.

What I will try to do in the chapters that follow is look at some of the questions that people have asked about language and some of the answers that have been proposed to them. However, before beginning, we should address the issue of what 'language' itself is. What is its 'essence', as it were? There is good reason to believe that only if we can find a satisfactory answer to that question can we proceed to find answers to other questions that might also interest us, e.g. how language relates to human bodies and minds, how different languages relate to one another, how languages are learned and so on.

## 1.1   Some traditional views

We owe much of our current understanding – and misunderstanding – of language and languages to people who lived in

Greece and Rome about two millennia ago. The Greeks were very interested in language. They debated such issues as whether language was a natural phenomenon or the gift of a beneficent deity, whether or not languages were 'regular' in the way they were organized and what the 'true' meanings of words were. Greek philosophers were interested in the world around them and tried to apply their philosophical systems to their own language. But the Greeks were interested in literature and rhetoric too and Greek study of language soon found itself tied closely to the study of the written forms of language and the arts of persuasion.

The best known Greek grammar, the *Techne Grammatike* of Dionysius Thrax, was a brief 15 pages in length but it has had a tremendous influence on linguistic description in the Western world. It is in this grammar that we first find reference to the 'eight parts of speech' and to the idea that 'parsing' the words of a language, i.e., describing the grammatical characteristics of individual words, is somehow central to the study of the 'grammar' of that language. It is to Thrax too that we owe the definition of a 'sentence' as being the expression of a 'complete meaning' or 'complete thought' and to sentences themselves described in rhetorical terms as 'statements', 'questions', 'commands' and so on.

The Romans inherited Greek culture and interests and showed little capacity for independent thought in matters to do with language. They simply took over what the Greeks had said about Greek and applied it to Latin. If what the Greeks had said did not quite fit, they made it fit in one way or another. They also made the study of grammar central to the curriculum of their schools. Two Roman grammarians, Donatus and Priscian, wrote grammars, the *Ars Grammatica* and the *Institutiones Grammaticae* respectively, that became extremely influential. In fact, the grammars established a tradition of language study, with a particular set of interests and a vocabulary to go along with them, that continues right to this day. Many of the descriptions that we have of contemporary languages are phrased in terms derived directly from this Roman tradition. One unfortunate consequence is that there exists a strong tradition in which a language like English is described as though it were a somewhat deficient variety of Greek or Latin rather than as the living, changing language that it is. Most 'educated' people actually still pay an indirect homage to Greek and Latin – though they may be completely unaware of that fact – when they attempt to describe how the English language seems to work.

We can see that this is so if we consider what happens when we make any kind of grammatical statement about English. We will almost certainly use terms borrowed directly from descriptions of Greek and Latin as we describe the various parts of speech we find and try to explain how different types of phrases and clauses are combined to form sentences. But, as many of us are also aware, such parsing never seems to work as well as it should, because we cannot easily make English fit this classical mould. There is always the ambiguity of a word like *stone* in *an old stone wall* – is *stone* an 'adjective' or is it a 'noun'? It is an adjective if all the words that 'modify' nouns are adjectives, but it is a noun if all the 'names of things' are nouns. Here *stone* is like *old* in some ways – *old* is definitely an adjective – and like *wall* in others – *wall* is definitely a noun. The difficulty can be resolved only if you are free to decide that words may have intrinsic 'forms', e.g. be adjectives, nouns, etc., but be used in different 'functions', e.g. be used as 'modifiers', 'complements', etc. However, such a solution is not one that comes easily to a person who has been thoroughly indoctrinated into describing English within the traditional 'classical' mould.

We tend not to draw the right conclusion from such an example, the conclusion that we should describe English on its own terms. Instead, we are asked to consider that if English does not fit the classical mould, it must be because it is somehow 'deficient' or even 'degenerate' in comparison to Greek and Latin. This idea of degeneracy is also part of the same tradition. The 'rules' that appear to describe Latin apply to a fairly small part of the Latin language as a whole, to a body of plays, poems, letters and so on, written by a rather select group of people during a relatively short period of time. There were other kinds of Latin at that time, particularly the spoken Latin, or 'Vulgar Latin', of the Roman Empire, and this Latin was not at all uniform. Over the centuries too Latin itself changed in at least two directions, into Medieval Latin on the one hand and into the various vernacular languages such as French, Spanish, Italian and so on, on the other. However, in spite of all this variety and change there still remained a belief that somehow Latin had been 'fixed' for all time and that this fixed language quite properly set a 'standard' for all other languages either to emulate or to measure themselves against. Needless to say they were generally found to be lacking when this happened.

We know that languages change over time, but the tradition we have inherited assumes that such change is always for the worst, possibly because it takes us further and further away from Latin. This idea of degeneracy is also applied most strongly to the spoken varieties of language because the tradition is more comfortable with the written forms of languages than with their spoken forms. So even major world languages like English may come to be regarded as degenerate in comparison to Classical Greek or Latin, and certainly spoken English is generally less highly valued than written English.

For a great many people the study of language has become reduced to the study of 'linguistic propriety', i.e., specific bits of language behaviour which this or that 'authority' – often a self-proclaimed one – approves or disapproves (see Milroy and Milroy, 1985). The study of grammar has become the study of 'correctness', the learning of arbitrary rules the observance of which or the breaking of which can have important consequences for individuals. People are therefore encouraged to worry about whether they are using words 'correctly', without being given any clear idea of how you indeed might specify what is 'correct' and what is not. One consequence is that points of usage (see Crystal, 1984) are hotly debated, e.g. whether or not *like* may be used as a preposition, whether you should use *different from* rather than *different than*, whether *Can I open the window?* is a legitimate way of seeking permission and even whether or not a preposition is the right kind of word to end a sentence with. Much modern concern about language, therefore, has come to focus on issues that are not at all relevant to understanding how it works in any interesting way.

Another result of this emphasis on correctness is that conscious efforts may be made from time to time to halt or reverse the degenerative processes that seem to be at work in languages. In this view languages will become inefficient if certain people do not take it upon themselves to become their guardians (see Newman, 1974; Safire, 1980, 1984; Simon, 1980). One result is a strong tendency toward the adoption of 'prescriptivism' in linguistic matters. Grammars and books on language usage become little more than sets of caveats, series of warnings about things not to do and errors that must be avoided at all costs. 'Authorities' are established and appealed to but most of these, of course, as I have observed, are self-appointed. Occasionally attempts are made – some successful, some not – to establish committees and academies to set standards of proper linguistic behaviour. France has had such an academy since the seventeenth century; England almost had one.

Such attempts may result in efforts to control the admission of new words into the language, particularly borrowings, e.g. of English words into French, to regulate grammatical usage, e.g. to prohibit the use of *ain't*, or to insist that *like* should not be used as a preposition, to condemn slang (for slang, like hair-length and skirt-length, arouses the emotions!), to decide on matters of correctness in pronunciation and spelling, to promote a particular dictionary as though it were like a new version of the Bible, and, in general, to elevate the written variety of the language at the expense of the various spoken varieties. This last point is really not so surprising. Most of us are not at all aware of how we learned to speak, and speech comes relatively easy to us. But we may be very aware indeed of the pains we suffered in achieving whatever literacy we possess. What we have won with so much difficulty we must protect and prize.

People often have defensive, self-conscious attitudes toward their language. They seem to know intuitively that systems tend to become chaotic if left to go their own way undisturbed, and they regard their language as one such system in apparent danger. Effort is therefore required of them to stop this natural law of dissolution from taking effect. They fail to realize that countervailing forces are at work, because their language must also be considered within a 'functional' framework. Each language has certain functions to perform; it will continue to perform these functions so long as they are important to the survival of those who speak the language. There is, therefore, really no reason to believe that any language anywhere is in a desperate state because of its deficiencies as a language. Some languages are imperilled to be sure, e.g. Breton in France and Gaelic in Scotland, but their peril is a social one not a linguistic one.

In still other ways we can see how pervasive are misconceptions about language. For many people a language is little more than a collection of words, a kind of huge dictionary. Therefore, in order to learn a new language you must learn a new set of words for known things and processes, words often combined and pronounced in peculiar ways to be sure but words nevertheless. Some languages are actually said to have little or no grammar – even English on occasion! In such circumstances it should come as no surprise that we are periodically exhorted to increase our vocabularies so as to become successful and influential and that dictionaries become objects of reverence. When a dictionary does actually report on the language in a new but not radically different way – as did Webster's *Third New International Dictionary* in 1961 – it may be greeted by cries of outrage, the kind of cries once reserved for new translations of holy writ (see Sledd and Ebbitt, 1962). Many years later people still continue to discuss the 'correctness' of the principles that went into the writing of that dictionary and it is safe to say that the reviews that greeted the *Third International* have affected in one way or another how editors have gone about compiling every subsequent unabridged dictionary of the language (see Burchfield, 1985).

## Further investigation

1   We use the word 'language' in such expressions as the 'language of poetry', the 'language of flowers', the 'sign language of the deaf' and 'computer language'. In this book we are concerned with 'natural language'. How do these other languages – and any others you can think of – differ from what we are concerned with?

2   What do people understand by the word 'grammar'? You should examine any definitions you can find, survey written views on the subject of grammar and consult the opinions of people that you know. Is there any consensus?

3   Find a grammar of English that offers definitions of the 'parts of speech'. Apply these definitions rigorously to each word in the following sentence: *Right then his newly-built sand castle was fast disappearing under the advancing water.* Compare your results with those of someone else and also try another set of definitions.

4 How might a 'prescriptive' grammarian attempt to 'correct' each of the following sentences? What argument or arguments might be advanced in each case to justify the 'corrected' sentence as being a 'better' sentence than the one given here? Assess the merits of these arguments.

> The mission of the USS Enterprise is to boldly go where no man has ever been before.
> Hopefully, the weather will clear up tomorrow.
> It's me who gets the blame for everything.
> Harry and Sally love one another.
> Who did you get that from?
> You are taller than me.
> Nobody said nothing.
> Those kind of people get on my nerves.
> If I was you, I would resign.
> None of the guests have arrived.
> Finding the door unlocked, an opportunity to escape appeared at last.
> Don't do it like he does it.
> He seems quite disinterested these days.
> She was one of those students whom everyone said would succeed.

## 1.2 A more promising approach

The immediate issue confronting anyone who wants to make a serious, scientific study of language and its place in the world is that of deciding what the important questions are and what data exist that bear on these questions. Every discipline is defined by the questions its practitioners ask and the kinds of data they regard as providing genuine evidence about these questions. Moreover, a scientifically-oriented discipline requires that we ask only questions for which we can expect to find genuine answers. That is, the exercise must not be a purely speculative one in which claims are advanced merely to counter other claims, but where there is absolutely no hope at all of testing any of the competing claims. We will find for example that it is possible to make certain scientifically testable claims about language use in relation to certain areas of the human brain but none at all about which language Adam and Eve used in the Garden of Eden.

We can see how important it is to find good questions about language by looking at a few that we might be tempted to consider. How are the sounds of speech produced and understood? What are the exact physical limitations of speaking and hearing? How do words combine in sentences in order to achieve the meanings that sentences have? What are the basic units of language? Are they sounds, syllables, words and sentences? If so, what exactly is each of these units? How does language work in communication, e.g. between two people in a conversation? How do children acquire language? What kinds of learning are involved? How does language break down, e.g. as a result of injury to the head? How do languages change and vary over space and time? Why do they change and vary in this way? Do all languages share certain characteristics? If so, why? Is it possible to find in the animal world anything that resembles the languages that humans speak? Could we possibly teach animals to use a language? If not, why not?

Each of the above questions is a useful question to ask and each is answerable within certain limitations. That is, we can provide some kind of answer to each that accounts for the data that need to be accounted for in a way that allows us to provide testable evidence for any claims we make. Of course, different questions require different kinds of investigation and data. Perhaps, too, the questions above are themselves not of equal importance, but there happens to be no shortage of data bearing on parts of all of them. For example, we have masses of information about children's use of language.

The key issue in any serious linguistic investigation is finding the data that are relevant to answering an interesting question, i.e., one that furthers our knowledge and understanding of language. By themselves data are almost valueless in the absence of one or more questions that arise from a researchable hypothesis. A serious researcher must always have in mind some idea that can be proved or disproved. The idea itself may actually have emerged from looking at masses and masses of data but it can be proved or disproved only if stated in the form of a hypothesis and then systematically tested against data. As we will see, it is testing the various hypotheses about children's language that has advanced our understanding of how children acquire language, not just simply collecting more and more data.

As our understanding of language develops and changes new questions will occur to us and become answerable and old questions and answers will be revised or even rejected. The issue of the ultimate origins of language is a good example. The origins of language seem to be hidden in the impenetrable past and, in general, it appears to be impossible to say anything scientifically useful on this issue. Yet from time to time a faint glimmer of possibility does arise and the issue does get looked at once more, but usually for a short time only. However, it gets looked at again not really because we suddenly discover more data, but because someone has a promising new theoretical insight that seems to allow data long in existence to be looked at in a way that might tell us something new about the problem.

Linguists are agreed that asking good questions is the cornerstone of any worthwhile linguistic endeavour. They agree too on the importance of finding just the right data that bear on the questions. The better the data the greater the certainty about the answers. In this way linguistic study has a strong empirical component, i.e., it has a great respect for anchoring its conclusions in evidence from the real world. The answers to questions that linguists ask will therefore have a strong empirical basis or be labelled quite clearly as speculative in the absence of such a basis. This requirement follows from the need to be scientific, i.e., to use procedures that other investigators can also use in order to seek independent confirmation of any claims that are made. If such independent confirmation is not possible, then there has been a failure in the procedures that were used. Speculative conclusions, on the other hand, still remain to be confirmed or refuted. If some chance exists of doing one or the other, we can think of them as being hypotheses that remain to be tested, e.g. certain hypotheses about the origins of language; however, if there is no chance of testing them at all, they are quite useless and completely 'unscientific', e.g. the aforementioned speculations about what language Adam and Eve spoke in the Garden of Eden.

Science itself goes far beyond data collecting. Science is concerned with theory building, i.e., with making very general statements about phenomena in the real world. Any findings that linguists wish to present must be presented within a general theory about how languages work. Any such theory also requires explicit statements concerning both the underlying assumptions and the units and operations employed in the theory. Consequently, linguists must constantly ask themselves what the various statements they make about language really mean. They must constantly examine and re-examine their claims both about languages in general and about specific languages. How do languages work? How does a specific language work? There should also be a considerable 'sameness' to the two answers. We can see how these principles would work if you found yourself wanting to write a description of some 'exotic' language. It would be enormously helpful if you knew something about how languages seem to work. However, if you thought that you should really try to make the language fit some Latinate grammar you knew, or that all you had to do to understand the language was to compile a dictionary, or that linguistic propriety in the language should be your concern, your endeavours would be almost worthless.

A theory is also an abstraction. A good theory about language does not merely offer descriptions of particular linguistic events or individual uses of language, but tries to offer an account of language events and uses at a more general level. To use an analogy, an airline timetable describes more than the route of a particular aeroplane on a particular day; it describes a whole system of flights. Similarly, a chessboard and the rules of chess are not designed for one particular game of chess but for all possible games of chess. We must note, however, that a language system, i.e., a grammar, is much more difficult to characterize than either an airline timetable or the rules of chess. The system was not designed consciously by one or more people and the possibilities it allows appear to be infinite. Moreover, a linguist must try to reconstruct the whole system from data that are fleeting and partial at best. We need only consider how difficult it would be to try to reconstruct the timetable of a particular airline from occasional visits to airports and flights across the country or even to figure out the rules of chess from a few photographs taken of random games in progress. It is just such a problem that confronts a linguist who tries to write a grammar of a language. The linguist can observe only so much, but the grammar that results must go far beyond those observations and, if it is to be quite thorough, should cover every aspect of the language.

Most linguists share many of the same assumptions about language and there is widespread agreement on most of the major questions. There are, of course, also certain disagreements. Such disagreements have sometimes been well publicized, particularly those in which the best-known of modern linguists, Noam Chomsky, has been involved. However, this publicity conceals the fact that the areas of agreement among linguists are much greater than those of disagreement. It is the relatively small shifts within linguistics, the sometimes over-eager dissemination of new and still untested ideas, and a decided preference for reporting findings that appear to eclipse previous work rather than to confirm or disconfirm it that have captured public attention. The continued shared assumptions and the undisputed findings tend to be overlooked. It is these that are really our concern in the pages that follow.

## *Further investigation*

1  Which of the following are 'answerable' questions about language? How are they or aren't they?

Is Basque an 'older' language than English?
Are English and Chinese vastly different languages because they are written so differently?
Is Latin the 'ancestor' of French?
Is it possible to show that English and Albanian are 'related' in some way?
Do 'primitive' people speak 'primitive' languages?
Is *He didn't do nothing* ungrammatical because it is illogical?
Is English an inherently 'sexist' language?

2  Discussions of language often become debates about 'correctness'. What is a 'correct' scientific claim?
3  Most linguists agree that language is fundamentally speech not writing. A few maintain that language can be realized either through speech or writing. What merit, if any, do you find in this second view?

## 1.3    A variety of possibilities

As soon as you begin to look at any language closely to see how it works, you are forced to recognize that it must be systematic in its organization, i.e., it must have a grammar, for otherwise speakers using it could not possibly communicate with one another. Speakers rely on the systematic nature of language in order to say things to one another that will not be misunderstood. For example, speakers of English rely on the fact that *pin, bin, tin* and *din* begin with four different 'sounds' and that these same four sounds occur over and over again in the language to distinguish sets of words like *pan, ban, tan* and *Dan* and *pail, bail, tail* and *dale*. There are other sounds too, e.g. those at the beginnings of *ran, van, man* and so on. We can also combine some of these at the beginnings of words but not others: *bran* is a possible English word but *mran, rtan* and *ptan* are not. There must obviously be a 'system of sounds' in English and we might ask ourselves what that system is.

Speakers of English also rely on 'words', which we may regard as being built in some way out of the sounds I have just mentioned, occurring in particular orders to indicate certain 'meanings': for example, an object referred to as a *houseboat* is not the same as an object referred to as a *boathouse*, and *Jack kissed Mary* is different in meaning from *Mary kissed Jack*. So there seems to be a system of words and their possible arrangements as well as a system of sounds and their possible arrangements.

We should attempt, therefore, to describe the systematic nature of any language that interests us. Just how does it work? Actually, it appears that every language is made up of two largely independent but nevertheless interrelated systems, one of sounds and the other of meanings. This characteristic of all languages – and therefore of the fundamental nature of language as a phenomenon – is often referred to as 'duality'. Languages have been described (Martinet, 1964) as being 'doubly articulated' because they contain two systems that operate together.

There are also units of various kinds in the two systems, not just one kind of unit in each, and these units are arranged in complex patterns, hierarchies and relationships. In the system of sounds there are the component parts of sounds, the sounds themselves (sometimes called 'phonemes'), and the possible groupings, or 'clusters', of these sounds, especially 'syllables', and 'tone groups'. In the system of meanings there are the units of meaning (sometimes called 'morphemes'), special clusters of these meanings (sometimes called 'words') and the various phrase and clause groups that the 'syntax' allows.

Before the development of modern linguistics serious students of languages had found a need for units with which to describe language and had used terms like *sound, syllable, word* and *sentence* in their work. However, they never clearly defined such terms and the definitions that did exist made appeals to intuition rather than to specific, verifiable, defining characteristics such as actual articulations, specific grammatical characteristics or the various possibilities and impossibilities for combining and recombining elements in a language. (A considerable part of language instruction in schools is actually devoted to attempts to develop in children the 'correct' intuitions about sounds, syllables, words, etc. with little recognition of how ill-founded and necessarily vague is much of that instruction.) If we are to investigate language in a scientific manner we must spell out how we are to go about that task and employ a set of concepts and principles that do not depend on appeals to intuition. Consequently, linguists have made considerable use of such concepts as the 'phoneme' and the 'morpheme' and the principle of 'contrast' in their work and paid considerable attention to their actual status in language study.

The phoneme is now a 'classical' unit in linguistics. *Pin* differs from *bin,* so the sound that the letter *p* represents contrasts with the sound that the letter *b* represents. The contrast is a phonemic one because it produces a difference in meaning, because *pin* refers to an object you might prick yourself with and *bin* to an object you probably put things in. A phoneme is a recurrent contrastive unit in the sound system of a language. The phoneme at the beginning of *pin* also occurs at the end of *cup,* after the *s* in *spin,* and – once only because we are considering sounds not letters – in the middle of *happen.*

If we apply this method of investigation to English we will find that there appear to be about 40 phonemes in English – *about* because different decisions as to what does or does not constitute a phonemic contrast produce different inventories and because we can really speak only of individual varieties of English as having phonemes and there are numerous varieties each with a slightly different system of sounds, e.g. Cockney English, what we might call BBC English and Texas English. Some of these phonemes we will also want to call 'consonants' and some 'vowels', and still others we may be uncertain about. But we can do this only if we have established some principle that will allow us to distinguish consonants from vowels – and once again I am not talking about spelling!

On further investigation we will find that we can describe the phonemes themselves as being combinations of even smaller articulatory events, such as lip closure, use of the nasal passage, activity in the vocal cords, exact placement of the tongue and so on. The phoneme at the beginning of *pin*, for example, is articulated through a combination of lip closure followed by a sharp release of that closure together with a slight puff of air. There is also a concurrent lack of activity in the vocal cords during the initial part of the articulation. We will also find that when we use that same phoneme as the second sound in *spin* that it lacks the puff of air that it has in *pin*.

There are also restrictions concerning how we may combine the various phonemes in English, restrictions to do with the allowable sequences of vowels and consonants, the structure of syllables, the shapes of possible words and the patterns of omission and combination of sounds that are possible in higher level sequences. *Trem* is a possible English syllable or even word but *tmre* and *trme* are impossible.

At the level of meanings we can investigate how individual minimal bits of discrete meaning, called 'morphemes', occur and vary. English uses an *-s* ending on a class of words that we can call 'nouns' in order to indicate 'plural', as in *cats, dogs* and *judges*. However, these words have different pronunciations (or 'allomorphs') of this plural ending: /s/ in *cats*, /z/ in *dogs* and /əz/ in *judges*. The plural ending has entirely different phonological shapes again in nouns like *oxen* and *children*, is not an ending at all but a vowel change in *feet* and *mice* and is actually nothing at all in *sheep* (*one sheep, two sheep*).

We also use morphemes to construct 'words' of various kinds. Both *cat* and *cats* are words and so are *place, replace* and *replacement*, and *houseboat* and *boathouse*. It may even be possible to use word-making processes of this kind to decide how words themselves fall into certain classes, e.g. 'nouns' are words that also have a 'plural' form (*cat, cats*), 'verbs' words that have a 'past tense' form (*bake, baked*) and 'adjectives' words that have a 'comparative' form (*big, bigger*). Many words, however, allow no change in form at all, e.g. *but, until, very, must* and so on. These must, therefore, be words of a different kind from *cat, bake, big*, etc.

We also do not talk by simply stringing words together one after the other like putting beads on a string. We arrange them in 'phrases' and 'clauses'. These phrases and clauses have a 'constituency structure'. For example, at the phrase level we can say *the boy* but not *boy the, can go* but not *go can*, and *at the end* but not *the end at*. These are respectively a 'noun phrase', a 'verb phrase' and a 'prepositional phrase' and each has its own structure. At the clause level we can say *John stroked the cat* but not *John the cat stroked, Do you want an apple?* but not *Want you an apple?* and *The pizza you ordered is here* but not *The you ordered pizza is here*. Again we can see here that English puts 'objects' after 'verbs' and not before them, that we cannot 'invert' *you* with *want* to form a question but must use another type of inversion and that a 'relative clause' must follow the noun phrase to which it is attached, not precede it. Only certain 'syntactic arrangements' are possible in each language and we must try to find out what these are.

One kind of description of a language therefore can consist of statements about the kinds of characteristics that I have just mentioned. I have touched on these only superficially by way of illustration. In practice the difficulties are legion. However, we can be sure that the results will look nothing like any kind of description of the language that you will see in the kinds of 'grammars' you are likely to find in a school classroom or even in many colleges and universities. The focus in the above approach is also on the spoken language and what is described is the language that speakers actually use. There will be no value judgements, i.e., no 'prescriptions' of the order that many speakers do this or that but should not do so. The end result will not be a 'prescriptive' account of the language, an account which will almost certainly focus on a specific written variety, but a 'descriptive' account of the actual spoken language.

Such an approach to language owes much of its undoubted success to investigators having certain ideas about what they are likely to find in a language before they attempt an analysis and also having the skills that the approach requires. It assumes too that certain kinds of units and contrast exist and are discoverable, i.e., it assumes the existence of certain kinds of units and systems in *every* language. It also assumes that certain matters will always be of importance. For example, so far as phonology is concerned, it assumes that there will always be a 'consonant–vowel' distinction in the system of sounds, almost certainly a 'voiced–voiceless' contrast within the consonants themselves, a set of vowels distinguished from one another through differences in 'tongue height' and 'frontness-backness', a possible set of 'nasal' vowels contrasting with the 'oral' vowels and so on. The exact contrasts and the various details for a specific language will have to be worked out rather carefully, but the major characteristics of the language will not likely be very different from those of other languages.

In this view, therefore, any statement that a linguist makes about a language, whether about its sounds (a phonological statement) or about its meanings (a grammatical and/or semantic statement) is tantamount to a claim that the language 'works' in a certain way or possibly even about how the minds of the users of that language work in using the language. Linguists realize that phonologies and grammars make such claims. They must, therefore, be interested in both the basic units of language and the possible arrangements of these units. They may also be interested in why there are such units and arrangements. That is, they may be interested in those characteristics that all languages appear to share either because it is in the nature of every language to have such characteristics or because it is in the nature of every human to be able to use only languages of a certain kind.

Linguists, almost without exception, assume that any new language they investigate will have units and arrangements of these units that are very much the same as those that have been found in the languages they have looked at before. They also assume that they will be able to describe what they find within the general systems of description that they have developed for other languages. The overriding assumption is that languages and/or language users are everywhere much the same; therefore, languages and language users do not vary in all possible ways. They also assume that nothing new and startling is likely to be found in investigating a previously uninvestigated language. On the whole, new and startling ideas in linguistics have come not from such investigations but from asking new and interesting questions about language, particularly in recent years about the English language. We will now look at some of these questions.

### Further investigation

1   How many different single phonemes can we place before *-at* in English words? Here are some examples: *cat, bat, fat, chat* (*ch* is a single phoneme). Now try to complete the list. Go on to develop similar lists before *-eet, -up, -ip* and so on. Combine your lists. The result is a list of English phonemes that can occur initially in English words. Now follow the same procedure for single phonemes at the ends of words: *pi-, re-, be-, sa-* and so on. Again combine the lists. Then combine the two resulting lists of the possible beginnings and endings. You should now have a list of 23 English consonant phonemes if you cannot find in this way the sound that occurs in the middle of *pleasure*, and 24 if you can. (Kreidler (1989) is a good help here and in the next case too.)

2   Now try to find the English vowel phonemes using a similar procedure. Use testing frames like *b-t, p-ck, s-p* and so on (but avoid a final *r*). (Note that we are discussing sounds, so that both *bit* and *bite* are good examples in the first case.) You should be able to find a dozen or so vowel phonemes in this way.

3   How do we make English nouns 'plural'? With *one cat* and *two cats* we add /s/, but with *one dog* and *two dogs* we add /z/. How do we make the plurals of *judge, test, cow, box, man, woman, child, ox, criterion, sheep* and *gentleman*? Remember we are concerned with sounds not spellings. (Huddleston (1988) is a good help here and in the next few cases too.)

4   How do we put English verbs into the 'past tense'? From *we bake* to *we baked* we add /t/ and from *we beg* to *we begged* we add /d/. What do we do with *grab, kiss, pray, crash, sing, see, blow, creep, spend, sit, hit* and *go*?

5 Many English words contain 'suffixes'. Here are some words that end in *-ly*: *beastly, bravely, cowardly, hastily, kingly, manly, quickly, quietly, sisterly, tidily* and *worldly*. How 'correct' is the following generalization about these words: there are actually two *-ly* suffixes here, one added to nouns to form adjectives and the other added to adjectives to form adverbs? Test this generalization against further data.

6 Each of the following phrases or sentences is ambiguous:

French language teacher.
Old men and women.
He kissed the girl in the bus.
They took her flowers.
She commented on the page.
He took down the name.

Try to specify exactly why each is ambiguous. Do not be content with offering a simple meaning paraphrase but try to provide a grammatical explanation.

7 Assume that there is a strong grammatical relationship between the sentences in each of the following pairs. Explain as precisely as you can exactly what the grammatical differences are. You will need a 'vocabulary' to do so. Pay attention to that vocabulary for what it allows you to say.

John went to the cinema yesterday.
Did John go to the cinema yesterday?

The boy ate the apple.
The apple was eaten by the boy.

He gave some money to his friends.
He gave his friends some money.

She gave her sister some advice.
Did she give her sister any advice?

## 1.4  Still wider considerations

One observation that we can make about the procedures that I have just discussed is that they are concerned with trying to discover what we might call the 'basic organizational units' of language and their possible 'combinations'. This is because linguists try to account for the systems that underlie the actual phenomena they observe rather than just the phenomena themselves. They cannot and do not disregard the actual phenomena because linguistics is an empirical science, i.e., one that has a healthy respect for data. However, we can see this concern for systems that underlie those data in the terms that linguists use. They use terms like *data, s* (or *surface* or *superficial*) *structure* and *performance* to describe the actual observations they make; on the other hand, they use terms like *facts, d* (or *deep* or *underlying*) *structure* and *competence* to describe the systems they postulate to exist 'behind' those observations.

Linguists are interested in what the nineteenth-century German language scholar Wilhelm von Humboldt called *innere Sprachform* and what the great Swiss linguist Ferdinand de Saussure (1959) called *langue*, i.e., the language habits of all speakers of a language, rather than in what the latter called *parole*, i.e., the individual uses and variations we observe. Therefore, they are concerned with trying to make some sense of the abstract language system (*langue*) to which all speakers of a language are assumed to have access because they actually do use it unthinkingly and unhesitatingly. They are not really concerned with particular instances of language (*parole*), which may be imperfect in any one of several ways because of the situations in which people actually use the language, e.g. while tired, in a hurry, with interruptions, for working out ideas and so on.

Linguists must also construct hypotheses about the general structure of any language from observations made on just a few individuals, sometimes even on just one individual, in widely varying circumstances. The result is a rather interesting paradox: a grammar of a language – a claim about *langue* – may be based on observations from a single individual who must necessarily have certain idiosyncratic linguistic uses – an instance of *parole* – but such idiosyncrasies can safely be ignored because we must regard the grammar itself as a statement about matters that appear to be common to all speakers of the language.

In recent years a number of linguists have used the terms *competence* and *performance* to refer to something like the distinctions between *langue* and *parole*. Competence has taken on the additional meaning of the knowledge of the language system that every speaker is presumed to have, and performance the additional meaning of those things that the individual actually does in attempting to make use of that knowledge in communication. In both sets of distinctions a dichotomy exists between some kind of 'inner form' and 'outer substance'. The inner form is an abstraction – the language knowledge that resides in both individuals and groups of individuals – behind the outer substance of observed behaviour – the actual language usages of particular individuals on specific occasions.

It is our language competence, for example, that enables us to produce sentences that we have never produced before and never heard anyone else produce either. That competence also enables us to recognize that certain sentences are 'ungrammatical', e.g. *Can you to go? I wanted he to do it, The book were taken by the boys, The apple that he ate the apple was sour* and so on. In performance we do make various kinds of 'mistakes' but these are of a different order from the above examples of ungrammaticality. We restart sentences, change our minds in the middle of one grammatical construction and turn it into another, make a slip of the tongue, repeat something, hesitate or interrupt ourselves, or just simply get confused and so on.

Prompted in considerable part by the work of Noam Chomsky, linguists have made their discipline very theory-oriented in the sense of trying to understand what it means to be competent in a language and to acquire that competence (see Newmeyer, 1987). In particular, many linguists seek now to try to make statements about what they perceive to be the essential nature of language. What exactly is language? It is obviously a form of human behaviour that conforms to certain principles but just what are these principles and why do they exist? One possible answer to the last of these questions is that they exist because of the kinds of minds that humans have. Human minds are constructed in a way that has allowed them to become the animals with language. Moreover, that language must be language of a particular kind. Other kinds of language might have been possible but the human mind has developed in such a way that only one kind of language, with of course numerous variations, has resulted. So humans are uniquely endowed to use a certain kind of language. Linguistic investigation should focus on this unique endowment and its consequences.

Once we begin to investigate language from such a perspective it appears that certain aspects of language appear to be more important than others, i.e., they become more central in understanding how language is so special. For example, the actual words a language uses seem to be far less interesting than the syntactic possibilities for their use. It is the ability to construct and comprehend new sentences – admittedly to be filled in with words which eventually must be pronounced and understood – that is at the heart of human language ability. You cannot learn either your first language or a new language without learning some words, but language learning and language use involve far more than merely learning and using words: you must discover how you can use these words in sentences.

Such being the case, linguists should focus their attention primarily on syntax if they are to achieve an understanding of language. Other matters may be important and cannot be entirely ignored, e.g. how words and their pronunciations relate to that syntax, but some matters that have often been the focus of linguistic investigation may safely be excluded for a while. For example, concerns about speakers' beliefs, intentions and attitudes do not appear to be very relevant to a programme of linguistic investigation that focuses on syntax. Moreover, while the social uses of language may be interesting in their own right, they tell you virtually nothing about the essential nature of language if syntax plays the role it appears to play.

The approach to linguistic investigation just described is most clearly associated with Noam Chomsky. Chomsky has set out his views on the subject matter of linguistics in a series of books published since 1957 (particularly Chomsky, 1957, 1965, 1976, 1981, 1986). The precise details of these views have changed considerably over the years as Chomsky has developed his underlying theory and responded to critiques of that developing theory. Over more than three decades though Chomsky has actually managed to stay ahead of his critics and forced them to speak to the agenda he has proposed for linguistics, quite a remarkable achievement in any discipline.

Chomsky has always been concerned with trying to discover what the essential characteristics of language are, how these relate to the study of the human 'mind' and how human beings acquire language in childhood. One of his earliest publications (1959) was actually a scathing attack on B. F. Skinner's views (1957) on this last subject. Initially, Chomsky conceived of language as a generative system. Knowing a language is equivalent to knowing a set of rules for producing sentences in that language, in fact knowing a finite set of rules for producing an infinite set of sentences. The rules themselves were of two kinds: one kind 'generated' underlying or deep structures for sentences and the other kind 'transformed' these structures into superficial or surface structures. As a consequence this grammatical model for language became known as the 'transformational–generative' model and the grammars that resulted as 'transformational–generative grammars'.

For many years much effort went into trying to specify the rules and rule schemata that were necessary in such grammars. As we will see too in chapter four, numerous experiments were also conducted to investigate their 'psychological reality'. Until recently most of the discussion of Chomskyan linguistics has been conducted within this framework, known in its later development as Chomsky's 'extended standard theory'. Most of the criticisms of Chomskyan linguistics are actually criticisms of work done in this mould.

It is this version of Chomsky's theory that relates a 'passive' sentence such as *The banana was eaten by the chimpanzee*, to its 'active' counterpart *The chimpanzee ate the banana* by, among other things, a 'passive transformation' which moves the original 'deep subject', *the chimpanzee*, into a *by* phrase and then moves the original 'deep direct object', *the banana*, into the now vacant subject position. It is the same theory that derives *I want to go* from a deep structure in which *I to go* is the object of *I want* and a transformation removes the *I* before *to go* because the two pronouns make 'identical reference' when the two underlying clauses become one. In contrast the sentence *I want him to go* derives from a deep structure in which *he to go* is the object of *I want*. In this case the *he* is not deleted because it is not identical with the *I* in *I want*. Furthermore, in this case when the two clauses become one the *he* of *he to go* actually becomes the object of *want* and therefore must ultimately be pronounced as *him*.

Chomsky has continued to develop his ideas and his most recent publications carry his initial programme in new directions.

His interest now is in 'universal grammar', i.e., in what ways all languages must be alike because if they were not alike in such ways children could not acquire them. In such a view all languages make use of certain principles which children must 'know' before they come to the task of acquiring language. These principles are therefore 'innate', i.e., inborn, and part of the genetic make-up of human beings.

Furthermore, close inspection of different languages reveals that the principles that operate in language appear to operate nowhere else in our lives. For example, they seem to be quite independent of our visual abilities, our intelligence, our artistic and musical abilities, our logical and mathematical abilities and so on. It is as though we had a separate language 'faculty' or 'organ'. In fact, the claim is that all of these aforementioned abilities, including language ability itself, are best viewed as discrete. Such a view is now often referred to as a 'modular' view of the structure of the mind (see Fodor, 1983). In this view, each module is discrete and the human mind is not a unitary system in which every process is somehow related to every other process virtually all the time, but is rather a set of subsystems that work with considerable independence of one another.

In this view then there is a language 'module' within the mind. Consequently, the human mind is genetically programmed to acquire only a language of a certain kind. The claim is that there is no other way you can explain why all languages are alike in certain respects and how with so little data available to them children are able to 'figure out' what is possible and what is not in language. Children 'know' and do not have to 'learn' that linguistic operations involve the manipulation of grammatical structures rather than the manipulation of words. That is, children know that you make questions like *Is Mary happy?* by inverting verb phrases of a certain kind with subject noun phrases and not by inverting the first and second words of a sentence (because while such a rule would succeed with *Is Mary happy?* derived from *Mary is happy*, it would fail completely with *Is your mother happy?* derived from *Your mother is happy*, in that the result would be *Mother your is happy?*). Similarly, they know that to form passives they must move structural units like subject and object noun phrases, not simply words that occur before and after verbs.

There are other principles too that must be known rather than learned. For example, only certain kinds of structures can be moved in sentences and these movements are bounded or constrained, e.g. the movements that allow *what* and *which* in the following sentences to occur where they do: *What did he want?* and *The book which he borrowed belongs to John.* Noun phrases can express only a limited number of relationships with verbs, i.e., they can fill only certain 'roles' so that we know who did what to whom in both *The girl kissed the boy* and *The boy was kissed by the girl.* There must be a set of principles that allow us to relate nouns and pronouns in order to achieve correct understanding of sentences like *John likes him* and *John likes himself.* There must also be still another set so that we know that in a sentence like *She wants to go, she* is the subject of both *wants* and *go* but that in a sentence like *She wants her to go, she* and *her* refer to different people and *her* is at the same time both the object of *wants* and the subject of *go*. In this view these are some of the facts about English that we must be prepared to explain.

Chomsky's latest theory, called 'government and binding', claims that principles such as these are somehow built into human beings. When children come to the task of acquiring their first language, what they must do is just apply this 'knowledge' they have of such principles to the actual language data that confront them. They will have to make various decisions to be sure. In some cases they will have to set what have been called 'parameters' to the principles, e.g. they will have to figure out just what kinds of movements the particular language that they have encountered allows. If that language is English, they will have to set the movement parameter in one way and if it is some other language in another way. They will quickly set the parameters for the various sets of principles and once the parameters are set most of the actual data of whichever language it is they have encountered will then fall neatly into place. Naturally, they will have to learn the specific words and sounds people use in that language but there are likely to be innate principles operating here too that will help them.

This approach to language is one that treats language as a unique phenomenon in the world. It arises from trying to specify what language is like while at the same time insisting that any such account of what it is like must also explain how it is that most three-year-olds are able to use the first language they encounter as easily as they do. There must be certain kinds of principles in both languages and speakers that permit this to happen. Sometimes these principles have been called 'principles of mind'. Today then, there is considerably less emphasis than there once used to be on trying to write grammars that consist of masses and masses of 'rules'. Attempts, too, to investigate the 'psychological reality' of any proposals that are made are also very differently framed, because it is no longer the psychological reality of rules and transformations that is an issue but rather the psychological reality of the modules, principles and parameters.

Numerous linguists working within the programme of linguistic investigation set out by Chomsky hold such a view as the one just outlined. It is not the only view that you find today within linguistics as a whole or even within the area known as 'generative linguistics' (see, for example, Bresnan, 1981; Gazdar *et al.* 1985), but it seems safe to say that no linguist today can ignore Chomsky's ideas and that anyone who adopts a different approach to linguistic issues will almost certainly be called upon at some time to defend it against attacks of being wrongheaded, trivial, etc. In other words, there is a dominant paradigm in linguistics, one that says that at the heart of the discipline is the issue of trying to define what language is and why it must be so.

Investigations into language therefore tend to be highly 'theoretical'. Only certain kinds of questions are likely to be deemed to be appropriate and the data bearing on these questions may not be readily at hand. Certainly you cannot expect to find the data you want just from making masses and masses of random observations in the hope that something relevant to your concerns will turn up. A linguist must go out and look for data relevant to deciding some issue or other. Fortunately, much of the relevant data can come out of the knowledge of the language that the linguist already has. Is this sentence ambiguous and, if so, in what way? Is this sentence a paraphrase of that sentence? Why is this sentence grammatical and that sentence ungrammatical? Which structural elements in this or that sentence can be moved and which cannot? Why do young children say things like such and such but not things like something else? Answers to questions such as these may allow an investigator to focus on general principles of language organization and lead to hypotheses about the structure of the human mind and the process of language acquisition. In Chomsky's view that is what linguistics is all about.

## Further investigation

1   Examine the following sentences:

John is eager to please.
John is certain to please.
John is easy to please.

Although these sentences appear to have the same structure, they are really quite different. Try to show these differences by asking such questions as who is eager, certain, etc. and who is doing the pleasing or is being pleased.

2   Examine the following data:

| | |
|---|---|
| Here he comes. | Here comes he. |
| Here John comes. | Here comes John. |
| Away it sails. | Away sails it. |
| Away the ship sails. | Away sails the ship. |
| Down he went. | Down went he. |
| Down Peter went. | Down went Peter. |
| Outside she stood. | Outside stood she. |
| Outside Mary stood | Outside stood Mary. |

Are some of these sentences 'good' and others 'bad'? Can you work out a 'rule' that accounts for any differences you find?

3   In the following sentences look at the words *John*, *he* and *himself*. How do you know who is being referred to in each case? Try to relate your understanding to the grammatical structure of each sentence to see if you can discover one or two simple 'rules' or 'principles'.

John imagined himself kissing Jane.
John imagined him kissing Jane.
John imagined him kissing himself.
John imagined himself kissing himself.
John asked what he could do.
He asked what John could do.
He asked what he could do.

John asked what John could do.
He believed him to be the rightful owner.
He believed himself to be the rightful owner.

4  Let us assume that we can change certain 'echo' questions into
'wh-' questions, i.e., questions like *He is doing what?* into
questions like *What is he doing?* by moving a 'wh-' word or
phrase to the front of the sentence and 'inverting' the subject
and verb. Here are some examples:

He has gone into which room?
Which room has he gone into?
Into which room has he gone?

He has asked for what?
What has he asked for?

He has been asking to go to where for a long time?
Where has he been asking to go for a long time?

You were led to understand that John believed he had seen
who in town today?
Who were you led to understand that John believed he had
seen in town today?
You have bought a picture of what?
What have you bought a picture of?

However, we cannot do the same thing with these 'echo'
questions:
You have bought John's what? (What have you bought
John's?)
John was questioning his statement that Fred likes what?
(What was John questioning his statement that Fred likes?)
He has found the book I gave to whom? (Whom has he found
the book I gave to?)
Why not? This is the kind of problem that attracts linguists
today.

## 1.5   Further issues

One of the most important reasons for inquiring into the nature
of language is to find out exactly what it is. Language is a worthy

subject of study for this reason alone, as an end in itself. Since language is a unique phenomenon in the world – how unique it is being a matter of some controversy as we will see in the chapters that follow – the properties that make it unique are of considerable interest. How does language differ from other systems of communication, both human and non-human? Language is also used by people, and the two – language and the people who use it – are not separable, although attempts to separate them are made from time to time. Language must be related in some way to the physical and mental capacities that people have and also to the functions they make it serve. But how special are these relationships and functions? Is there anything like them anywhere else in the world?

Linguists have always been interested in making generalizations about language. Leonard Bloomfield (1933), regarded by many as the seminal figure in structural linguistics in North America, believed that it was possible to make useful inductive generalizations about language. If linguists worked with enough languages, they would find certain kinds of phenomena occurring time and time again and they might expect the same phenomena to recur in still other languages to which they gave their attention. They might also expect their investigative procedures to keep on working in the new situations because languages resemble one another in certain ways. For example, we may claim, as we have seen, that they all have phonemes, morphemes and grammatical structures. They depend on contrasts between units to make distinctions. They make use of classes of words like nouns and verbs. They have ways of making statements, asking questions and issuing commands and requests. However, this is obviously a very different programme from the one pursued by someone like Chomsky; nevertheless, it is a programme for linguistic investigation and one that was extremely influential in linguistics for a long time.

The assumption that all languages are alike in certain respects is really basic to all work in linguistics. It may even be behind attempts to describe English as though it were a variant form of Greek or Latin! It is certainly behind the accounts of language offered by any school or tradition in linguistics, whether Saussurian, Bloomfieldian or Chomskyan. Saussure and Bloomfield believed that all languages are structured; so does Chomsky. They differ in what they have perceived to be the important structures and how these operate. No linguist begins the task of describing a language without some assumptions concerning what is likely to be found – and most bring many assumptions to the task. And that is really how it must be, for working without assumptions would be like working in the dark without tools and in a place you did not recognize in some way. The important thing to acknowledge in evaluating linguistic work is the particular light the linguist uses to illuminate parts of that darkness. Different lights may also be expected to illuminate different parts, not all of which may be of equal interest.

The emphasis on looking exclusively at language itself for generalizations has led some linguists on a search for what we can call 'language universals', i.e., those properties that all languages are assumed to exhibit. These properties are more specific than such general characteristics as 'duality', 'contrast' and so on. The properties, or universals, are of interest because there seems to be no other reason for them but accident, i.e., all languages share certain characteristics by chance, or monogenesis, i.e., all languages are alike in certain ways because of descent from a common ancestor which existed at some distant point in time, or design i.e., all languages are alike because it is in the nature of language itself or of the human mind itself that they must be so. Today, most linguists seem to favour one version or the other of this last reason. They do not entirely disavow the second, but since there is presently no conclusive proof either for or against monogenesis, they find it relatively uninteresting. They reject the first reason as quite improbable because the kinds of evidence we find suggest that the similarities among languages cannot be attributed to chance.

The anthropological linguist Joseph Greenberg (1963) has long been interested in language universals. He has listed numerous ways in which languages resemble one another. One kind of universal is the *if-then* variety, i.e., if a language has one characteristic, then it must have another. For example, according to Greenberg, if a language has inflections e.g. the *-s* on *cats*, then it also has derivations, e.g. the *-ness* on *kindness*; if verbs agree with subjects or objects in gender, then they also agree in number; if a language has a dual number, i.e., a grammatical way of grouping entities by two, then it also has a plural, i.e., in this case a way of grouping entities into a category of more than two; if a language has a category of gender, then it also has one of number; if adjectives follow nouns, then the adjectives must carry all the inflections of the nouns they follow; if descriptive adjectives generally precede nouns, then nouns will follow, but if they generally follow nouns then some may also precede; and so on.

There are also greater-than-chance possibilities, e.g. languages with normal subject-object-verb word order are overwhelmingly 'postpositional', employing suffixes to express relationships rather than independent prepositions. In comparison, languages with dominant verb-subject-object word order are always 'prepositional'. In declarative sentences subjects almost always precede objects; languages with dominant verb-subject-object sentences have the adjectives after the noun with overwhelmingly more than chance frequency; and so on. To these universals we can add further ones such as that nasal vowels are overall less frequent in any language than oral ones, with the actual inventory of nasal vowels never exceeding that of the oral vowels. And, finally, the total phonemic inventory of any language must fall in the range of between ten and 70 phonemes with the greatest number of languages showing distributions around the mid-point of that range, i.e., having about 40 phonemes, as English does. One characteristic shared by all these universals is that they are formal in the sense that they make reference only to the actual linguistic forms employed by speakers of a language; they are not concerned with functional matters, i.e., what utterances are used to communicate, nor with the characteristics of individual speakers.

Another way of classifying languages and looking for patterns among them is to classify them by 'type'. Typology studies developed in the nineteenth century, particularly in Germany. For example, one division among languages places them into either an 'analytic' type in which you use small words to construct sentences, e.g. Chinese and Vietnamese, or a 'synthetic' type in which there is hardly any distinction between sentence and word, e.g. many native languages of the Americas. The more frequent variation of this principle postulates three types of language: 'isolating', 'inflectional' and 'agglutinative'. Isolating languages – Chinese and Vietnamese again – tend to employ monosyllabic words in constructing sentences. Inflectional languages, e.g. Classical Greek and Latin, employ inseparable inflections on words to do much of their grammatical work, e.g. Latin *amo* 'I love' is comprised of *am-* 'love' and *-o* 'first person, singular, present tense, indicative mood'. Agglutinative languages, e.g. Turkish and Kiswahili, combine words with sets of stable affixes to produce complicated phrases, e.g. Turkish *adamlara* 'to the men' is comprised of *adam-* 'man', *-lar* 'plural' and *-a* 'to'. In this view English is a kind of hybrid with small isolated words like *a*, *not* and *very*, minor complicated inflectional systems like *sing, sang, song, sung* and agglutinations in words like *judgemental* and *helplessness*. This approach to language typology raises several interesting issues. How did the different types come into existence? Can a language of one type change into a language of another type? If it can, how does it do so? How important really are such typological differences? Might they not just simply be somewhat misleading surface characteristics of language that divert our attention from more profound matters?

As we have seen, language universals are also the central concern of Chomsky's work in linguistics. He too is interested in properties that might be common to all languages, believing that these derive from the structure of the human mind. His assumption is that the human mind is structured in such a way that it can use only languages of a certain kind. Moreover, that structure is innate, being a biological given. Language itself is species-specific. In this view, therefore, the task that the linguist confronts is one of explaining the universal principles that are involved in the construction of utterances in any language. These principles will also be the same for all languages and for all speakers.

As Chomsky has refined and developed his theory over the years, the principles that he has seen as universal have changed somewhat. Whereas at one time rule schemata, transformations and a deep-surface distinction in the organization of sentences seemed to be of paramount importance in any consideration of universals, now the focus has shifted to trying to specify a general set of principles having to do with permissible structures, movements and dependencies of various kinds among the parts of utterances. The emphasis on universals has been strengthened, so it is not surprising that Chomsky's grammatical approach is now often more likely to be referred to as 'universal grammar' (see Cook, 1988) than as 'transformational–generative grammar'.

Chomsky's ideas concerning universal grammar have produced considerable changes in linguistic investigation. New areas of concern have been opened up and old issues have been re-examined in a new light. As we will see, Chomsky's ideas touch on almost every issue that is important in the study of human language. Whereas it is still possible to approach linguistic issues without necessarily subscribing to Chomsky's views about language or what the central task of linguistics is, it is not possible entirely to ignore his views. Indeed any independent theorizing must always acknowledge, either directly or indirectly, Chomsky's work and views on any matters connected to that theorizing. In a real sense Chomsky has established almost the entire agenda of current linguistic investigation.

However, what is not covered in this agenda is not without interest. Language is used by real people in real-life situations. Consequently, it is legitimate to ask questions about those people and their situations: about their physical limitations as users of language; about how they use language to get through their daily lives; and about the almost endless yet not unsystematic variation in the observed use of language – the different dialects we hear, the way individuals vary their speech almost moment by moment, the slips of the tongue they make, the attempts at self-correction, the way they pursue topics in conversation, and so on and so on. There are obvious relationships between language and physical, psychological and sociological factors (see Crystal, 1987; Newmeyer, 1988), and although these relationships may not be in some way as central as the relationship between language and the human mind – the relationship that Chomsky puts at the heart of linguistic concern – they are every bit as important in other ways. After all, we could not live if we did not have functioning hearts, but knowing that people who live have functioning hearts does not tell you anything about the quality and purpose of their lives. Language is used for living and there is no reason to assume that we must delay trying to understand how it is used in living and how it relates to the quality of the life we live until we know exactly what it is we are using.

The position that I will adopt in the chapters that follow is that language is almost certainly a unique phenomenon. We will investigate many of the special characteristics that appear to confirm its uniqueness. Chomsky and his followers focus mainly on the structural characteristics of language in order to show what they consider to be unique about language. I will take a somewhat broader approach as we investigate different facets of both language and its use.

## Further investigation

1   Schleicher believed that 'isolating' languages changed slowly into 'agglutinating' ones and these in turn into 'inflectional' ones. In Schleicher's view languages were natural organisms that grew in accordance with definite laws, so languages 'developed' and eventually 'grew old and died'. How might you go about testing such an idea?

2   There is general agreement among linguists that all languages have sentences constructed from subjects (S), verbs (V) and objects (O), e.g. *Dogs chase cats* is SVO. Theoretically, S, V and O can occur in any one of six orders: SOV, SVO, VSO, VOS, OVS and OSV. However, in practice more than eighty per cent of languages are basically either SOV or SVO in their ordering, most of the rest are VSO, a very few are VOS, and the OVS and OSV orders are extremely rare. What hypotheses do such data suggest?

3   In a famous essay on the French language, awarded a prize in 1783 by the Berlin Academy of Sciences, the French philosopher Antoine Rivarol wrote that 'French first designates the subject of the sentence, then the verb that is the action and finally the object of this action; this is the logic natural to all men.' He went on to declare that on this account French was 'an instrument of pure reason,' that 'French syntax is incorruptible', and that the result for French 'is that admirable clarity which is the lasting foundation of our language. What is not clear is not French.' Would Rivarol be a serious candidate for a similar prize today?

# 2

# *Do only humans talk?*

Our experience tells us that only humans use language but we also know that humans are part of the animal world and animals certainly do communicate with one another. What could we possibly learn about both language and animal communication if we try to compare the two? Certain animals appear to have some of the physical, social and intellectual characteristics that humans possess – although we appear to possess them in much greater measure – and we might well ask too how these characteristics relate to any ability to use language. There is even a fairly widespread belief that we may be able to learn interesting things about language itself if we were to look closely at how certain other animals communicate among themselves or try to teach certain animals to communicate with us and perhaps even with one another. In such a view it would be erroneous just simply to declare that language is a unique human attribute and that studies of animal communication and attempts to teach animals some form of language can tell us nothing about language itself. What we cannot do is simply assert that language is unique to humans and leave the issue there; we must try to prove that it is indeed unique – if we can – by thoroughly examining any capacities that animals might have for language or any form of human-like communication.

Two issues arise immediately. How do we account for language within an evolutionary perspective and why is it that only humans appear to have linguistic ability? Language actually appears to pose a serious problem within evolutionary theory in that there is still no adequate explanation of how it originated within the total history of human development. It was a most significant milestone in that development – perhaps even the most important one of all – but if we find nothing even remotely resembling language in those species that are closest to humans, its exact origin in our species is something of a mystery, but not one, as we will see, that has been ignored.

According to evolutionary theory, new species arise when, through processes of change and differentiation, an adaptive variation increases the chances of survival. Charles Darwin himself saw no problem in explaining how language fitted into evolution: it was a successful adaptation made by humans. It certainly dramatically enhanced their chances for survival in what must have been a very dangerous world. Darwin maintained that there was no fundamental difference between humans and the higher mammals in their mental faculties. Humans differed solely in the much greater power they possessed to associate sounds and ideas. In such a view any differences between humans and animals are largely quantitative. Any examination of the history of nineteenth-century linguistics with its focus on historical matters and on language change quickly reveals how mutually supportive were evolutionary theory and linguistics during the era in which they were both developing. Of course, some linguists did raise their voices in objection to this close alliance; Max Müller for one objected that language was a serious obstacle to Darwin's theory because he saw no continuity at all between non-language and language.

There are some key questions we might ask. In what ways are language and the various communication systems of other species alike? In what ways are they different? Are any differences that do exist between language and the communication systems that certain animals employ simply 'quantitative' differences, i.e., differences of degree, or are they 'qualitative', i.e., differences of kind? Are humans just better in some ways at doing certain things, or are they completely different in a way that places the kinds of language abilities they possess quite out of reach of members of other species? But then again how do you decide what is a qualitative difference rather than a quantitative one?

It is necessary therefore to look at the kinds of evidence we might bring to bear on the issue of the possible relatedness of language to systems of animal communication and on various attempts to teach animals to use language in one way or another. We might also usefully examine some of the different claims that have been made concerning what is really so unique about language. Is it the human articulatory apparatus alone? Is it greater brain size and/or a particular type of internal organization of that brain? Is it the feature of language which I referred to in the last chapter as 'duality', i.e., the existence of parallel and independent systems of sounds and meanings? Is it merely a much greater ability to manipulate abstract symbols in extraordinarily complex ways? Is it therefore just a greater cognitive ability, or perhaps a cognitive ability of an entirely different order?

There seems to be little doubt that language use does involve an ability or a set of abilities that we do not find in other species. The evidence we find around us is quite clear on that issue: no other species uses language. We cannot 'talk' in any meaningful sense to any other species of animal, not even cats, dogs and certain pet birds! Nor can they 'talk' to one another. But can certain animals acquire some – or even all – of the properties we associate with language if we patiently set out to see that they do acquire them? We may even define the central issue as being that of the 'continuity' – or 'discontinuity' – in the world between animals and humans. What essentially is the relationship – if any – between the song of a nightingale and an aria from *Madame Butterfly* or between a dog barking at a stranger and a sign that says *Beware of the dog*? Are we forever doomed from communicating meaningfully in two-way interaction with animals, even the 'smartest' of them? Are humans not only 'talking animals', but the only possible talking animals?

## 2.1 Mainly of birds and bees

Animals do communicate with one another, within species at least. But just how limited is that communication and how does it compare with all the opportunities that talk offers us? Communication within other species appears to be completely determined by the genetic make-up of the particular species, i.e., on the kinds of 'collective memory' that the species hands on genetically from one generation to the next. As such, any system of communication that does exist is both highly predictable and, as it turns out, severely limited. As we would expect too, almost no variation exists in the kinds of communicative behaviour that we observe. However, there are several issues that do merit special consideration.

We know that innate patterns of behaviour are not activated at random. As well as being highly specific, they are also extremely functional. Many such behaviours have to do with the marking of territory, e.g. certain kinds of birdsong or the behaviour of cats and dogs when they urinate to lay claims to certain spaces. Fireflies show where they are by glowing. Display behaviour may also occur, particularly as part of a courting ritual, as anyone who has observed the struttings of a peacock can readily attest. There are even ritualistic displays of submission, e.g. of inferior animals rolling over to expose their soft underbellies and throats to superior animals. Anyone who has lived closely with animals soon comes to recognize such behaviours and to interpret, although not always accurately, various movements, chirps, whistles, bellows, grunts, hoots, croaks, barks, etc.

Such behaviour must often be 'triggered' in a way that is very narrowly prescribed. If a particular species has an instinct to flee from danger, cues as to what is potentially dangerous must be available if flight is to occur. If mating is to be successful, cues to suitable partners and possible rivals must exist to set off the appropriate response, e.g. possession of the partner or aggression against the rival. Very specific cues often act as the triggers. Female silkworm moths attract male moths by exuding minute traces of a rare chemical compound bombykol. The scent of blood produces deliberate searching movements in sharks. The blue strip on the belly of a male fence lizard arouses fighting behaviour in any other male fence lizard who sees it. The cheeping of turkey chicks arouses brooding behaviour in turkey hens, even when the actual noise of the chicks comes from a tape recording inside a stuffed skunk, a natural enemy of the turkey. The red belly of a male stickleback arouses aggressive behaviour in other males. A small stick painted red underneath will also induce the same behaviour in a male stickleback but a small stick painted red on top will not. The same red belly will attract female sticklebacks to a nest that a male has constructed.

Observers have recorded many different instances of such behaviour. Records show that this kind of animal behaviour is almost entirely predictable if you know certain things about the circumstances the animal finds itself in because it must react instinctively, i.e., in a fixed way, in those circumstances. For example, a particular set of circumstances inevitably brings on pecking, mating, fighting or some such behaviour. To some extent humans behave like this too, e.g. human babies exhibit sucking and grasping movements when objects are presented to their mouths and hands, and all humans prefer animals with large eyes, high domed heads and a general roundness or chubbiness to those that are small and beady-eyed or slit-eyed. (You only have to look at the way that animals are shown in cartoons to see examples of how artists exploit this human reaction there.) In the vast majority of cases, however, human behaviour seems to be under 'voluntary' control rather than to be instinctively induced. Not only do systems of human law recognize this fact but also our experience of human language tells us that you cannot easily predict what people will say.

Over the years investigators have looked closely at various systems of animal communication in order to see how they work and sometimes to compare them with language. One of the great pioneers of ethology, Konrad Lorenz (1952) studied the system of calls that jackdaws employ as part of his overall study of these birds. He found that jackdaws have a very limited number of 'holistic' calls at their disposal, e.g. a 'food' call, a 'danger' call, a 'let's go' call and so on. A food call brings other birds to a source of food, a danger call alerts them to the presence of a possible predator and a let's go call induces a whole flock of birds to change location. There is no 'talk' or 'conversation', as we understand these terms, among the birds and there is no variation in the calls. Like some other kinds of behaviour that the birds show, the calls are instinctive to the species. The birds do not 'learn' the calls in the same way that we learn names and telephone numbers. Rather, every jackdaw 'knows' the proper calls because that is what part of being a jackdaw is.

Other species show the same limitations in their communicative behaviour. North American cicadas also have four discrete signals: one of alarm, another a congregating signal and two male courting calls. Monkeys and chimpanzees in the wild also have a few discrete calls. Cuckoos reared in isolation from one another or deafened or exposed to the songs of other birds still sing like cuckoos, still another indication of the innateness and invariance of communication systems in non-humans. There are really very few exceptions. One is the bullfinch. Apparently, a bullfinch reared with a canary will sing like a canary and even pass on canary song to its own young. But this is neither a large variation in behaviour nor one that is commonly found.

Dolphins have been of interest to people for many years now, particularly the Atlantic bottlenose dolphin, and a considerable body of knowledge and a still more considerable body of folklore have gathered around them (see Lilly, 1967; Russell and Russell, 1971). Highly trainable, social and playful sea mammals, dolphins make a wide variety of calls, clicks, whistles and yelps in their natural environment, many of which seem to be motivated by a need to communicate. However, rigorous investigation has shown that the total range of calls is actually very limited and that dolphins do not use them for anything that might resemble human conversation but rather in order to monitor one another's positions, locate objects in the water and perhaps express a limited range of emotions.

In one interesting experiment (Evans and Bastian, 1969) two Atlantic bottlenose dolphins, Buzz, a male, and Doris, a female, were taught to press one of two paddles for fish after a light was switched on in their tank so as to provide either a continuous signal or an intermittent one. A continuous signal required the dolphins to press one paddle in order to be rewarded with fish; an intermittent signal required them to press the other paddle for a similar reward. After this training an opaque screen was used to separate the dolphins in the tank. Both dolphins had access to a pair of paddles but only Doris could see the light. Fish were then fed to the dolphins only after both dolphins pressed the appropriate paddles. Doris therefore had to 'tell' Buzz which paddle to press. The dolphins achieved better than ninety per cent success in several thousand attempts during which Buzz was able to hear Doris. Her calls were also observed to differ as the light signal differed, i.e., according to how the light was turned on. Consequently, it is safe to say that the two dolphins were able to communicate the information that would ensure that they would be fed. However, when the opaque partition was finally removed and the dolphins were reunited, Doris continued to exhibit the same kind of vocal behaviour even though it was now completely redundant. Furthermore, she continued to do so even after Buzz was removed from the tank! The results would appear to indicate just how effective 'conditioning' can be with an 'intelligent' animal rather than that dolphins have access to a communication system that they can employ when necessary.

Honey bees use both non-symbolic and symbolic forms of communication. In a hive they are receptive to the smell of returning foragers and of the nectar they bring with them, and they are able to judge its kind and quality immediately. They have a system of communication that allows returning bees to communicate the exact location of food sources and also the location of possible new homes when a swarm is seeking to move. Karl von Frisch (1950, 1953, 1962, 1967) and Martin Lindauer (1961) have offered explanations of how Austrian bees 'dance' in order to communicate with one another

A returning foraging bee performs a dance either on the vertical side of the hive or on a horizontal surface outside to tell the bees in the hive where a possible source of food is located. One dance, a long and vigorous dance, indicates a good food supply; another dance, a short and weak dance, indicates a poor food supply. The direction of the food source is indicated by lining up the axis of the dance with the food source and the bee uses the location of the sun as a reference point even on overcast days. Outside the hive this procedure presents no problem. Inside the hive, if the axis of the dance is vertically up, the food source is located in the direction of the sun, if vertically down it is directly away from the sun, and if at an angle from the vertical, it is at that angle from the sun. That is, the bees substitute gravitational direction for the sun's direction. The amount of buzzing that accompanies the dance correlates with the distance to the food source and the amount of tail-wagging correlates with the quality of the food.

Still another dance has at least two variant forms: if the food source is near, i.e., within about ten metres, the bee performs a round or circular dance; if the food source lies beyond that distance, then the bee performs a tail-wagging or sickle dance in the form of a figure-of-eight. Some investigators believe that if the dance occurs inside the hive the other bees actually 'read' it through their feelers and that if it occurs outside the hive they use both their feelers and exactly what they see of the dance. However, there is some controversy as to exactly how they 'read' the dance in either case.

All bees appear to share the same basic system. In some kinds of bees the dance is more developed than others and interesting 'dialect' differences have been reported. Italian and Austrian bees can live and breed together but seem to misinterpret each other's communications about food sources. Italian bees never go far enough to look for food in response to a message from an Austrian bee, whereas Austrian bees consistently overfly food sources that Italian foragers report. The sickle dance is also exclusive to Italian bees and Austrian bees do not respond to it.

The communication systems of a number of other species have also been examined but almost without exception in nowhere near the detail of those just mentioned. The range of species is large: crickets, grasshoppers, doves, finches, mynah birds, prairie dogs, whales and various primates to name but a few. None employs more than three dozen holistic signs at most, e.g. the vervet monkey and the Japanese monkey, and most have fewer than a dozen. If that is so, then there really does not seem to be much to gain from following this line of investigation, since animal communication systems do not appear to bear even the slightest resemblance to language. However, it might be appropriate to find out what kinds of capacities other species might exhibit for acquiring aspects of human language. If in nature animals do not use anything that appears to resemble language, what kinds of abilities would they display if we deliberately gave some of them the opportunity to learn language from us? And if they did learn something what would we make of the results of that learning?

## Further investigation

1 Most of us have had some experience of close contact with animals, particularly with cats and dogs. Try to specify exactly how such animals communicate (and what they communicate) with each other and to us (and us to them).

2 Look at work that tries to understand how dolphins and whales communicate, particularly how they must do so under water. What can we learn from such work? Anything more than that they are 'intelligent' sea mammals, somewhat mysterious, but lacking entirely anything that resembles language?

3  Honey bees are said to be 'sociable' creatures. Some investigators regard the development of sociability as a critical prerequisite to the development of language in the human species. In this view, increased sociability led to language, since a language-less species must be limited in the social contacts that are possible among its members. How interesting is this idea? (Note that other investigators have regarded such things as the development of the controlled use of fire and of bipedalism, i.e., walking on two legs, as 'critical' in the same way.)

## 2.2  Talking apes?

What would happen if we tried to teach a language to members of another species? What would they learn? And what might the results tell us about language? There have actually been many such attempts to establish some form of communication between humans and other species (see Bright, 1990, for a popular account). Most stop at instructing animals like horses and dogs to obey certain commands, but a few attempt to go far beyond this. Several even try to employ some kind of system that will enable the animal to express certain 'wants' or even to convey certain kinds of information to humans.

One of the most famous instances of an animal that appeared to be able to communicate all kinds of information to a human was Clever Hans, an eight-year-old stallion that belonged to Wilhelm von Osten in Germany (Pfungst, 1911). In a series of amazing performances in 1904 von Osten and Clever Hans seemed to establish that the horse knew a great number of things and that it could communicate that knowledge to observers through a system of head movements and hoof tappings. It appeared that Clever Hans could do simple additions, change simple fractions to decimals or decimals to fractions and tell observers the day of the month. Rigorous tests, however, proved that the horse knew nothing other than how to respond to subtle visual cues that either von Osten or other handlers were uncon-sciously providing to him. Clever Hans failed to respond when his eyes were covered or if someone around him did not know the answer to the question that he had been asked. There was no doubt about the horse's cleverness but no part of it had to do with being able to use language in any way. Clever Hans turned out to be a spectacular failure, but the twentieth century has seen a number of well publicized experiments in which deliberate attempts have been made to teach certain animals bits and pieces of language. Predictably, the results have generated considerable controversy.

Since primates are our nearest 'relatives' in the animal world – but with a 'separation' dating back some five to ten million years depending on the species – it is not surprising that from time to time people have attempted to teach an occasional captive primate to use language. The chimpanzee, our closest 'relative' in nature, has been the usual beneficiary of this kind of attention, but a mature chimpanzee has to be treated carefully, being many times stronger than a mature human being.

Chimpanzees and humans share numerous anatomical and physiological characteristics, as we might expect from two species that share approximately ninety-nine per cent of their genetic material. They also have certain similarities in blood chemistry that are not found anywhere else in nature, and carry some of the same parasites. Sociable creatures, chimpanzees are also animals that recognize themselves in mirrors, pictures and films, and they have excellent colour vision. Like all apes they have considerable cognitive ability: they are able to solve simple problems, they use simple tools and they show many examples of co-operative behaviour (see Goodall, 1986). There is, however, no resemblance at all between the kinds of communication that chimpanzees employ in the wild and language. A captive chimpanzee must be taught everything she – the experiments have generally used females – is to learn. The two best-known earliest attempts to find out if chimpanzees could learn language actually involved bringing them up like human children.

In 1931 the Kellogs (Kellog, 1968; Kellog and Kellog, 1933) 'adopted' a seven-month-old chimpanzee, Gua, as a companion to their ten-month-old son, Donald. They treated Gua like a typical middle-class baby, giving her her own bed and highchair, dressing and undressing her, bathing and feeding her and establishing household routines for her. The chimpanzee and the boy were brought up together as though they were siblings and the Kellogs kept a record of their joint development over a span of nine months. Gua was the more agile of the two. Donald, perhaps surprisingly, the more imitative. The boy's imitating of the chimpanzee was actually one of the main causes of the eventual abandoning of the experiment, because the presence of the chimpanzee appeared to be retarding the boy's development. At the end of the experiment the Kellogs reported that Gua understood 95 words and Donald 107 words. The chimpanzee would, for example, extend her arm in response to an instruction to *Shake hands*, sit on *Sit down*, point to her nose when told *Show me your nose* and emit a food bark when asked *Want some milk?* or *Want some orange?* However, Gua never learned to say anything and an attempt to teach her the word *papa* failed utterly. But she was extremely responsive to tactile communication, reacting promptly and correctly to even the slightest touch. On the other hand, Donald much preferred to react to words and by the end of the experiment had developed an obvious preference for language.

In 1948 the Hayes (Hayes, 1951; Hayes and Hayes, 1951) brought another chimpanzee, Viki, into their childless house when she was only a few days old to see if they could teach her to speak. But teaching Viki to speak was not at all easy; in fact it was almost impossible. At 18 months Viki could say *mama*; a few months later she added *papa* and still later *cup*. A fourth word *up* was a still later addition to Viki's vocabulary. However, her pronunciation was always very poor and she did not use her few words for their exact referents: they were mainly attention getters in the first two cases and a request for water in the third.

When she was five years old, Viki was given some psychological tests requiring her to sort pictures. These tests showed that she could apparently make a few basic distinctions between pairs of concepts such as 'animate' and 'inanimate', 'red' and 'green', 'large' and 'small' and so on. But she never made much progress in responding to language. Most people who met Viki apparently regarded her not so much as a severely retarded child but as a chimpanzee who had acquired a few interesting bits of human-like behaviour as the result of a long period of intimate contact with humans, i.e., as something like a really clever house dog. It is of some interest to note too that during the picture-sorting tasks referred to above Viki unhesitatingly placed a picture of herself with humans. However, a picture of her chimpanzee father went into the 'animal' file. The socializing experience she had undergone had not been without its effect on her! But there was no real bridging of the language gap that exists between human beings and animals in her case, just as there had been none with Gua.

The next major development in this line of work came as a result of a radical shift in emphasis. The Kellogs and the Hayes had tried to teach chimpanzees as though they were the investigators' natural infants. In such circumstances chimpanzees must learn to behave like children and cannot capitalize on some of their peculiar strengths. They cannot profit from their agility and dexterity and they are not encouraged to imitate gestures, something which they do well. Instead, attempts are made to teach them to speak, something which they do very badly. As we will see later, there is also good reason now to believe that 'speaking' is a task which is almost certainly impossible for them anyway, both anatomically and cognitively. Apes do vocalize in the wild when they are excited, but such vocalizations have properties that are entirely different from those of human speech and these cannot be refashioned to produce human speech.

When, in June, 1966, Allan and Beatrice Gardner, two comparative psychologists, adopted their chimpanzee Washoe, who had been born wild in Africa, she was approximately a year old. They decided to teach her the 'sign language' of the deaf (Gardner and Gardner, 1969, 1971) and bring her up in an environment which would suit her rather than themselves. Washoe was therefore taught a version of Ameslan, American Sign Language, the communication system of the deaf, not the finger-spelling form in which words are spelled out letter by letter but the form that employs holistic signs to express concepts and relationships.

While Ameslan is only partially based on English, it can apparently be used to 'say' anything you can say in English. Some of the signs are highly iconic. For example, the sign for *drink* is the thumb extended from the fist to touch the mouth; for *smell* it is the palm held in front of the nose and moved slightly upward several times; for *cat* it is the thumb and index finger moved outward from the corner of the mouth; and for *up* it is the arms, and possibly the index finger as well, pointed upward. However, most of the signs are completely arbitrary.

Washoe learned her signs in various ways: through instrumental conditioning, her reward being tickling, which she enjoyed immensely; from moulding of her 'hands'; with repeated prompting; and by deliberate imitation. She also learned her signs in a particularly rich environment. Kept in a trailer in the Gardners' back yard, Washoe had few constraints placed on her behaviour, continual human companionship during her waking hours, lots of games and activities and a constant flow of signs in her presence. The Gardners attempted to create an environment that resembled that of a particularly fortunate child. No actual spoken language was employed in Washoe's presence, but expressive sounds were permitted. She therefore lived in a rich, naturalistic setting that provided very strong incentives to communicate.

Washoe made remarkable progress in her ability to communicate. After less than two years she had learned to use 38 signs correctly. She did not use a particular sign for a particular object only. For example, she used the sign *dog* not only for a dog but also for a picture of a dog, a drawing of a dog and even when she heard a dog bark. She therefore applied the signs she learned to classes of objects and events rather than just to the particular objects and events associated with the learning of the signs. Washoe's signs were not always exactly like those made by the human deaf – she was after all an animal not a human – and the trainers themselves were not entirely proficient in Ameslan. Her signs were sometimes immature or 'babified' as are the signs of deaf children, but deaf adults who have seen films of Washoe easily understand her signing and deaf children are reported to be especially captivated by what they see of Washoe's signing behaviour.

In three years Washoe's repertoire of signs had increased to 85 signs, the acquisition of each sign being confirmed through rigorous 'double-blind' testing procedures devised to ensure that the investigators were actually testing what they claimed to be testing. Washoe also used signs in combination, combining as many as four or five signs at a time. The Gardners reported combinations of signs such as the following: two signs like *hurry open, more sweet, listen eat, you drink* and *Roger come*; and three or more signs like *key open food, Roger Washoe tickle, key open please blanket* and *you me go in*. These combinations are not unlike the 'telegraphic' speech that very young children use for a while.

An examination of how Washoe used specific signs showed that she rapidly extended such a sign as the one for *open* from use with a particular closed door, to closed doors in general and then to a variety of closed containers such as cupboards, refrigerators, boxes, jars and briefcases. Eventually, she extended it to water taps (*open drink*) and even to pop bottles. Likewise, Washoe extended the sign for *more*, initially a request for more tickling, to anything that she enjoyed, for example, to swinging and grooming, to favourite foods and extra helpings of these, and still later to requests for repetitions of events. The union of the signs for *water* and *bird* in *water bird* also was Washoe's way of referring to a duck. Such semantic development is not unlike that which occurs in young children, so there are some very interesting parallels between Washoe's 'language' behaviour and the language behaviour we observe in young children.

But what of Washoe's syntactic development, since syntax seems to lie at the very centre of language ability? Were Washoe's signs ordered in such a way as to demonstrate that she had a solid grasp of syntactic relationships and processes? The example *Roger Washoe tickle* is of particular interest. Who was to do the tickling, Roger or Washoe? Would the sign sequence *Washoe Roger tickle* be quite interchangeable with the first sequence in making the identical request or would its meaning be quite different? Linguists ask such questions about Washoe's performance since they do not regard language ability as merely the ability to learn a set of signs but as the ability both to learn such a set and to manipulate the signs in syntactic arrangements that contrast with one another.

There is no doubt that Washoe's performance showed that she had considerable ability to sign, even in quite complex situations. But the signing in such situations appeared to be unordered. On different occasions Washoe used the following combinations of signs at a locked door: *gimme key, more key, gimme key more, open key, key open, open more, more open, key in, open key please, open gimme key, in open, help, help key in* and *open key help hurry*. Syntactic ordering of any kind seems to be absent and the signs themselves appear to be combined at random. Human language is not randomly organized in this way and young children very soon show that they are aware of this fact.

Washoe also did not apparently initiate questions, even though questioning was very much part of her environment – perhaps questioning is what humans do and chimpanzees merely have to respond! It is not at all surprising that Washoe's trainers 'understood' her: they were encouraged to be generous in their responses and they were committed to the success of the total experiment. Such 'generous' interpretations actually occur repeatedly in studies of animal communication, i.e., the investigator provides the 'best possible' interpretation of the animal's behaviour. More 'objective' analyses quite often show that there is considerable 'over-claiming' as a consequence.

A number of linguists have been particularly harsh in their criticisms of the claims made about Washoe's ability to use language. Some have gone so far as to deny that what Washoe knows is anything like what humans know. In this view Washoe may not even know some version of Ameslan. The Gardners have also been criticized for their selective use of data, the aforementioned generous interpretations and their apparent lack of theoretical concern. However, the Washoe experiment and others like it certainly captured public attention for a while.

The Gardners themselves have not been vitally interested in many of the issues that I have just mentioned, preferring to let each investigator define language as the investigator sees fit. They point out that linguists do not themselves agree on what language is. In a 1975 paper, for example, they argued that the failure of linguists and psycholinguists to devise a behavioural definition of language is an obstacle they were trying to avoid by obtaining observations of the acquisition of sign language by young chimpanzees that could be compared with observations of the acquisition of spoken language and sign language by human children. They pointed out that any theoretical criteria that can be applied to the early utterances of children can also be applied to the early utterances of chimpanzees and that if children can be said to have acquired language on the basis of their performance, then chimpanzees can be said to have acquired language to the extent that their performance matches that of children.

While the Gardners recognize the possibility that animal communication and human language may be two distinct and non-comparable types of phenomena, they believe that some aspects of communicative behaviour show a continuity between non-humans and humans. Like many other investigators of animal communication, they have also pointed out that as soon as they demonstrate that an animal can perform a particular 'language' task demanded by linguists, then these same linguists say that that task is not enough and insist on the completion of some further task, in effect constantly putting language out of reach of the animal. The Gardners say that they prefer their results to be judged for what they are – an initial attempt, remarkably success-ful, at 'two-way' communication with a member of another species. *Two-way* is important, because Washoe obviously initiated communication in considerable quantities during the course of the Gardners' investigation.

By 1970 Washoe had grown too big to handle and was sent to live with other chimpanzees in an ape colony. Later, in 1974, she was given a young male chimpanzee, Loulis, to bring up after her own infant died and she soon apparently taught him some 20 or more signs with his favourite being the sign for 'hug'. Other chimpanzees have also been taught in conditions similar to those Washoe experienced, particularly in Oklahoma (Fouts *et al.* 1982, 1984). Some use signs only to humans, others use them to both humans and one another, and there is even some evidence that certain chimpanzees have created new signs and novel combinations of signs independently, e.g. a pygmy chimpanzee, Kanzi, brought up in a quasi-natural environment and exposed to both spoken language and a signing system (Savage-Rumbaugh, 1986).

In still another well known experiment the psychologist David Premack (Premack, 1970, 1971; Premack and Premack, 1972, 1983) used a wild-born six-year-old chimpanzee, Sarah, to investi-gate the intellectual potential of apes. Premack wanted to find out what Sarah could do if she were taught to communicate through a system that employed certain logical concepts. In contrast to Washoe, who lived in a very free environment, Sarah was taught certain things and then she was tested to see how much she had learned; all the teaching and testing took place in a highly constrained laboratory setting. Premack deliberately set out to shape Sarah's language-like behaviour through the use of strict training procedures that limited the occurrence of undesired behaviours. Sarah was taught to place well over a hundred metal-backed plastic tokens of various sizes, shapes and colours onto a magnetized board mounted on a wall. She 'wrote her sentences' on this board vertically top-to-bottom by arranging the tokens in specified orders. Each token represented a word (*Sarah, green, banana* and so on) or was a 'logical-syntactic' operator (*is the same as, is different from* and so on).

Like the Gardners, Premack avoided the problems inherent in trying to teach his chimpanzee to speak. In this view while speech may be a property of language, it is not one absolutely necessary to language. Such a view was in agreement with Premack's general approach to language, one that allowed him to define it for his own purpose. For example, Premack asked what kinds of operations does language typically allow; he then conceived his task to be one of devising schedules that would eventually allow the chimpanzee to perform these operations by using tokens on the magnetized board. The actual teaching was carried out by means of very sophisticated techniques of 'reinforcement' designed to shape Sarah's behaviour toward certain goals. Appropriate behaviours from Sarah were rewarded by foods of various kinds. Once a desired goal was achieved it was then tested, and on these tests Sarah usually achieved a success ratio of about eighty per cent regardless of the kind of behaviour that was tested.

Premack required Sarah to perform a variety of operations. One was a naming operation which Sarah performed by placing on the board a plastic token that correctly named an object, e.g. *Mary, Sarah, apple* and so on. An increasingly complicated set of operations required Sarah to use several plastic tokens in sequence to indicate certain states in the real world, e.g. *Mary give apple Sarah*. A four-sign sequence such as this one was built up through the use of previously mastered two-sign and three-sign sequences. Both 'yes-no' questions, i.e., questions that can be answered with either a *yes* or a *no*, and 'wh-' questions, i.e., questions that require the supplying of some information other than *yes* or *no*, were also built up using real objects: the first as '*X*' *is (not) the same as* '*Y*' *question* (where '*X*' and '*Y*' were actual objects and *is (not) the same as* and *question* were represented by tokens), with the answer being either *yes* or *no*; the second as either '*X*' *is not the same as question*, with the answer a choice between objects available to Sarah, or as '*X*' *question* '*Y*', with the answer either the token for *is the same as* or the one for *is not the same as*. Other operations involved an *if-then* pairing, a metalinguistic task that required responding with an appropriate token to the token for *name of* in the presence of an object, and an identification task that required Sarah to classify objects according to either colour, shape or size.

One particularly interesting task involved the processes of compounding and deleting, therefore control of the structural, i.e., grammatical, components in the system that was being used. First of all, Sarah learned to construct sequences of tokens such as *Sarah insert banana pail* to describe her placing a banana into a pail and *Sarah insert apple dish* to describe her placing an apple into a dish. Then she learned *Sarah insert banana pail Sarah insert apple dish* (compounding) followed by *Sarah insert banana pail insert apple dish* (deleting the second *Sarah*) with Sarah as the subject doing the insertion. Finally, she learned *Sarah insert banana pail apple dish* (deleting the second *insert*). Further work with the verb *withdraw* substituted for *insert* showed that Sarah was also able to transfer or generalize what she had learned, a structural principle involving compounding and deletion.

According to Premack, Sarah mastered a wide variety of tasks. She could name, compose sentences, ask questions and classify objects by colour, shape and size. She could also use plurals and negation, and she acquired some understanding of quantification. Her syntactic abilities covered conjoining and of course the kind of compounding and deletion I have just mentioned.

Premack's results and claims seem to be considerably more interesting and controversial than those of the Gardners. However, it is not easy to explain why Sarah should be about equally successful – or equally unsuccessful – in scoring at about the eighty per cent level on the various tasks. It would be much easier to explain either almost perfect learning, complete failure or some kind of gradation in success according to the difficulty of the task. In similar circumstances once young children learn to use a particular structure they use it without a similar twenty per cent error rate.

Secondly, Sarah almost never initiated communication or gave any kind of response that she was not required to give. However, all her learning occurred in very controlled situations keyed to very specific tasks and she was not encouraged to be spontaneous in her behaviour. She was also not encouraged to construct 'sentences'. Sarah's task was to learn something and be tested on her learning, so she almost never played with her 'language' the way Washoe played with hers when she was left alone. Of course, the circumstances under which the two chimpanzees lived and the methods of training they experienced were very different. Sarah lived in a wire cage with a cement block wall, few toys, very little exposure to humans and almost no opportunity for spontaneous social behaviour. She also received only one hour of 'language' training each working day of the week. These circumstances obviously differed greatly from those in which Washoe found herself.

Another difficulty has to do with the experimental conditions themselves. Sarah's performance with people she did not know was less satisfactory than her performance with people she knew. It fell to about a seventy per cent rate of success. Of course, both children and adults can behave in the same manner, their performances tending to decline too when circumstances are less favourable to them. Still the possibility exists that Sarah was reacting to non-linguistic cues from the people she knew, just as Clever Hans did. There is even the possibility that Sarah had learned whole response patterns that she produced on cue rather than a set of abstractions from which she selected a response appropriate to the circumstances.

It is this last point that causes greatest concern among linguists. Was what Sarah used 'language' in any interesting sense? Premack has argued that Sarah was using language because she had mastered some of the processes Premack regarded as being basic to language. However, the total range of these processes was severely limited, as was the number of items manipulated within the processes. Sarah also did not attempt to make connections among the 'sentence' types, e.g. to relate statements to questions, affirmatives to negatives and so on. Children do make such connections without instruction. Obviously, certain very basic characteristics of human language were missing from the system that Sarah was asked to acquire. Such shortcomings, however, should not be allowed to detract from Premack's accomplishment because Sarah did learn a lot about something in a very short time. In one sense we know what she learned and how she learned it, but in another sense we do not. We cannot know if she learned a form of language unless we know exactly what language is, and, as we have seen, we are still not sure what exactly language is or what it means to say that someone 'knows' a language.

In still another experiment (Rumbaugh, 1977) a group of psychologists in Georgia were able to teach a two-year-old chimpanzee, Lana, to interact with a computer using a language, which they called Yerkish, that employs a set of specially designed characters. Once again the learning took place in a highly constrained environment. Lana was able to use the keyboard of the computer to manipulate a set of about 75 such characters so as to provide herself with drinks, bananas, sweets, toys and even films. To get what she wanted, Lana had to press the correct keys in the correct order, e.g. *please machine give banana period* or *please machine make music period* but not the unacceptable *please machine make banana period* or *please machine give music period*. Lana achieved a high degree of success – which varied with the complexity of the task from sixty-five to a hundred per cent – in getting what she wanted. She was able to find the right keys and orders in which she had to press them and to read various messages that were presented to her in Yerkish on a screen. She was also able to recognize and erase incorrect messages. Intriguing though this experiment with Lana was, its results are probably less interesting than those of the previous two experiments because of its much more limited scope. However, once again it deliberately circumvents the problem of speech and does try to capitalize on the strengths of chimpanzees as 'language' learners rather than to point out their weaknesses.

Other animals than Washoe, Sarah and Lana have participated in similar 'language' learning experiments. The chimpanzee Nim (Terrace, 1984; Terrace *et al.* 1979), also appeared to have learned to use a lot of signs, but a close analysis of those signs showed that Nim really had not learned much at all and may indeed have been a rather 'dumb' animal. The case of Koko, a gorilla (Patterson, 1978; Patterson and Linden, 1981), has received a great deal of publicity. Patterson claims that Koko is very communicative, e.g. that she can sign *I love Coca-Cola* by concurrently hugging herself ('love') and signing 'Coca-Cola' with her hands. However, there is considerable scepticism concerning many of the claims made on Koko's behalf and much of the discussion of Koko's abilities – or lack of them – has been very emotionally charged. The debate concerning just how well chimpanzees and gorillas perform as 'language learners' is certainly far from over.

As I have indicated, one of the basic characteristics of human language is that humans speak. No other species has this ability. Neither Washoe, Sarah nor Lana was required to speak, so in that respect they did not demonstrate the ability to use language. It now seems that chimpanzees and gorillas will never learn to speak even if they do manage to acquire some of the other characteristics of language. So the attempt the Hayes made to get Viki to speak was foredoomed to failure. Quite simply, as Philip Lieberman and his co-workers (Lieberman, 1968, 1975, 1984, 1991; Lieberman *et al*. 1972) seem to have demonstrated quite conclusively, only humans have the kind of vocal apparatus that speaking requires.

The ability to produce the sounds of language depends on having a bent vocal tract and the three cavities of the pharynx, mouth and nose. A bent vocal tract is a concomitant of upright posture. A well-developed pharynx also requires that the larynx be located low in the throat. The use of the nasal cavity also requires a very flexible velum. To some extent chimpanzees share the upright posture of humans. However, the chimpanzee does not have the necessary long pharynx and its larynx is located high in the pharynx. The flexible velum is also absent. Very young children also have high larynxes. Having such a high larynx is extremely useful in infancy, because it enables a young child to swallow and breathe at the same time without choking. It has a strong survival value then. As the child gets older, the larynx drops, the pharynx lengthens and speech as we know it becomes possible. However, such a change does not occur in chimpanzees and the larynx stays high. Speech as we know it is therefore impossible to both a new-born human child and a chimpanzee of any age.

The vocal folds of chimpanzees are also not as flexible as those of humans and there are fewer neural connections between the parts of the mouth and the brain in apes than in humans. In one experiment Lieberman used a computer simulation to reproduce the possible 'vowel space' of a rhesus monkey. He found the vowel space to be quite limited in contrast to the vowel space available to humans. The deficiency resulted almost entirely from the unavailability of an adequate pharyngeal cavity. Lieberman concluded that the rhesus monkey lacks the full articulatory apparatus essential for the production of human speech and that the human articulatory apparatus is species-specific. Essentially then, only humans can talk.

Lieberman's claim is not accepted universally. For example, Jordan (1971) has expressed another view on the matter. Following an acoustical analysis of sounds actually emitted by chimpanzees, he concluded that chimpanzees are quite capable of producing sounds in the same frequency range as humans. In Jordan's view a chimpanzee cannot produce such sounds because it is constrained cognitively and its central nervous system is inadequate for speech rather than because it has a deficient articulatory apparatus. But the end result, of course, is the same: chimpanzees lack the ability to speak like humans.

Investigators who have been concerned with issues such as those just mentioned regard speech as a critical component in language rather than as simply an accidental or peripheral characteristic. In this view, then, the animal studies therefore fail on this additional count, just as they failed on the count of in no way demonstrating that animals can do with whatever 'language' they have been taught many of the things that very young children can do with language without any instruction at all.

## Further investigation

1  Although chimpanzees and humans are closely related species they are still quite different species. Try to find out exactly how they differ and where language fits into that scheme of things. (You will also find out in doing so how closely they are alike!)

2  What would you consider to be a 'critical' test of an animal's language capability?

3  Recently Premack (1986) has expressed the view that investigations of the capability of animals for human-like behaviour have over-stressed language; he says that most investigators were 'infatuated' with language. He says that other 'specializations' of behaviour are likely to be more important in understanding similarities and differences between humans and non-humans and mentions pedagogy, aesthetics, cognition, social attribution and consciousness. Do you see any problem with such a view, i.e., with trying to define these

'specializations' that Premack mentions? (Note how important the definition of 'language' was in Premack's work with Sarah.)

## 2.3   The 'language' issue

The linguist Charles Hockett has tried to specify (Hockett, 1958, 1963; Hockett and Altmann, 1968) a number of essential characteristics of human language, which he has called 'design features'. The exact features that Hockett has proposed have varied from time to time and not every linguist would agree that such an approach to understanding language within a communicative framework is at all useful. Certainly the result is a kind of definition of language which is very different from the kinds of definition we usually find in either dictionaries or in books written by other linguists. However, it does merit our attention.

Since, according to Hockett, all the languages that humans speak possess this set of design features, it might be useful to compare any system of communication that animals use with the set in order to see which features such a system shares and which it lacks. Insofar as any system of animal communication fails to exhibit one or more of the named features it is at least that much different from language.

A key design feature of language is that it makes use of the 'vocal-auditory channel': i.e., language is speech. It is produced by the mouth and received by the ears. Many other species also use the vocal-auditory channel or just the auditory part of that channel, e.g. crickets. Still other species use quite different channels: visual (sticklebacks), tactile (bees?) and chemical (certain insects). Humans also use other channels to supplement what they communicate through speech; we also react to gesture, touch, smell and taste as well as sound. However, language is essentially speech. It is well to remember too that it is almost certainly the case that all existing writing systems ultimately derive from spoken language.

Human language is broadcast at large but allows speakers to be located. It is neither narrowly beamed to a specific receiver on the one hand nor broadcast in such a way that the source is completely unclear on the other. Anyone within earshot can hear what is said and can usually tell exactly who is speaking. Hockett calls this design feature 'broadcast transmission and directional reception'.

Speech itself is also 'rapidly fading'. The channel does not get cluttered up but remains open for use and re-use. A system that used smells would quickly become unserviceable because smells stay around for some time and mingle with other smells. A system that used concrete objects would create problems of storage and manipulation to keep the channel clear and it would also be extremely cumbersome, as Jonathan Swift pointed out in *Gulliver's Travels*. However, rapid fading requires that different kinds of memory must be available to process and store the fleeting signals used in the system. Humans do have such memories.

A fourth design feature is 'interchangeability'. Any human being can be both a sender and a receiver of messages once linguistic maturity has been achieved. In the animal world communication is often sex-linked, e.g. only male crickets chirp, or is restricted in some other way, e.g. only worker bees dance. Senders also have 'total feedback', in that speakers can monitor what they say. Just how much feedback bees get from their dancing is quite unclear. In the absence of feedback to their own voices human beings can sound quite strange, which is one of the reasons that makes teaching deaf people to speak so difficult or makes a person who has become deaf sometimes hard to understand. One interesting consequence of the presence of these last two features in human language is that people can also talk to themselves.

'Specialization' is a sixth design feature. Speech has no other biological function than communication. However, many animal communication systems are just as specialized, and possibly even more so in their narrowness. Bee dancing is obviously highly specialized. 'Semanticity', still another design feature, refers to the meaning content of the system: the system allows its users to say something. Language actually allows speakers to say anything they wish to say. On the other hand, the chirping of crickets probably lacks semanticity entirely and the bee dance has a very limited semantic content indeed, being about little more than possible food sources at the most. Human language, in contrast, is infinitely open, because people can introduce new topics at any time and the means for discussing these topics are always available.

The actual signals used in human language also possess the design feature of 'arbitrariness'. They bear no resemblance at all to the things they stand for, being almost completely non-iconic. The word *cat* has a completely arbitrary relationship to the animal named, as anyone can attest who knows how cats are named in other languages. In contrast, a bee dance directly represents to a considerable extent the quantity, distance, direction and even quality of the food source in the execution of the dance itself. A bee dance is highly iconic.

'Productivity' is a very important design feature. Language is infinitely productive in the variations that can occur in what is said. We constantly produce novel sentences and understand such sentences from others. A bee dance is also productive as bees pass on information about new food sources. However, you might well argue that to use a single term *productivity* to cover both types of behaviour is not particularly revealing and actually serves to reduce what is really a qualitative difference to a quantitative one.

The design feature of 'discreteness' refers to the fact that the system is made up of elements that are clearly distinguishable from one another. For example, *bin* and *pin* are clearly differentiated in their initial sounds in English. There is no sound intermediate between the initial sounds and there are no permissible gradations in these initial sounds, i.e., the sound that occurs is either a *b* or a *p*. Language is 'digital' rather than 'analogical' in its inner workings. Bee dancing lacks this same discreteness as any largely iconic system must.

Still another design feature of language, 'displacement', allows people to construct messages about the past, present and future, and also about both real and imaginary worlds. In contrast, gibbon calls are always about something present in the environment and bee dances about something in the immediate past. The first never exhibit displacement; the second always do. Human language is quite unconstrained in this way because we can talk about the past, present and future, and both the real and the imaginary.

Human language is also passed on by 'traditional transmission' in that the specific language a child acquires depends on the linguistic group into which that child is born. No one is genetically programmed to acquire a specific language, although we might all be programmed to acquire some language. Bees are programmed to dance, and an Italian bee raised in an Austrian hive will dance the Italian bee dance not the Austrian one. All languages are equally learnable so far as children are concerned and we can learn – though often not always easily – two or more languages. However, as we have seen, not even very 'bright' animals easily learn new systems of communication.

'Duality of patterning' is generally acknowledged to be the most distinctive design feature of language. Every human language makes use of two largely independent subsystems, one of sounds and the other of meanings. This feature enables a small number of elements of one subsystem (the phonemes, i.e., roughly sounds) to be combined and recombined into units and patterns of meaning (the morphemes and syntax, i.e., roughly words and sentences) in the other subsystem. No other species has a communication system that possesses this feature.

The final two design features are 'reflexiveness' and 'prevarication'. Once again these features may be unique to language. Reflexiveness refers to the use of language to talk about language, i.e., the system can be used to say something about the uses and characteristics of the system. It allows us to develop a 'metalanguage' – words like *noun, verb, sentence* and so on – so that we can discuss the kinds of phenomena that are our concern in this book. In contrast, dogs do not bark about barking nor do bees dance about dancing. Prevarication refers to the possible use of the system to mislead others deliberately. Human beings tell lies, i.e., they conjure up alternative worlds, some of which are deliberately false. Bees, however, do not lie about possible food sources. However, we do find the occasional report of an animal using deceptive communication; Lorenz himself cites the example of his own dog, who mistook him for a stranger and then, according to Lorenz, 'pretended' that a stranger had been present. But the evidence for any such deliberate prevarication is not at all strong.

These design features are obviously not all completely independent of one another. Some could not exist without others. For example, it would be impossible to lie if the system did not possess the features of semanticity, displacement and productivity. Lies depend on meaning, in this case falsity of meaning. They are also usually about things that cannot easily be verified in the immediate context unless they are deliberately bare-faced. A productive or open system is required since closed systems employ limited sets of calls that are entirely functional and 'honest'. Of course, not all prevarication may be bad. In one sense a hypothesis is a kind of lie. It is a particular claim that may be true or false, but it is clearly marked for what it is, in contrast to most ordinary lies. And, if it is a genuinely scientific hypothesis, it must be quite obvious how it can be disproved.

The features may also be interpreted to have an all-or-none quality about them. A system is either productive or not, arbitrary or not. As noted above, bee dancing is productive, but that productivity is very different from the productivity of human language. The design features have sometimes been recast to recognize this inadequacy and to make the list more coherent, orderly and sensitive to degrees of difference. Such a recasting emphasizes the importance of the channel, the setting and the purpose of the various speech acts and the internal structure of the communication system itself – its duality, arbitrariness and productivity.

It is, of course, quite possible to define language in many different ways. The approach using design features within a communicative framework is just one of many possibilities. The features are stated at a level of generality that encourages investigators to look for features that quite different systems share because most features allow for considerable latitude, e.g. one instance of prevarication may be as important as pervasive lying. However, the discovery of a single system with duality of patterning would be a very important – even linguistically earthshaking – discovery! It is just this kind of generality that Chomsky has warned about. In Chomsky's view, language is unique to humans and it is an exploration of that very uniqueness that should lie at the centre of linguistic endeavour, not investigations of what he regards as spurious connections to other systems of communication found elsewhere in nature. Most linguists agree with Chomsky's views on this matter.

## *Further investigation*

1 Compare Hockett's definition of language through the use of 'design features' with other definitions of language that you know. How useful is it?

2 Assess the various systems of communication that investigators developed for use between humans and apes according to Hockett's 'design features'. Were the investigators using 'language' in Hockett's sense?

3 If Hockett's 'design features' are useful in describing language, then we might assume that they evolved as our species evolved. A speculative issue you might address is the possible order in which the various features evolved.

## 2.4 The 'continuity' issue

In recent years a serious interest has developed in 'ethology', the study of animal behaviour in its natural setting rather than the study of such behaviour in the laboratory, the kind of behaviour that has long interested certain psychologists, for example. The natural behaviour that is studied can be of various kinds: behaviour brought about by 'releasers' or 'triggers' in the environment; the use of gestures, displays and other kinds of communicative behaviour; bonding and various forms of social organization; dominance and the assignment of space or 'territory'; the use of 'tools'; and so on. In particular, the behaviour of primates, our closest 'relatives' in nature, has come under very sharp scrutiny. It is not surprising, therefore, that certain investigators have been concerned with the language capabilities of these animals.

But may not any such capabilities that have been shown to exist only *look* like language? This is a possibility we must entertain in that there is something like a five-million-year separation between humans and chimpanzees, our nearest 'relatives' in nature, and, of course, a much greater separation from any other species. Are any abilities we claim to discover not something like the ability of B. F. Skinner's pigeons to play table tennis? Skinner's pigeons were able to knock a ping pong ball back and forward over a net and a photograph of this activity might well persuade some that the pigeons were actually playing table tennis. But playing table tennis requires that players keep score, be competitive, devise certain playing strategies and so on. The pigeons would also have to 'know' what they were doing. No one can claim that the pigeons were able to do any of these things. Similarly, language-like behaviour in the higher apes may be no closer to language than pigeon table-tennis playing is to Olympic competition in that sport.

All this is not to deny that the various animals mentioned above all learned something – many certainly learned to please their handlers – but that something does not appear to have been language. Nor did they learn what they learned in any way that resembles how children 'learn' language. We cannot even say that they learned a 'rudimentary form' of language because we have no idea at all of what a rudimentary form of language might be like, since it exists nowhere in the world.

It has become fashionable in some circles to regard humans as sophisticated primates or 'naked apes'. As I noted above, there are certainly many anatomical and physiological parallels between humans and primates. However, the psychological and sociocultural parallels are much more tenuous, even though many kinds of human and primate behaviour in these areas too can be shown to have common characteristics. Both humans and primates yawn, bare their teeth, scratch, cry out in pain, bristle with fear or anger, gesture and menace one another. Both differentiate sex roles, bring up their young in systematic ways, tend to 'know their places' in groups and are conscious of their territorial rights. We know too that both humans and some primates, in this case chimpanzees, are meat-eaters, food-sharers and tool-users, the zoologist Jane Goodall (1986, 1990) having witnessed chimpanzees eating a variety of meats, e.g. young monkeys, bush pigs and baboons, sharing food, and using sticks and chewed leaves as simple tools to collect termites and sponge up water. Some ethologists go so far as to see the primitive animal in just about everything people do, 'civilization' in this view being but the shallowest and frailest of veneers over an unchanged and possibly unchangeable 'animal' nature. Freudian psychiatry with its emphasis on instinctual patterns and deep-seated desires is another older variation on this same theme.

There are several difficulties with accepting this kind of biological determinism uncritically, of possibly over-emphasizing the 'continuity' of behaviour between animals and humans. The first concerns the vocabulary that is used to discuss both human and animal behaviour. It may be just as inappropriate to apply terms used for describing animal behaviour to human behaviour as vice versa. Certainly, extreme caution is necessary in talking about an animal's 'intentions', or about anything presumed to be going on in its 'mind', or about its 'intelligence'. It is possible to talk with a high degree of certainty about fixed instinctual patterns of behaviour in some animals because such patterns are clearly demonstrable. However, humans constantly transcend instinct because of their cognitive and linguistic resources. Humans are products of culture as well as nature. To say that nature nearly always gets the better when there is a conflict or that its 'laws' are immutable is either to deny that humans can change their lot through 'intelligent' behaviour and the resource that language provides, or to refuse to refine evolutionary theory to accommodate what humans have actually achieved. Another danger in the use of the same vocabulary is that of 'anthropomorphism': animal behaviour is seen in human terms from a human perspective. Semi-popular accounts of what animals can do have long suffered from anthropomorphism. Dolphins and chimpanzees have merely been the most recent beneficiaries – or victims!

Still another difficulty concerns any definition of natural behaviour that we attempt. As we make more and more observations of the behaviour of any species we notice more and more variations. Behaviour becomes more intricate rather than less intricate. For example, bee, dolphin and chimpanzee behaviour becomes more complicated to explain as the number of observations increases. But the greatest variation of all is in the patterns of behaviour that humans evince. 'Natural' human behaviour must be behaviour that is characteristic of all humans, but the weight of evidence from anthropological investigations is that few, if any, universal characteristics exist. I need cite only the example of movement and gesture, for which universal patterns have been assumed to exist among all humans. Evidently there are no universal facial expressions, gestures, stances or movements. People do move, manipulate and position their bodies and body parts in a wide variety of ways, but no single movement or gesture has the same communicative significance everywhere. Movements and gestures vary in their meanings according to the cultures in which they are found. They are learned behaviours.

Another difficulty concerns the level of generality at which investigators have attempted to state relationships between animals and humans. It is really of little interest that both consume oxygen; it may be of more interest that there are certain anatomical and physiological relationships between primates and humans, as, for example, in brain organization and blood chemistry. We know that medical researchers have long used rats, dogs and monkeys in their work because of their numerous resemblances to humans. But most psychologists have denied that these animals also share psychological characteristics with humans, except for a very few characteristics which they have been able to manipulate and extrapolate from in their laboratories.

It would be of very considerable interest indeed if the properties that essentially characterize language could be shown to exist elsewhere in the animal world. But if, as Chomsky (1967) has pointed out, the level of connection that is usually established between language and animal communication allows you to say no more than animal walking is like speech in showing some purpose and internal principles of organization, such an observation is completely vacuous. In Chomsky's opinion it is not any resemblance that language shows to other communication systems that is important but rather what especially characterizes language itself, i.e., what language really is and not what it is like. To use another example, walking, swimming and flying are all forms of locomotion, but little can be learned about any one of them from stressing what all have in common as forms of locomotion. Walking is neither swimming nor flying; it is walking. The real issue concerns what walking itself is, what the principles are that go into it. Similarly, the real issue is what language itself is, what its organizing principles are.

Speaking itself as an activity often looms large in definitions of language, as is deciding whether or not any other species is capable of acquiring language. But language ability is more than just the use of speech; it involves the complex manipulation of sets of signs. It is quite obvious that species other than the human species can manipulate signs and engage in complex forms of signing behaviour. What is crucial in this regard is whether any other species has the capacity to handle the syntactic organization of human signing in which finite systems of principles and operations allow users to create sentences out of an infinite set of possibilities. Only humans appear to have this capacity; it is almost certainly species-specific.

One consequence is that all languages are alike in certain respects, all children acquire language in very much the same way and all languages are equally easy – or difficult – for those who acquire them as children. Everyone learns a language and uses it in much the same way for much the same purposes and with relatively little variation in either time or space. If this is so, language is inherently different from any kind of communication system found in any other species. Eric Lenneberg, for example, argued (Lenneberg, 1967) that any similarities noted between language and animal communication rest on superficial intuition and are spurious rather than real, logical rather than biological.

In this view the experiments with the chimpanzees tell us nothing at all about what language is. Similarly, experiments with the speech capacities of various vocal tracts tell us nothing. Such experiments can show us only what kinds of limits prevail in certain species and under what conditions. Constructing definitions of language cannot tell us anything either, nor can specifying sets of design features. If language must have a speech component, must allow anything that can be thought to be talked about, must be efficient yet possess a certain amount of redundancy and must allow for two-way communication among those who use it, then language is unique to the human species.

However, if language is no more than a system for manipulating signs rather than objects, then many species would have some kind of language. Since different investigators draw the line between these two extreme positions in very different places they come inevitably to very different conclusions. But you can also argue that all such attempts to specify what language is are misguided. You find out what language is, not by making definitions and saying how they apply, but by looking closely at language and seeing what kinds of principles you require to account for your observations.

## Further investigation

1 Lord Monboddo, an eighteenth-century British philosopher and dilettante, considered that orang-utans were really some kind of primitive humans who had never succeeded in 'discovering' language. Other people have claimed that at some time in the past humans 'invented' language. Does it make any sense to use 'discover' or 'invent' in such a context?

2 Linden (1974) views the language experiments with chimpanzees as revolutionary in their implications for understanding our (i.e., humans') place in nature, declaring in one rhetorical flourish that 'the chimpanzee in the temple of language is really Darwin wreaking havoc in the temple of Plato'. How would you propose to continue research in this area? What new questions would you want to pursue? Why? How?

3 In assessing her 30 years of work with chimpanzees, Goodall (1990) mentions that because of their lack of language, chimpanzees seem to be 'trapped within themselves'. The implication is that with language chimpanzees would be able to give full expression to something inside them. Consider the following questions. If a chimpanzee could talk what would it talk about? What would a cat talk about if it could talk? You should be aware that some philosophers consider the following question to be completely meaningless: What is it like to be a cat?

4 Many investigators have found work with great apes to be extremely rewarding and their devotion to their work and to the apes is considerable. In every case there has been the inevitable language barrier. You might look at how different investigators have attempted to cross or ignore that barrier.

# 3

# *Are we 'wired' for language?*

As I indicated in the first chapter it is a fundamental assumption of modern linguistic approaches to the study of language that what we should be concerned with is speech rather than writing. Some readily observable facts can be cited to support this assumption: while speaking is universal, writing is not; the written forms of all languages are based on their spoken forms not vice versa; in the history of the human species the development of speech preceded the development of writing; and, finally, each human individual usually learns to speak before learning to write. Linguists therefore consider the 'primacy' of speech to be a virtually undeniable fact about language. We should not be surprised then to observe a 'phonetic bias', i.e., a strong emphasis on speech, in much linguistic investigation. None of what I have said though denies the importance of writing because writing certainly is important; it just does not happen to be central to 'linguistic' concerns, although it may well be central to other concerns and indeed it too may have significant linguistic characteristics.

It is of considerable interest that human communication in the form of language depends on sounds pronounced within mouths and perceived by ears rather than on some other sensory system or systems, particularly the gestural–visual system. As we have seen, other species communicate through visual systems (e.g. sticklebacks), or combinations of visual and call systems (e.g. certain birds and animals) and so on. Although humans have extremely good vision, such vision being necessary in their ancestors to ensure survival among trees and on the savannas, the part of human communication that depends on gesture and vision – facial expression, posture and movement – seems very much underdeveloped for communication in comparison with the part that shows no such dependency, language itself.

Humans everywhere do use gestures either to supplement speech or to replace it entirely on occasion; hand waves, blows, kisses and shrugs, for example, may communicate at times much more effectively than words. This universal use of gestures has led more than one investigator (see Hewes, 1975, for a comprehensive bibliography on this general topic) to consider that language itself grew out of 'primitive' gestural systems, i.e., that gestures were the precursor of language as we know it now. However, most such ideas on this matter are highly speculative and address few of the issues that must be confronted if you are to make any very serious attempt to explain the ultimate origins of language. (I will make reference to some of these issues from time to time.)

Communication systems that employ gestures and depend on vision also have serious limitations. If the communication system makes extensive use of the hands, then the hands cannot be used for activities like carrying and climbing. If there is little or no light, the gestures may be misinterpreted or cannot be seen at all. If the potential users are out of view of one another communication is out of the question. Gesture inventories themselves must necessarily be quite small because of limitations of production, recognition and memory. (The sign language of the deaf does overcome many of these limitations but does so by being language-based.) We know too how ambiguous gestures can be. On the other hand, language allows speakers to use sounds in order to send any one message 'selected' from an infinite set of messages and it also allows listeners to figure out which message was sent with a very high degree of confidence. Information theorists have calculated that the 'channel' that sound provides for communication is vastly superior to the one that vision might have provided: its carrying capacity is enormous.

Humans have, of course, developed a special means of very efficient communication that does employ vision: they have developed various writing systems. However, as I have said, such systems are always based on the spoken language in one way or another and individuals almost always acquire their knowledge of one or more of them after they have learned to listen and speak. Certain writing systems – English is sometimes cited as an example – apparently cause some of their learners considerable problems. They are said to be difficult to learn and sometimes the difficulty is attributed to the complexity of the visual and cognitive processes that are involved in acquiring a thorough knowledge of the details and abstractions of the system. (However, there may also be a strong cultural component in the actual learning process itself because although the Japanese writing system is acknowledged to be one of the most 'difficult' in the world, Japanese children are reported to be highly literate!) On the other hand, children acquiring their first language usually experience little or no difficulty, even in situations in which some are severely handicapped.

## 3.1   Are mouths and ears important?

The fact that language makes use of sounds in systematic ways differentiates it quite clearly from all other kinds of communication systems. Other species communicate in different ways, e.g. visual, tactile, chemical, olfactory or auditory. Humans alone use the vocal–auditory channel in a very special way and alone appear to have the ability to do so. Humans are also unique in the vast auditory memories they have. However, as we saw in the previous chapter, the communication systems of certain other species seem to exhibit some of the same general characteristics that provide some kind of foundation for the human system. These characteristics may be present only in greater quantity in language, so that the human system is only 'quantitatively' different from other systems of communication. On the other hand, language may have unique characteristics and be 'qualitatively' different from all other systems. We will consider this second view.

As a broad characterization, we can say that language makes use of sounds produced with air originating in the lungs and flowing out of the body through the windpipe and then through the mouth and nose. Human ears then perceive these sounds. Lungs, windpipes, mouths, noses and ears do not exist for speech alone; speech is not even their primary function. Lungs, windpipes and mouths exist for breathing, mouths also for eating and ears for monitoring the environment. Speech is a secondary 'overlaid' function of all of these organs. That is, while we can say that humans have 'speech organs' we must remember that these are not organs whose primary purpose is speech.

One of the most discussed speech organs is the larynx because of its function and also its unique positioning in humans. The adult human larynx is placed low in the respiratory tract in comparison with the larynxes of other species and even in comparison with the position of the larynx in the human infant. The human larynx 'drops' between infancy and adulthood. A high larynx is useful in that it allows for concurrent respiration and ingestion of food, so babies rarely choke to death (in contrast to adults). However, a high larynx severely restricts the kinds of sounds that can be made in the vocal tract above the larynx. Lieberman (1984, 1991) claims that language as we know it requires a low larynx and that the human infant is quite incapable of speech. However, as even Darwin himself observed, that same low larynx does exact its price on humans, as thousands choke to death each year when food 'goes down the wrong way'.

One very interesting issue is to try to find out when in the history of the human species the particular arrangement of organs that we have finally came about. There are several intriguing problems to consider here because chimpanzees, for example, and many other animals have the same organs. However, the human organs are uniquely related to one another. Students of human evolution are not at all agreed as to how and when the modern human (*homo sapiens sapiens*) arrangement occurred. One current view is that it is a relatively recent phenomenon (see Lieberman, 1984, 1991). An important corollary of such a view would be that language as we know it is a fairly recent phenomenon, perhaps as recent as 30,000 or 40,000 years.

When we examine what happens in speaking in some detail we discover some very interesting things. The normal breathing rate is about a dozen breaths each minute and, in the absence of speech, inhalation and exhalation each occupy about half of this time; moreover, any interference with this rate and with the regularity of inhalation and exhalation when not speaking soon causes certain types of distress, e.g. hyperventilation. However, in speaking, we inhale very rapidly and exhale very slowly but this fundamental change in breathing associated with speaking does not cause us any problems. Normal speech also occurs at a rate of between 200 and 300 syllables each minute and involves movement in perhaps a hundred different muscles in the production of about eight 'phonemes', i.e., sounds, each second. Consequently, we must have the means for co-ordinating the various parts of the articulatory apparatus in ways that are quite irrelevant to their basic functioning in breathing and eating, ways too which must be highly 'automatic', i.e., be beyond any kind of conscious control.

Linguists usually begin any consideration of the use of sound in language with consideration of the various events that occur in the upper respiratory tract during the production of speech. They tend to focus on how the sounds of language are articulated rather than on how they are perceived. Such an approach is quite defensible. Most such articulations can be observed, and it is also quite possible to see and feel much of what happens in the vocal apparatus. On the other hand, ears, or at least what happens within them, are almost completely inaccessible to any such observation.

Various other procedures and devices can also be used to observe what happens in speech, but linguists generally find it quite easy to justify not using many of them in their day-to-day work on languages. Laryngoscopy, spectrography, dynamic palatography, electromyography, ultrasonics, cineradiography and so on could all be used. However, most linguists – and I include many phoneticians here – tend to argue that the really important facts about the sound systems of languages cannot be detected from just simply noting what such instruments record or allow you to observe. Such devices do provide valuable data on certain physical events, e.g. which parts of the articulatory apparatus are in motion, what air pressures exist in various cavities, what electrical discharges are occurring as muscles move and so on. However, it is important language facts that underlie these events. These facts are abstractions such as the phonemes I mentioned in the first chapter, and no device, no matter how sophisticated it is, can identify a phoneme. The observable events are realizations of abstractions but we cannot easily use them to tell us all we need to know about these abstractions. Hence the failure so far to produce computer programs that will allow even very sophisticated computers to 'speak' messages from written text in a completely naturalistic manner or to capture in writing what you say to them.

Speech does not consist of a series of events that can be clearly discriminated one from the other in a purely mechanical way. Actual speech is a series of overlapping events, and understanding it requires a considerable amount of mental activity on the part of a listener, just as it involves a considerable amount of both mental and physical ability on the part of the speaker. Speech is a continuum because the tongue does not move from one fixed position, instantaneously as it were, to another, stop, then go on to a third, stop again, and so on. Nor does any other part of the body involved in the production of speech. Every study that has examined speaking through the use of devices such as those mentioned above has confirmed this fact. The individual sounds of speech about which we speak so casually are really mental constructs realized in waves of physical activity, but they are not those waves of activity themselves.

The phoneme is a mental construct. It is a reference point in an abstract system. That is where its 'reality' is. When we say that the first sound in *pin* is the phoneme /p/ we are making a claim about how the minds of speakers of English work and not merely a statement about a specific sound we find to occur in English. An essential part of the /p/ phoneme in English is that there is a whole set of other phonemes that contrast with it, e.g. /b/ in *bin* and /f/ in *fin*. In a real sense part of the 'reality' of the /p/ in English is that it is neither /b/ nor /f/. However, at the same time we must not forget that the abstract system itself can exploit only the actual sounds humans can make and therefore that the physical capabilities of humans do play an important role in speech. These capabilities are also different from those of other species. It is important therefore to look at what those capabilities are.

The human vocal apparatus (see Denes and Pinson, 1963) produces sounds much as does a trumpet. That is, a stream of air is forced through a series of chambers – in the case of speech these are the throat, the various parts of the mouth and sometimes the nose – and these chambers act as resonators. In the average adult male the throat and mouth have a length of about seven inches, measured from the vocal cords to the lips. A pipe of such a length, even a soft bent pipe in this case, produces a basic concentration of 'frequencies', called a 'first formant' at about

500 cycles per second (500Hz), within the total speech range of 50 to 10,000Hz (one cycle per second equals one Herz). The greatest concentration of this kind of energy lies in the range of 100 to 600Hz. Other similar concentrations, i.e., formants, characteristically appear at intervals of roughly a thousand cycles per second in pipes of this length, and so it is with speech. The second and third formants at approximately 1500Hz and 2500Hz combine with the first formant to give the sounds of speech their recognizable character.

Modifications within this pipe, in this case modifications in the vocal tract, shift the first formant and also alter the characteristic relationship of the formants to one another. The sounds of speech achieve their individual characters from the specific modifications used in their production. Such modifications also produce 'noise' of different kinds, i.e., sounds that lack the kinds of concentrations mentioned above. Since women and children also usually have shorter vocal tracts than adult males, their voices are characterized by formants with higher frequency concentrations and greater separation of the formants. In addition, women and children tend to have 'higher' voices, i.e., they speak or sing in a higher vocal register because their vocal cords are generally shorter and thinner than those of men and also vibrate considerably faster, at 200 to 300Hz rather than at 100 to 150Hz.

We can identify English vowel sounds by their first three formants. The first two formants alone provide most of the information a listener needs in order to identify vowels correctly; the third formant eliminates any possible ambiguities that would exist if only the first two formants were made to carry all the necessary distinctions. A three-dimensional system of this kind is much more efficient than a two-dimensional system, particularly when there is so much individual variation in voices from speaker to speaker within each sex, and across the sexes and various ages. It is also possible to say what the average frequency concentration (in Hz) of the three formants is for all English vowels. For example, for the vowel in *beet* it is 270, 2290 and 3010 for men and 310, 2790 and 3310 for women, and for the vowel in *boot* it is 300, 870 and 2240 for men and 370, 950 and 2670 for women. It is of some interest also to note how easily we learn to calibrate 'typical' male, female and child pronunciations when there is actually a very considerable range in the frequencies we must deal with.

It is of some interest too that 'unround' and 'round' vowels of similar height, as in *beet* and *boot* – these are both 'high' vowels, the first is a high 'front' vowel pronounced with unrounded lips and the second a high 'back' vowel pronounced with rounded lips – have formant structures that are clearly very different and therefore readily distinguishable by the human ear. It is also the second formant that is particularly responsible for this distinctiveness (see Wang, 1971). Round front vowels and unround back vowels of the same height are nowhere near as distinctive, so it is perhaps not surprising that we find many languages in which front unround vowels contrast with back round vowels but in which roundedness in front vowels and unroundedness in back vowels are either infrequent or entirely lacking. Moreover, we never find the latter characteristic without finding the former, i.e., if there are round front vowels and unround back vowels there must also be unround front vowels and round back vowels. English is a good example of a language with only unround front vowels and round back vowels, and French of a language with both unround and round front vowels and round back vowels. The vowel systems of languages therefore appear to owe some of their characteristics to what ears can hear and clearly distinguish. Humans do not use all the possibilities that the vocal tract offers them.

Speech is both produced and heard. In some ways it seems surprising that speech is heard at all because it has so little intrinsic power and is so fleeting. It has been calculated that if 15 million people were to speak in an auditorium – necessarily a rather large one! – without the assistance of amplification, they would collectively generate only a single horsepower of acoustic energy. Similarly, a hundred people hammering energetically on steel plates would produce only enough acoustic energy to light a single 100 watt light bulb if that energy could be converted to electrical power.

The human ear, however, is an extremely sensitive instrument and is well able to respond to sounds of very low and subtly different degrees of loudness and to very small differences in frequency. In fact, it is so sensitive that in ideal conditions the ear can detect differences not much greater than the random movements of individual molecules of air. The weakness and fleetingness of speech also have advantages for communication.

As previously indicated, sounds can coexist without losing their individual identities and they also disappear very quickly. The result is that more than one person can speak at a time, the human voice can be heard against other noises and the vocal–auditory channel does not get cluttered up with old information. Instead, the auditory channel constantly maintains its availability to all who seek to use it and allows considerable freedom in that use. Of course, what this implies too is that humans must have some kind of ability to detect certain kinds of sounds, to process them and to remember them. Consequently, 'hearing' does not occur in the ears alone.

The ear is also important to the voice, not only because people usually talk to one another rather than to themselves, but also because they monitor their own speech. Speakers listen to what they are saying. They not only feel the movements of their own speech organs but are also aware of the sounds they are making, even to the extent of being sensitive to the conduction of those sounds through the bones in the head. Such feedback is very important to the production of coherent speech. Anesthesia, deafness, drugs and deliberate speech delay through experimental procedures can seriously disturb the mouth–ear link. The congenitally deaf do not speak normally because they cannot hear and monitor themselves in addition to not being able to hear others.

We measure the loudness of sound in units called decibels (db). It has been estimated that a whisper source at four to five feet is about 20db, night noises in a city about 40db, quiet speech about 45db, conversation on the telephone or at a distance of three feet between 60 and 70db, loud shouting about 85db and a pneumatic drill at a distance of three feet about 90db. Humans experience hearing discomfort beginning at about 110db and actual pain begins at about 120db, which is often the sound level of amplified rock music listened to at close range.

When we hear a sound there is also a subtle relationship between its frequency and its loudness. A sound of a particular frequency must have a certain loudness before we can hear it at all. There is a hearing threshold for each sound. Whereas ninety per cent of humans can hear a pure tone of 1000Hz at 30db in ideal conditions, none can hear a pure tone of 100Hz at 30db. Less than fifty per cent can hear a pure tone of 10,000Hz at 30db. However, if the intensity of a pure tone of 100Hz is increased to 55db and one of 10,000Hz is increased to 65db, then over ninety per cent of humans can hear these tones at the new levels.

People also vary in their hearing thresholds, revealing different abilities to detect sounds. Whereas ninety per cent can hear a pure tone of 1000Hz at 30db, only twenty-five per cent can detect a similar tone at 10db. However, people are fairly consistent in reacting to loud sounds, e.g. any sound within the normal frequency range of human speech that achieves a loudness of about 140db causes very considerable pain. While the hearing threshold varies considerably, the pain threshold is apparently more uniform.

The frequency and loudness of sounds are related in still another way. Listeners will judge a 'pure tone', i.e., a sound with a single unchanging frequency, of 100Hz at 50db to be as loud as a pure tone of 1000Hz at 30db and one of 10,000Hz at 20db. However, at 90db the first two tones will be judged to be still equally loud whereas the third will not be perceived to be as loud as the other two. At 60db the tone at 1000Hz will be judged to be a little louder than the tone at 10,000Hz, and the tone at 100Hz will be perceived to be considerably less loud than either of the other two tones.

The human ear is also capable of detecting variations in pure tones of as small as two or three cycles per second in tones below 1000Hz. Altogether as many as 1000 differences are distinguishable in ideal experimental conditions. Together with the approximately 300 perceptually different levels of loudness that are distinguishable in the same conditions, this total number of differences would allow for the existence of as many as one third of a million potentially distinguishable pure tones. So it is from a potential range such as this that we fashion our ability to recognize the many different human voices that we eventually come to discriminate, once again with a large contribution from human memory.

Speaking and listening nearly always occur in less than ideal conditions because all kinds of noises exist in the environment, the tones of speech are not pure tones, and individuals may differ considerably from one another in their realizations of the different contrasts, as we saw in just what qualities they give to the vowels in *beet* and *boot*. A particular language therefore exploits only a very few of the great many possibilities within the total acoustic 'space' that is theoretically available. The human ear is most sensitive to differences of sound when the tones are 50db above the hearing threshold and within the frequency range of 500 to 4000Hz. It should come as no surprise then to find that the sound systems of languages make maximal use of exactly the acoustic space the human ear prefers to use when it might also have used other parts of the space.

The individual sounds of speech vary considerably in their loudness. In English the vowels are 'stronger,' or louder, than the consonants, with the low back vowel in a word like *talk* the strongest vowel of all. High vowels, front or back, as in *beet* or *boot*, are 'weaker' than low vowels, possessing no more than a third of their loudness. This difference in vowel loudness is mainly attributable to the first formant, which is stronger in low vowels than in high, the mouth being more open in their production. The strongest consonant is the initial consonant of a word like *red*, but it is no stronger than the weakest vowel. However, it is more than twice as strong as the initial consonant of *ship*, six times as strong as the initial consonant of *no* and over 200 times as strong as the weakest consonant of all, the initial consonant of *thin*. It should not be surprising therefore that words containing this last sound cause certain children difficulty in both listening and speaking.

People, of course, have two ears not one. Having two ears allows us to locate sound sources and to perceive the environment as a rich auditory texture in the same way that having two eyes allows depth and richness of vision. Experiments (Kimura, 1967; Shankweiler, 1971; Studdert-Kennedy and Shankweiler, 1970) which delay the arrival of sound for a fraction of a second to one ear but not to the other result in listeners incorrectly locating the source of a sound. Creating a slight delay in arrival in the right ear moves the apparent sound source further to the left; however, a slight increase in the loudness of the signal to the right ear will move the apparent source of the sound back to the right again. Such binaurality, together with the accompanying ability to move the head very slightly in order to compare very small differences in sounds, is not only important to people in locating a sound source but is also important in allowing them to focus on specific sounds and types of sound. Humans can actually localize a sound source to within about ten degrees. They can also pick out one voice from a number of voices or hear two or more sounds concurrently without those sounds necessarily blending into one another to form a single sound. In like circumstances two or more colours always blend to form one. These abilities, of course, are not abilities of the ear itself (or the ears) but of the central nervous system, i.e., the brain, since it is our brains that are really responsible for what we hear.

There is at least one further interesting consequence of binaurality in humans: for most people the right ear appears to be more responsive to speech sounds than the left ear, which in turn appears to respond better to musical and environmental sounds. The right ear is also more adept at perceiving consonants than the left ear. If the stimulus word *top* is presented to the right ear while the stimulus word *pop* is presented to the left ear, listeners will tend to report hearing the first word rather than the second. However, presenting *pop* in one ear and *pip* in the other produces only random results, since there seems to be no ear preference for vowels. These last findings may turn out to have an explanation for, as we will see in the following section of this chapter, an important fact about language is that some of its functions are 'lateralized' in the brain, i.e., located on one side rather than the other.

The human ear is an amazing instrument. It can detect subtle differences in frequency and loudness, distinguish between pure tones and 'noise', i.e., sounds composed of randomly assigned frequencies, and catch exquisite differences in timing, as, for example, the different onsets of 'voicing', i.e., vibration in the vocal cords, at the beginnings of *tan* and *dan*. The brain obviously plays a very important part in any such activity, but we must not underestimate what the ear itself does. It could handle a communication channel of enormous complexity. That it is not required to do so is an interesting fact. Therefore, the constraints on language systems that people use are not imposed solely by the 'peripheral organs', the mouth and ears. The constraints are mainly central, arising from characteristics of the brain, the nervous system and the mind, whatever the latter is. They are therefore constraints within the 'language organ' itself rather than within the speech organs.

The brain must somehow guide the mouth and ears in what they do. Certain properties and relations must be present if a particular message is to be produced or received. To take one obvious example: a child, a woman or a man will all pronounce a word differently, e.g. the word *cat*, yet they will all be perceived to have said the 'same word'. Just about every one of its parts may be shown to be physically different in each case, but in each case the overall relationship of the parts of the word and the relationship of those parts to a kind of base line demonstrate a pattern which is recognizably the 'same' at some level of abstraction. The linguist is interested above all in this abstraction because this is where the truly important facts of language are presumed to be located.

We can readily confirm that the kinds of acoustic information that the ear and the brain must process are often limited in serious ways. We know that people are more hesitant in identifying vowel sounds than consonant sounds. They usually perceive the latter to be quite clearly one sound or another, but they must assess the former in relation to other vowels in the surrounding message. We may be quite sure that what we are hearing is *pat* not *cat*, but we may not be so sure that we are hearing *pat* rather than *pot* and we may need to hear some other words containing other vowels, e.g. *pet, put* and *port*, before we fully trust our judgement. The same sound, that is 'same' so far as its acoustical properties are concerned, may even be identified differently in different environments (Liberman *et al.* 1952). Even consonant sounds can be so affected. For example, exactly the same noise burst produced by a speech synthesizer before *eep, oop* and *op* may be identified as a *p*-like sound in the first two cases (*peep* and *poop*) and a *k*-like sound in the last (*cop*). While your ears are extremely sensitive to the various frequencies, loudnesses and relative durations used in speech, how your brain interprets what your ears 'hear' is another matter.

Speech also turns out to be remarkably resilient. Experiments (Miller, 1951) using either treated samples of ordinary speech or artificially synthesized speech have shown that if we omit certain kinds of loudness usually present in speech, the message can still be understood. It seems to make little difference to the intelligibility of speech that certain very loud or very soft sounds are not transmitted at all; the message remains clearly intelligible in the absence of the two peaks because the majority of its 'information' is packed between those peaks. A small amount of peak-clipping can actually make a message more intelligible rather than less intelligible because the consonants become more discriminably different as the loudness of the vowels is reduced. On the other hand, centre-clipping, i.e., cutting out sounds of middle intensity, leads to unintelligibility and distortion.

Other kinds of 'filtering' and 'masking' sometimes have little effect too on the intelligibility of speech, e.g. eliminating certain frequencies, interrupting by regularly excising minute parts of a message along the time axis, varying the loudness levels of the different frequencies that are present, changing the fundamental frequency of the voice, slowing down or speeding up the message with or without accompanying changes of frequency and even systematically delaying parts of the signal. Experiments show that hearing speech is relatively impervious to many such experimental changes. So far as the need to hear your own voice while speaking is concerned, however, we know that a delay of as little as one-fifth of a second in hearing your own voice can seriously disconcert a speaker, putting the speaker's speech production out of phase and inducing hesitations, repetitions, stammering and sometimes shouting.

Normal speech is massively 'redundant' and contains much more information than listeners really need in order to decide what is being said. Consequently, speech can be used in situations that contain different kinds of potential hindrances to communication. It can be used over the telephone, over poor radio links, by the partially deaf, in noisy surroundings and so on. If it were not so redundant it could not be used in such circumstances. But listeners do not merely perceive the sounds of language without any direct involvement of the mental processes; they must interpret what they hear. This interpretation occurs centrally in the brain not peripherally in the ears, because it is the brain which guides and for the most part controls what it is the ears hear, just as it controls what it is the mouth says. In this view, then, language is essentially a mental rather than a physical activity.

## Further investigation

1  Try to find out as much as you can about how voice quality relates to such factors as age, sex and social class, and possibly

to which language someone speaks. Are any differences you find attributable to learning, i.e., are acquired rather than innate?

2  Try to explain in as much detail as you can everything that happens in your vocal apparatus when you pronounce a word like *cool*. What differences are there between pronouncing *cool* and pronouncing *keel*, *coop* and *fool*? Say these four words over and over again in sequence and changing the order from time to time and consider exactly what kinds of 'instructions' are involved in pronouncing them.

3  The comic operas of Gilbert and Sullivan contain a number of well-known 'patter' songs in which the words are sung very quickly. Try to listen to one or two of these (and sing them too). How easy (or difficult) is this? Why?

4  Listen carefully to the sounds in your environment on different occasions. What exactly do you hear? How do you recognize what you are hearing for what it is?

5  Try to listen to two things at the same time, e.g. words and words, words and music, two different languages. (The ready availability of recorders and ear phones may allow you to control which ear hears which.) Try to find out why you 'hear' certain things but do not 'hear' other things.

6  The fact that certain birds, e.g. parrots, can utter comprehensible speech does raise important questions about the need for the human larynx (a bird has a syrinx). How do such birds actually produce the sounds they do?

7  One of the reasons we recognize speech is that it is considerably 'redundant'. So is writing. Look at these two sentences:

Th– c–t s–t –n th– m–t
– –e –a– –a– o– – –e –a–

One of the conclusions you might draw here is that vowels seem to be more redundant, i.e., omissible, than consonants. From the same sentence you can omit the two *the*s and still understand it but you cannot omit any of the other words. (This is the principle you use in sending telegrams.) You can also omit every third letter and still understand a lot:

Th– ca– sa– on –he –at.

How useful is this concept of redundancy in trying to understand how people understand speech (and writing)?

Remember that if there were no redundancy at all then there would be no room for 'error' in sending messages because each sound or letter would be critically important to getting your message across.

## 3.2   The puzzle of the brain

During the production and reception of speech, signals are being sent through the central nervous system. These signals originate in the brain in the case of speech and eventually cause various muscles of the jaw, larynx, mouth, tongue, lips and so on to move. In the case of listening, some of the activity must also proceed in the opposite direction, i.e., from the periphery to the centre. However, in both speaking and listening, it is the brain that exercises control of the various activities of the nervous system.

Experiments have shown that the brain itself is particularly well adapted to controlling the muscles used in speech. We know that the 'motor' activities of the lips and tongue are regulated by areas of the brain much greater in size than those that regulate the motor activities of many other parts of the body. (It is of some interest too that the areas of the brain that regulate the motor activities of the hands and fingers are also large in contrast to those that regulate the feet and toes.) The muscles of the tongue and lips in humans are also much more developed in their neurology than they are in any closely related species. In fact, such development is far in advance of any development required just simply for breathing and eating. We do not even need the kinds of teeth we have if teeth existed solely for eating – and we also have too many of them for the kind of jaw we have, hence all those compacted wisdom teeth we suffer from!

Speaking is particularly sophisticated in the very fine signalling that is involved in its production and programming. Minute differences must be produced and sequenced with exquisite timing. Listening requires equally fine detection abilities. We know that one essential way in which *den* and *ten* are articulated differently is that in *ten* there is a delay of as little as four hundredths of a second in 'voicing' the vowel, i.e., in setting the vocal cords in motion after the tongue is removed from behind the top teeth to articulate the *t*, but there is no corresponding delay after a similar removal of the tongue to articulate the *d* in *den*. Such movements are controlled through the nervous system and normally articulated speech requires a large number of them each second, all finely co-ordinated. Therefore, the nervous system is actively involved in the production of speech. It is, itself, of course, directly under the control of a very sophisticated central resource, the brain.

As we find out more and more about the neural transmission of language signals, we come to a better understanding of how the structure of the system itself imposes limitations on both the production and reception of speech. The system has characteristics that limit its capability; it can do only so much and it must do what it does in certain ways. For example, everything else being equal, electrochemical neural impulses take longer to travel over long nerve fibres to effector cells in the system than they take to travel over short nerve fibres. Impulses that must travel over thin nerve fibres also travel slower than those that must travel over thick nerve fibres. Facts like these are inescapable and we must recognize them when we give serious consideration to how the brain is involved in the production and reception of language. The brain's instructions to the various speech organs must be programmed in a way that allows for the desired sequences of movements to be realized. Yet the various signals do not all travel at the same speed to the effector cells because their neural pathways differ considerably in both length and width. Therefore, the brain must have the ability to take such differences into account in issuing the instructions it sends out to the various body parts.

While the brain is obviously important in the production and reception of speech, much still remains to be discovered about its internal structure and functions. We know that the importance of the human brain does not derive exclusively from its absolute size. Elephants and whales have larger brains, and the brain of a mature blue whale is actually about five times larger than the brain of an adult human. On the other hand, a dwarf's brain may be very small indeed. The Neanderthal brain was also at least the same size as the modern human brain. What modern humans do have though is the best brain–body weight ratio of any species.

The importance of the human brain seems to derive mainly from its complexity, i.e., the massive number of cells – perhaps ten billion – and the connections among those cells, the alternative pathways that are available within it, the large expanses of surface areas within the brain that fold onto one another, the brain's enormous redundancies and an overall asymmetry. It has often been said that human brains are qualitatively different rather than quantitatively different from the brains of other species and there seems little reason to doubt such a claim. However, only a very small part of the human brain seems to be directly involved in language activity. The lower part of the brain, the 'stem', controls functions such as the beating of the heart and respiration; it is the upper part of the brain, the 'cerebrum', that is involved in the 'higher' processes, with language being by far the most interesting of these.

A brain is a difficult object to study. It is impossible to probe into and experiment on a living human brain for linguistic purposes alone. Any understanding of the relationship between language and the brain must be gained in indirect ways, usually from the incidental and accidental effects of research and experimentation primarily conducted for medical reasons. Or it must be gained through trying to relate particular kinds of linguistic evidence to evidence produced by post-mortems, as in the case of 'aphasia', i.e., language loss or deficiency brought about by brain damage through accidents, tumours, strokes, etc. Millions of people suffer varying degrees of such damage, which is also often accompanied by other physical and intellectual deficits.

Aphasia can affect language ability in a wide variety of ways (Goodglass and Kaplan, 1983). It can lead to a total loss of ability to use language or it may affect just one or more types of language ability, e.g. naming objects, recalling words, repeating something that was just said, using certain sounds, comprehending writing and so on. Aphasia may result in what sounds like a 'foreign' accent or some kind of 'word salad' being produced instead of coherent speech. It also sometimes produces effects that appear to be less like problems of retrieval, i.e., the ability to get something that is known out of the head, than like problems of programming in the gaps, confusions and production difficulties that occur. The aphasic condition itself may be permanent or it may prove to be only temporary. In some cases it is actually intermittent, coming and going.

The various symptoms of aphasia have proved to be difficult to classify. Broad classifications such as receptive aphasias and expressive aphasias have sometimes been used. So also have classifications employing linguistic labels, e.g. agrammatism. However, no classification is entirely satisfactory because of the wide range of symptoms that exist, their range of severity and their relationships to deficits of other kinds, for example, to the previously mentioned physical – particularly motor – and intellectual deficits.

Since aphasia results from brain damage, it should be possible to relate specific language deficiencies to particular kinds of damage as these are revealed, for example, through the findings of post-mortems on aphasics. The findings should lead to a gradual increase in understanding how the brain functions with regard to language. Such evidence from aphasia should provide a growing body of knowledge about such matters as the storage of linguistic information in the brain, the possible localization of the various language functions, any inter-relationships of these functions and perhaps even the 'reality' of the grammars that linguists propose. More than a century of work has produced a considerable amount of evidence on some of these topics, but much remains to be discovered before truly definitive statements can be made. Many people believe that brain research is still in its infancy and that most of the discoveries are still waiting to be made because of the difficulties that researchers inevitably confront in this kind of work.

One of the most important discoveries in the history of research in aphasia was made in the early 1860s by a French physician, Paul Broca. He discovered that a particular kind of language loss was associated with damage to a particular area in the brain. This area, part of the left frontal lobe (located a short distance above and in front of the left ear) has since become known as 'Broca's area'. Broca's aphasia, or agrammatism, is the best understood of the various aphasias. Its symptoms are certain kinds of expressive and motor difficulties that affect the ability to speak. There is a loss of articulation and grammatical skills but not of vocabulary and comprehension skills. People suffering from Broca's aphasia can comprehend speech that does not contain too many small 'grammatical' words and this is the kind of speech they themselves use. It is as though they prefer to send and receive 'telegrams'. A sentence like *The girl that the boy is chasing is tall* is just too difficult to produce or comprehend with its use of *the, that, the, is* and *is*, for only *girl, boy, chase* and *tall* 'stand out' for such aphasics. People suffering from this kind of aphasia may well understand much that they hear but may experience considerable difficulty in trying to make themselves understood.

In the 1870s Carl Wernicke identified another area of the brain, now known as 'Wernicke's area', that is associated with another kind of aphasia. Damage to Wernicke's area, the posterior part of the left temporal lobe (around and under the left ear) results in receptive or sensory aphasia. People suffering this kind of aphasia retain control of articulation and grammar but not of vocabulary. The result is that they lose the ability to comprehend both speech and writing and to monitor their own utterances effectively. One consequence may be nonsensical talk.

It soon became apparent that damage to the left side of the brain more often resulted in aphasia than damage to the right side. About seven out of ten people who suffer damage to the left side of the brain experience some type of aphasia, but perhaps only one person in every hundred who suffer damage to the right side is similarly afflicted. It is now generally accepted that the two halves of the brain function quite differently in human beings and that for most people language is located in some way in the left side – or left hemisphere – of the brain. Language is not distributed equally between the two hemispheres. Moreover, within the left hemisphere it is located toward the front rather than toward the back.

We know from the use of 'dichotic' listening tests that the right ear in adult humans is dominant for speech sounds. If in such tests either one set of digits is presented to one ear and a different set to the other, or one message is presented to one ear and a different message to the other ear, listeners will overwhelmingly report hearing what was presented to the right ear rather than to the left ear. But for tunes presented in this way the favoured ear will be the left one. It may even be that the left side of the brain is responsible not only for language but also for other 'higher intellectual' processes too, e.g. reasoning. On the other hand, the right side of the brain is said to be 'visually–spatially' oriented so that its 'preference' is for non-speech sounds, music, melody and perhaps even emotional expression. So 'lateralization' of the brain may extend well beyond language alone.

Language therefore appears to be lateralized in the brain with the left hemisphere dominant. Some investigators believe that this preference for processing language in the left hemisphere is present at birth. They say that it is possible to show that three-week-old human babies display greater electrical activity in their left hemispheres than their right hemispheres when they are presented with human sounds. On the other hand, musical sounds produce greater activity in the right hemispheres of the same babies.

This kind of lateralization of function is almost entirely unknown ouside the human species. While it is common for the right sides of brains to control the left sides of bodies and vice versa, it is extremely rare for one side of the brain to control a function of the body as a whole. Something like lateralization has been shown to exist in a few other species, e.g. the chaffinch, because chaffinch birdsong seems to depend on the bird's left brain hemisphere being intact (Nottebohm, 1970), and some other primates (Newman, 1988). However, any connection between chaffinch birdsong and human language seems quite tenuous and the evidence from the non-human primates is slim.

The human brain is also not symmetrical. The left hemisphere is usually larger than the right and this difference is said to be present at birth. Apparently, the left hemisphere takes the lead very early in language acquisition (Entus, 1977), and the vast majority of humans end up being left-hemisphere dominant so far as language is concerned. The left hemisphere may also control many learned movements, e.g. movements used in working with tools. It may not be surprising then that humans are the world's best tool users as well as the world's only language users.

A young child who experiences damage to the left side of the brain may lose all ability to use language for a while but usually can re-learn – or re-acquire – what was lost by using the right side of the brain. However, it is widely believed that the right hemisphere remains available in this way only until the early stages of puberty. Early brain damage followed by such a switch-over also usually produces few or even no discernible negative results so far as language ability is concerned. The right side of the brain there-fore can do anything that the left is able to do but is usually not required to do so and possibly cannot easily do so after about the first decade of life. Unfortunately, we know very little about what brings about this inability to switch from one hemisphere to the other. In some views the process of language acquisition seems to begin at roughly the same time as lateralization starts to establish itself and is complete at the end of that process. Hence, there is a widespread belief that there is a 'critical age' beyond which it is difficult and sometimes impossible either to overcome certain kinds of brain damage or even easily to acquire a new language.

This critical age is generally said to be the years between two and the onset of puberty (perhaps 14). We do have evidence (see Curtiss, 1977) from one child, Genie, who was closely confined and almost totally isolated from people and language until she was nearly 14, concerning how slow language development is after this age. Genie found it very difficult to learn language with-out considerable coaching. One thing that tests did not show was left-brain dominance as a result of whatever learning occurred; in fact, the tests revealed right-brain dominance. One possible expla-nation is that the left side of Genie's brain failed to get the stimu-lation it required at a critical period in her life so that at the age of 14 Genie's brain proceeded to use the right side for language, the side that she probably used most during the period of her long confinement.

The left hemisphere also controls the right side of the body. If language is a localized function in humans, then the possibility exists for an interesting relationship between handedness prefer-ence and language dominance. Humans are predominantly right-handed with well over ninety per cent showing such a preference. (There is also some evidence, for example from the tools they used, that late pre-humans, e.g. Neanderthals, were also right-handed.) They are also predominantly right-footed and right-eyed, though to a somewhat lesser extent. It is well known too that aphasia is often accompanied by physical disturbances such as paralysis in the right side of the body and that strong and per-sistent interference with handedness preferences can disturb language development. An interesting question concerns people who are naturally left-handed: do they exhibit left dominance or right dominance so far as language is concerned?

While the evidence from aphasics consistently supports the connection between right-handedness and left dominance for language, it seems to show that left-handedness is associated only to a limited extent with right dominance. Damage to the right side of the brain rarely produces aphasia in right-handed people, but does so significantly more often in left-handed people. However, damage to the left side of the brain produces aphasia with just about the same incidence in both right-handed and left-handed people. Less than one third of naturally left-handed people appear to be right dominant so far as language is concerned, or give evidence that both hemispheres are involved in their use of language. Even if we add to these people those who have substituted use of the right hemisphere for the left because of injury or disease experienced in early life, no more than one adult in 30 or 40 is right dominant for language. Humans, there-fore, are overwhelmingly left-hemisphere dominant for language.

Even though for the vast majority of people language is localized in the left hemisphere there is considerable difficulty in further localizing specific linguistic functions. As I have observed, Broca's area is associated with certain motor and expressive difficulties and Wernicke's area with certain receptive and sensory difficulties. However, injuries in other areas of the left hemi-sphere can produce similar effects and, conversely, injuries that might have been expected to produce a particular kind of aphasia sometimes do not. Broca's aphasia and Wernicke's aphasia tend to be general labels that cover a wide variety of symptoms, so that not all cases of each are alike. In fact, patients diagnosed as having either aphasia may exhibit quite different symptoms (Schwartz, 1984).

Maps of the brain that try to associate particular areas with specific language functions have only a limited usefulness. They are often based on experimental procedures, e.g. electrical stimu-lation, that tend to produce very general, and often ambiguous, results. The brain is excruciatingly complex, much more complex than any existing 'maps' can indicate. Brain systems also appear to be highly redundant and there is a considerable 'plasticity' within the brain that allows functions to be taken over when parts die or in some way cease to be serviceable. Brain cells are not replaced like skin cells; brain cells die and already existing cells must be pressed into service if the brain is to maintain its capabilities. This plasticity of the brain makes attempts at localization of specifics extremely difficult. Human brains are obviously alike in many respects, but it is an interesting problem at what point they differ among individuals in their internal structures. Certainly the evidence from aphasia suggests a wide range of individual variation.

The localization hypothesis for language has been much discussed for a century or so, i.e., that we should be able to specify exactly which parts of the human brain are involved with particular language functions. However, this kind of claim about extreme localization is now considered unlikely to be valid. More 'holistic' views concerning how language functions are related to brain structure are now in vogue. Such views are necessary because of the plasticity I have just mentioned, i.e., the ability of the brain to adapt itself to trauma if that trauma is not too great. But perhaps we do not have to be either extreme localizers or complete holists. There seems to be reason to believe that there is a place for both views. Certainly the finding that the right hemisphere can be substituted for the left if the left is damaged in the first years of life argues for holism, as do the various kinds of repairs adults can make for later traumas. But it is also true that very small lesions can produce drastic language deficits, so there is also strong evidence for some kinds of localization.

In recent years brain researchers have offered a variety of hypotheses to account for how language might be stored within the brain and how the brain might function with regard to language. For example, one proposal (Pribram, 1969) is that linguistic information is not stored as a series of wholes, i.e., in the form of discrete units, but is stored 'holographically'. This suggestion obviates any need to be concerned with extreme localization but we must recognize it for what it is, little more than an analogy, until we have reliable confirming evidence. The suggestion does not generate hypotheses that are easily subject to experimental investigation.

Other proposals have tried to relate memory of linguistic information to such things as RNA molecules, proteins and amino acids in the brain, but the various searches for 'engrams', i.e., the actual physical correlates or neural memory traces, of specific bits of linguistic information have been quite unsuccessful. There must be units and structures of some kind in the brain that are srongly connected to language but these may well be characterized by a massive redundancy. The human brain can afford such redundancy and language use may indeed require it. The whole language system does not usually break down until extreme old age and sometimes not even then, but, when it does break down, it does so in a fashion that seems to testify to this redundancy. It is bits and pieces that disappear randomly, not whole systems that disappear overnight as it were.

Certain work by the psychobiologist Roger Sperry (Sperry, 1964; Sperry and Gazzaniga, 1967) has resulted in considerable attention being given to the non-dominant hemisphere of the brain. The two hemispheres are connected by the corpus callosum, a bundle of nerve fibres. These fibres are sometimes severed surgically in treating varieties of severe epilepsy. The result is a 'split brain', i.e., a brain whose two parts are made to function quite independently of each other. Studies of split-brain patients indicate that the non-dominant hemisphere controls certain visual and spatial capabilities, is the locus of musical and artistic abilities and plays an important part in emotional behaviour. Apparently, too, the dominant hemisphere controls the non-dominant hemisphere in a variety of ways through the corpus callosum. Split-brain patients lack this control and cannot integrate certain kinds of visual and linguistic information. Most normal humans learn to use language to control their emotions but split-brain patients cannot control their emotional and affective behaviour through language use.

If the non-dominant hemisphere is surgically removed, the result is likely to be a loss of emotional response together with some of the patient's musical and artistic ability, but little or no language impairment. There may, however, be some deficiencies in how language is used in narratives and in understanding sequencing, in inferencing and in determining the plausibility of cause-and-effect relationships (Brownell *et al.* 1986; Gardner *et al.* 1983). Surgical removal of the dominant hemisphere, however, always has drastic consequences for language ability. A few commonplace expressions sometimes remain, particularly highly emotional expressions such as curses, and there is likely to be evidence of comprehension of a considerable amount of speech and of knowledge of how the world works, e.g. knowledge of social conventions. But full expressive speech capability is lost. The non-dominant hemisphere obviously knows certain kinds of things that it cannot communicate through language: artists of all kinds have frequently spoken of knowledge that is too deep for words. Split-brain research confirms the fact that while different ways of knowing do exist, language nevertheless provides the principal way of expressing such knowledge.

The brain still remains much of a mystery and many of its properties and processes are obscure. If the live brain resists investigation and tells us little about language directly, the dead brain tells us even less, particularly about linguistic functioning. Language certainly begins and ends in the brain but, as for many beginnings and endings, we can make little more than educated guesses about the facts. We do know that language itself is extraordinarily complex. The human brain is even more complex. We understand some of its gross characteristics. However, any connections we then proceed to make between what we know about those characteristics and language itself are largely conjectural. They depend on taking many things on trust, not least of which are beliefs about what language is and how useful one or another analogy is so far as the functioning of the brain is concerned. Some linguists believe that our growing knowledge of language will offer insights into the structure and functioning of the brain and can be used to guide some types of brain research. Such may be the case. But we must also remember that brain research conducted for other purposes than linguistic ones may provide linguists with insights into language structure and functioning, insights that may be very useful in understanding just what language is. But whichever view prevails, it seems impossible to deny that human language and the human brain are extremely interesting not only in their own right, but both together because of their interrelationship.

### Further investigation

1  Try to account for the fact that people who receive messages sent at very high speed by Morse Code actually do not understand what they are receiving at the time.
2  There are numerous reports in the literature of 'abandoned' or 'feral' children (like Genie). They vary in quality and

usefulness. You might try to find one or two of them and see why this is so.

3 Aphasia is an interesting topic, but not one without certain problems. Examine some of the kinds of aphasia you find described and assess the definitions that are given for their precision. Examine any of the 'maps' of the brain you find and the positioning there of Broca's area and Wernicke's area. Do the maps always agree on the precise locations of these areas?

4 'Cross-modal' connections are said to be very important in language. There is the connection between listening and speaking but there are also the connections between listening and speaking on the one hand and reading and writing on the other (and within the latter between reading and writing). Failure to make cross-modal connections can have serious consequences for individuals. What kinds of language problems can you see as possibly arising from such failure?

# 4

# *Does the mind matter?*

As we saw in the previous chapter, it is the human brain that is in control of language: it controls both what we say and hear and how we say and hear. The mouth, the ears and the nervous system have certain inherent limitations that constrain the possibilities for language, but the brain is really the key to it all. We must be concerned with the brain if we want to understand just how it is we can attend to, perceive and process the various language stimuli that come our way, and also how we go about producing what we say. There are likely to be certain central constraints in the brain – it must have some kind of internal structure – but, as we saw, such constraints are extremely difficult to investigate. There are serious limits on how we can use probes, rays and other forms of physical manipulation and experimentation in order to find out how the brain works. Instead, we must investigate these workings inferentially and be prepared to accept the consequences that attend such a mode of investigation, particularly the possibility of drawing entirely the wrong conclusions.

## 4.1 'Behaviour' and 'mind'

In general, the 'higher' the mental or psychological process we want to investigate the more difficult that process is to study, the greater the ingenuity required and the less confidence we can place in our results. For example, remembering, or memory, is much more difficult to investigate than attending, or attention. These higher processes are often referred to as processes of the 'mind' rather than of the brain. We will see that minds and their characteristics are at least as difficult to study as brains and their characteristics.

Psychology is sometimes defined as that branch of science that investigates 'behaviour,' with one goal being the prediction of that behaviour and possibly even its control. Sometimes, in its applications to human behaviour, psychology has been described as that branch of science that investigates the 'mind'. However, some psychologists deny the usefulness of mind as a concept in psychology. Noam Chomsky, who is, of course, a linguist, has constantly argued that linguistics itself is heavily involved in psychological matters even to the extent of being a branch of cognitive psychology. Mind is a key concept in Chomskyan linguistics and one of the fundamental goals of this approach to language study is exploring the relationship of language to mind.

It is not really surprising that how 'language' might possibly relate to 'mind' has become a central issue in modern linguistics. Language is possibly the highest mental 'process', or set of processes, of all. It is unique too in the sense that only humans possess language. But that uniqueness is itself a source of difficulty. If language is uniquely human, how far can you generalize findings about behaviour from animals to humans or proceed to apply any of these findings to language? The same difficulty arises with the study of mind if the human mind is different from any kind of non-human mind. Do we therefore have humans with their language capability and their minds on one side of a gap and every other species on the other side? Can we actually learn anything useful at all about either language or mind from studying other species?

For many years there has been a continuing debate among students of language between those who are 'behaviouristic' in psychological matters and those who reject such a view and who are 'mentalistic' in their orientation. Behaviourists believe that behaviour, both non-human and human, results from 'learning' in which certain kinds of stimuli are either 'reinforced' or not; they are extremely interested, therefore, in 'theories of learning'. On the other hand, mentalists believe that organisms, again both non-human and human, are structured in ways that allow them to acquire certain kinds of knowledge and no other kinds, the precise structures being innate in origin and in the case of humans obviously 'mental' ones.

It is of some interest to note that there was a time when most linguists were able to subscribe concurrently to beliefs in the uniqueness of language and the relevance of behaviouristic psychology to studies of language learning and use. It is possible to regard language as a kind of sophisticated system of stimuli and associated responses and to postulate that we learn language much as we learn any other set of habits, i.e., through building up associations and through successful reinforcement. In such a view, except for its complexity, language behaviour is not really different from the kinds of behaviours that rats and pigeons exhibit in laboratory conditions. The psychologist B. F. Skinner even went so far as to write a book entitled *Verbal Behavior* (1957), which claimed that principles derived from laboratory work on small animals and studies of vocabulary learning in humans could tell us all we need to know about language learning and use.

Many people have found such a view of language to be attractive. It encouraged a considerable number of linguists and psychologists to treat language behaviour just like any other kind of behaviour. They could apply the same principles and investigative techniques to laboratory rats, pigeons and humans (mainly college students as it turns out!) and, of course, avoid any kind of special pleading that language is somehow different. In this view language researchers need not begin their work by assuming that language behaviour is different in kind from all other varieties of behaviour. They could assume the opposite, that language behaviour is no different.

While not everyone agreed with such an approach to language and language behaviour, its first major critic was Noam Chomsky, who published a widely read, quite devastating review of Skinner's book in the journal *Language* (Chomsky, 1959). Chomsky denied the validity of Skinner's claims and asserted instead that language is a uniquely human possession. Moreover, in his view, behaviourist principles cannot explain even the simplest facts about language behaviour. Language is unique in that the human species is specially equipped to use language and the human mind is structured in a special way as a result of evolutionary development. This structure accounts not only for the resemblances among languages but also for the ways in which all languages are learned. The human mind is, as it were, programmed to acquire and use languages of a certain kind – in fact, just the kind that humans actually use.

Chomsky's mentalist views on these matters have now won over many linguists, perhaps even the majority. The result has been something like a revolution in linguistic thinking and investigation. Many influential psychologists have also adopted some or all of Chomsky's ideas. There is now a quite widespread belief that a close examination of the structure of language may reveal interesting facts about the structure of the human mind. Finding out how languages work may be equivalent to finding out what human minds are like, language serving as a 'window' into the mind. Chomsky is by no means alone in his belief that in a number of respects linguistics has become a branch of cognitive psychology.

Some current work on language and on associated mental processes also assumes that it is best to do such work independently of biological and neurological investigations. In this view you must know what language is like before you can usefully investigate how it might be present in minds and bodies, or even how it might be acquired. Consequently, the major emphasis in linguistics should be on specifying what language essentially is. Once you know what language is then you will know the kinds of questions you should seek answers to in biological and neurological investigations. Furthermore, social and cultural issues relating to language use are quite irrelevant, in that they do not touch in any way on the central issue of what language is.

One consequence of this overall approach is that for some investigators the computer has now become a major 'metaphor' in their thinking about language. Other metaphors have found some currency in language investigations, e.g. holograms, telephone switchboards, feedback servo-mechanisms, etc. Each was useful in its way but eventually abandoned once its limitations became all too apparent. We must remember that today the computer is only a useful metaphor; the mind is obviously not a computer, at least not a computer of the kind with which we are familiar. It might be another kind of computer though, but, if it is, just what kind remains to be discovered.

Linguists and psychologists who investigate language and language behaviour in a mentalist approach attempt to specify how the mind works and where language fits into the working.

Essentially, such investigations involve making hypotheses and testing them. Hence the importance of theory. This approach strongly contrasts with most older approaches in that it is essentially 'deductive' rather than 'inductive'. It requires investigators to look for interesting questions bearing on central issues, to make hypotheses and test these, and then to move on to still more interesting questions. It does not start with masses and masses of data and attempt to find out what you can do with the data. Both approaches use data, but whereas the second approach seems to say that all the relevant questions and answers about what you are studying can be found within the data, the first approach says that you must try to define the issues independently of any data you happen to have observed and then you must assiduously look for data bearing on those questions. If the questions are good questions, you will learn something important about language. On the other hand, you cannot hope to learn anything about language by just collecting data and hoping somehow that you will be able to make sense of what you have collected.

### Further investigation

1  How far do such activities as instruction in English grammar, spelling, reading and foreign languages make use of principles from behaviouristic psychology? What kinds of knowledge are being taught in this way?
2  In an 'inductive' style of reasoning you look at data and try to figure out how best to explain them; in a 'deductive' style some issue attracts your attention and you proceed to formulate an idea and test that idea against data that seem to be appropriate. Try to find instances of these two different styles at work over roughly comparable – they can never really be directly comparable – sets of data.

## 4.2  Taking in what we hear

Speech must be attended to and perceived if there is to be any possibility of communication. In the previous chapter I indicated that speech can function under very adverse conditions, e.g. that we can understand even severely distorted and mutilated speech. We also readily distinguish language sounds from non-language sounds. Experiments have shown that in very adverse conditions people can tell whether a human voice is present or not, whether it is a man's voice or a woman's voice and exactly the moment when a pure tone is substituted for either kind of voice. But they may not recognize either which language they are listening to (even if they know that language) or a change from one language to another, and they may be unable to distinguish sense from nonsense if they do happen to recognize the language.

There is also the well-known 'cocktail party effect' to be accounted for. We can follow one voice among many and our attention may also be caught by something relevant to us in another conversation to which we were paying no conscious attention. Like a voice-actuated recording device that works only when someone starts speaking, the human mind seems to be capable of attending to and perceiving information only when that information is somehow relevant to the attending mind. It also apparently ignores what is not relevant.

We are surrounded by masses of information with the potential to overwhelm us. We must therefore be selective in what we attend to because human attention itself is severely limited. We must choose among the myriad stimuli around us and focus on parts only. Attention is a kind of 'gate-keeping' operation for the mind. It allows only certain things in, but at the same time it must allow the right things in.

'Attention' and 'perception' refer to the immediate processing of the sensory experiences of organisms, the experiences of sight, sound, smell, taste and touch. Attention itself must be at least partly a 'bottom-up' process, i.e., there must be certain peripheral or gate-keeping operations which ensure that we are alerted to speech sounds and give us the initial ability we need to deal with them. 'Cognition' refers to the later involvement of the organism in processing these experiences. It is a 'top-down' process, i.e., central mental processes are responsible for making sense – if they can – of what the gate-keeping operations pass on to them. It is probably impossible, however, to say exactly where one kind of processing ends and the other begins. In this view, then, bottom-up and top-down processes are not mutually exclusive.

Speech has its own peculiar perceptual puzzles. The sounds of speech are not clearly discriminable from one another in the way that the letters we use in writing tend to be – the letters are not always clearly discriminable in handwriting – and they also vary considerably from utterance to utterance and from speaker to speaker. There are really very few invariants in the actual speech we hear around us. Yet we do not usually seem to experience much difficulty in understanding what others say to us even in poor conditions for hearing. There must be some special gate-keeping systems for speech, but there must also be a heavy involvement of central processes quite early. That is, there seems to be more 'top-downness' than 'bottom-upness' in attending to speech.

How do we learn to attend to and perceive speech? A simple answer is that we do so on the basis of experience. The British associationist psychologists such as Hartley, Mill and Berkeley believed that people learn to associate elementary sensations because such sensations tend to co-occur. People build up hierarchies of experiences that enable them to make more and more complex perceptions. The Canadian psychologist Donald Hebb (1949) went even further, claiming, for example, that when people notice the lines and corners of objects, sets of brain cells are activated. These sets of brain cells eventually form 'cell assemblies' which are brought into play in visual perception, and the availability of such cell assemblies increases according to the frequency with which they are used.

This is a kind of 'template' view of perception, one that maintains the importance of matching something in the world with some kind of stored inner representation of that thing. We do know that people and animals deprived of the opportunity to perceive certain kinds of things, e.g. humans born with cataracts and animals raised in the dark, experience difficulties in seeing for a while after they gain the ability to see. Some learning or experience is a necessary part of perception. However, template-matching is generally acknowledged not to be a feasible hypothesis for speech perception; the latter is not some kind of simple matching process.

Something more than learning and experience seems to be involved. There is a strong likelihood that organisms possess 'perceptual mechanisms' of different kinds which predispose them to perceive various things. Studies of animals such as frogs, cats, rabbits and monkeys (see Hubel, 1963; Hubel and Wiesel, 1962; Lettvin *et al.* 1959, 1961) show that their visual systems are organized in ways that help them to perceive very special characteristics in the environment. They have brain cells that respond to specific forms of information. These have been called 'feature detectors'. For example, frogs have detectors that enable them to perceive the edges between light and dark regions, any movements of such edges and changes in illumination. They also have a fourth kind of detector, one that allows them to perceive the movements of small dark objects in their field of vision, a 'bug detector'. They depend on this last detector for survival, because a frog will starve to death in the presence of freshly killed but motionless flies. Likewise, cats and rabbits have detectors that allow them to respond to angles and to motion in the environment.

There is considerable evidence therefore that the innate structures of organisms may predispose them to perceive certain kinds of things. Moreover, some of this evidence also suggests that if these structures are not activated early in life they may never become available to the organism. Human beings may also have very specialized systems of speech detectors (see Diehl, 1981). That is certainly one way of interpreting some of the phenomena of attending and perceiving mentioned above.

Gestalt psychologists make even stronger claims about perceptual matters, going much further than seeing the necessity only for detector systems. They claim that minds are innately disposed to search out patterns and to organize stimuli in the environment into patterns. That is the very nature of mind itself. In such a view special perceptual mechanisms and detector systems could be regarded as providing a necessary means for such pattern perception.

This last claim is not unlike one made today by many of those who are trying to account for the unique ability that humans have both to acquire and to use language. They acknowledge that people may indeed employ a variety of perceptual and processing strategies determined by the nature of the human organism, but they insist that people must be considered to have both an innate knowledge of the general form of all languages and the acquired knowledge of the special rules of the particular language that is being attended to. Such knowledge 'guides' them not only in their production of speech but also in their perception of it. Speech perception is under the control of a central language ability that all humans possess.

We do all kinds of interesting things as listeners. We automatically adjust our perception of the speech of others to accommodate individual variations in rate, intensity, pitch and so on, i.e., we normalize the speech of others, allowing even for the very different 'accents' we hear. Such an ability is particularly interesting when we consider the language of small children. There is no way children can reproduce exactly what adults say to them; their voices are entirely different and yet children too normalize and equate what they hear so that all pronunciations of *a* that they hear become the 'same', including their own. But then they must do this, we can argue, because that is the nature of language ability itself, to be concerned with the 'abstract' *a* and not with its various individual manifestations.

We perceive the units of language holistically and invariantly, i.e., as being this unit or that one. As I noted previously, the 'sounds' of speech come at us extremely quickly, sometimes exceeding 20 each second and often at more than twice the rate at which we can reliably identify individual sounds in a random sequence. We do not perceive the sounds we hear one by one, then somehow associate them with words, then work out possible sentences from these words, and finally supply meanings for these sentences, no more than we proceed in such a way when we read a page in a book – unless we are terribly poor readers! Our perceptual ability allows us to 'hear' all the significant bits and pieces in what is said to us as it is being said to us. It allows us to do this at a rate which suggests that it must be specially constructed for the purposes of speech recognition. It also does it in a way which suggests that it can handle various kinds of information concurrently and without difficulty. We hear sounds, we associate these with words we know, we understand how these words relate to one another and we work out the overall meanings all at the same time.

One explanation that we might advance to account for this ability is that humans have a special detection system for language, just like frogs have a bug-detector system. This would be an attractive solution, particularly if we could also show that no other species has such a system or anything like it. However, the evidence that humans are specially endowed in this way is not at all strong. What does seem unique about language is the way the human mind works, not that humans have some kind of unique detection system for language.

Another proposal is that we understand language the way we do because we process what we hear according to how we ourselves would say what we are hearing (see Lane, 1965; Studdert-Kennedy *et al.* 1970). That is, our understanding of what we hear is based on our ability also to be able to say – though not necessarily aloud – what we hear. This has been called the 'motor theory' of speech perception. The theory claims that as we hear something being said to us our articulatory apparatus is somehow involved in the act of perception: we somehow use the mouth to help us work out what is coming to us through our ears. What we cannot 'mouth' in this way we cannot 'hear'. This seems to be not an unreasonable idea. It might, for example, explain why it is we have so much difficulty in even hearing a foreign language: because we cannot articulate its sounds. However, a closer examination shows that the theory does not work. There is no evidence of any kind of muscular or neurological activity in studies that try to measure such activity, paralysis of the vocal organs or even a complete lack of them does not lead to a failure to understand speech (Lenneberg, 1962), and the theory fails to do justice to the abstract nature of language.

Another more sophisticated variant of this approach to understanding speech perception is called 'analysis-by-synthesis'. The idea in this case is that a person constructs a series of internal syntheses of an utterance and tries to interpret these syntheses. The process is a continuous one; there is a kind of constant hypothesis-testing of how what is being heard might be organized. It is as though we constantly sample the message and allow that sampling to guide us in deciding what we have actually heard. This explanation gives much more prominence to the mind, claiming as it does that we 'hear' by using the mind to guide the ears. What the ears perceive must be constantly tested against what the mind regards as being sensible to hear. But once again there are difficulties with such a view (see Thorne, 1966). It also requires a rather clumsy matching of external phenomena with internal abstractions, but it does at least try to come to grips with the issue that top-down processes are undoubtedly more important than bottom-up ones in language processing.

That view is very different from the associationist view because there is a great distance between a belief in some abstract and innate predisposition or knowledge that guides perception and a belief that the same perceptions are built up entirely from the growth of associations among stimuli. However, the actual evidence available to us does not really seem to support either position to the complete exclusion of the other. We need both receptor cells and perceptual processes, but it is debatable whether or not we are endowed with specific language-receptor systems. What we know – no matter how we define knowledge – also predisposes us to perceive certain things, as a wealth of studies which have explored ambiguous stimuli have shown, because it is clear that we often hear what we expect to hear, just as we often see what we expect to see.

As I have indicated, all kinds of sounds come to the ears and listeners must distinguish speech sounds from non-speech sounds, figure out how the speech sounds are organized and make some sense of those organized sounds. Listening and understanding require that people make sense out of what they hear. To do this they must have certain information that arises not only from their knowing the language in question but also from their knowing certain things about the real world. Listening and understanding are not passive activities that somehow precede interpretation. Such a two-stage model is quite inappropriate. Listening and understanding, i.e., the complete processing of language, require the active involvement of the listener at all stages of what is being said. The speech signals that reach the ears contain such a variety of 'information' and 'noise' that only a receiver actively committed to getting sense out of the signals, and with some fore-knowledge of how that message is probably constructed and what it is likely to be, could possibly succeed. And all this has to be done in real time, i.e., virtually instantly.

Experiments (Pollack and Pickett, 1964) show that people cannot identify individual words or even very short sequences of words when these are presented out of context even in optimal conditions. To achieve ninety per cent intelligibility, they must hear sequences of seven to eight words produced in no less than about two seconds. If listeners recognized words from their component sounds alone, they should have recognized even single words in such circumstances. Context is very important, even to the extent of affecting how we hear particular combinations of stressed syllables (Lieberman, 1967). *Lighthouse keeper* in *The life of a lighthouse keeper was formerly very lonely* and *light house-keeper* in *Our maid weighed 180 pounds, but the Joneses had a light housekeeper* have 'stress patterns', i.e., the vowels are pronounced slightly differently but mainly in degree of intensity, that are demonstrably quite different if we use a sound spectrograph to analyse all the component frequencies, intensities and timings. However, if we switch the pairs of words in the utterances electronically, listeners do not detect the switch or any change at all in the utterances. The syntactic differences of the two sentences appear to lead listeners to 'hear' stress patterns that are not actually there to hear.

If we present people with grammatical utterances, anomalous utterances and random strings of words of equal length in varying conditions of 'noise' (Miller and Isard, 1963), they will not be able to repeat the random strings presented in noise conditions which do not affect what they do when they hear and repeat the grammatical utterances; they will demonstrate an intermediate degree of success with the anomalous utterances in those same noise conditions. Therefore, it would appear that people use both syntactic and semantic clues in the processing of what they hear. Once again these results seem to indicate that a top-down process is at work, i.e., that the speech signal is interpreted and evaluated as part of the total process of perception; it is not perceived and then interpreted and evaluated in a kind of bottom-up process.

This top-down characteristic of speech perception and understanding accounts for a variety of phenomena. It explains why people will insist that certain sounds were actually present in utterances they heard even when we know that these sounds were deliberately excised from the utterances that they heard. Listeners, too, constantly ignore minor mispronunciations in what they hear, particularly when such mispronunciations occur at the ends of words rather than at the beginnings – as though they have already decided what they are going to hear and then proceed to 'hear' it. People force interpretations onto deviant utterances as though they were not deviant, seeking to make sense of them if they can. They overlook slips of the tongue, tolerate – and even attempt to fill – hesitations, and, in general, constantly strive to make sense out of what they hear. Some of the best examples to illustrate this phenomenon are utterances we hear from those who do not speak our language well. Such utterances often make sense only because we make sense of them. Unfortunately, sometimes that sense is not the sense that the speaker intended!

The assumption that what they are listening to makes sense leads listeners into occasional misunderstanding of what was said. For example, listeners frequently do not attend to many of the details of what is said to them because they are aware that speech is highly redundant. If it were not highly redundant, language would be very difficult to use; we would constantly misunderstand one another because it would be critical that we understood absolutely perfectly everything we heard. As it is, we need not understand everything because not every part of what people say is critical to understanding. Languages are structured in such a way that usually several kinds of signals point in the desired direction; if we miss one signal, there are still others available. For example, in the sentence *The boys played football, boys* is signalled as a noun by both the preceding *the* and its own *s* ending, and it also fills a position, subject, typical of nouns. So at least three signals operate to help us process that part of the sentence alone.

People also pick and choose what they want to hear according to strategies that have proved useful in the past but which may not be infallible. If they hear the words *man, drove* and *car* in sequence they may well assume that what they heard was *A man drove the car*. Similarly, the words *man, struck* and *car* may be heard as *A man struck the car* rather than *A man was struck by the car*, which might have been what was actually said. However, just catching a suggestion of the *by* between *struck* and *car* is likely to suggest the correct interpretation. The strategy here seems to be that unless some word like *by* is present, a verb like *struck* with an 'animate' noun before it and an 'inanimate' noun following it is likely to have that animate performing the action of the verb, in this case 'striking', on the inanimate that follows the verb. Both men and cars can strike all kinds of things, but, just as in speaking, many people tend to make a verb agree with the nearest preceding noun, so in listening they tend to treat the 'grammatical subject' of a verb as its 'conceptual subject' (with certain interpretations of how particular kinds of subjects relate to particular kinds of verbs more available than others). On the whole this strategy appears to serve them well, and, when it does not, there is usually enough redundancy elsewhere in what is being said to redirect the listener to the intended message.

## *Further investigation*

1  How do 'speech synthesizers' and 'voice-activated' recording devices work? What might we learn about language from trying to construct equipment of this kind?
2  The concept of 'noise' is very important in investigations of how we understand language. For example, sounds in the environment can mask what you want to hear, a 'foreign accent' can lead to communication difficulties and dropping a paper with writing on it into a puddle can smudge the writing. These are all examples of 'noise'. Find some more examples and consider the usefulness of this concept. How do we seek to overcome 'noise'?
3  In one view every sentence we hear is potentially ambiguous and it is context alone that allows us to decide what it 'means'. In practice, however, we rarely find a sentence to be ambiguous. Each of the following sentences is ambiguous in isolation but each can be clearly disambiguated if provided with an appropriate context. Supply such a context for each.

They have wounded people there.
Flying planes can be dangerous.
He kissed the girl in the bus.
It's too hot to eat.
He wasn't elected because he was rich.
John painted the house.

## 4.3  Memories are made of what?

Memory must also play an important role in language use. However, memory itself is not a unitary concept, because numerous different characteristics and processes seem to be involved in remembering. We should also probably exclude from consideration any characteristics that we believe to be entirely genetic in origin. It would seem to be inappropriate to describe as 'memory' any programme an organism must obey because it is an organism of a particular kind, i.e., bees do not 'remember' the bee dance.

As I have indicated, many linguists – and not a few psychologists – consider that humans are programmed genetically to acquire languages of a certain kind. If we believe that language is innate in humans, i.e., that humans can and will learn languages of only a certain kind, then it makes little or no sense to say that the basic characteristics of all languages are either learned or must be remembered. In exactly the same way a person does not 're-member' to be six feet tall. Memory refers to active learning and remembering. Innate knowledge is neither learned nor remembered in this sense; in fact, we may best regard it as providing some kind of guide to the organism in going about learning and remembering. As speakers of English, we must learn and remember the sounds, words and structural characteristics that are unique to English, but we do not learn that there must be sounds, words and structural characteristics in English – we are born with this latter knowledge!

There appear to be three different kinds of memory that might be of interest to us: a 'sensory-information store' of some kind; a 'short-term memory'; and a 'long-term memory'. The sensory-information store allows information gathered by the senses to be retained very briefly, only for a fraction of a second so far as vision is concerned. However, we can remember sounds a little longer than we can remember sights. This ability is very useful because it allows us to hold sounds briefly in that store, which is probably of fairly high capacity, until we are in a position to deal with them or decide not to deal with them. It is in this sense that we may regard hearing as a necessary prerequisite to understanding.

Short-term memory (see Miller, 1956) is a store of limited capacity in which we retain information during the processing of messages. This information comes from the sensory-information store, but the actual items themselves may vary considerably in size. The short-term memory can hold very little information; its capacity is about seven unrelated items, or 'chunks'. When we have about seven chunks of unrelated information in short-term memory and try to add more chunks, we must either reorganize the chunks that are already there by grouping two or more together as a bigger chunk, or squeeze out something to allow the new information to enter. We can provide the necessary space by rechunking, discarding or moving something into long-term memory. These are the various ways through which short-term memory achieves its turnover. Of course, we can retain items in short-term memory for a considerable time but we must 'rehearse' them to do so, i.e., we must continually remind ourselves about them. Items that we do not rehearse do not stay very long. The whole process of entry to and exit from short-term memory is one of 'easy in' and 'easy out' to ensure the necessary rapid turnover.

Long-term memory seems to offer fairly permanent and seemingly unlimited storage capacity for everything that we hold long enough in short-term memory to be processed, understood and deemed worth remembering. However, precisely how we store information in long-term memory is still much of a mystery. As I noted near the end of the previous chapter, the search for what has been called the 'engram', the neural memory trace of a linguistic datum, has been quite unsuccessful, and even less ambitious attempts at localization of systems have proved to be inconclusive. Information is most certainly stored in the brain, but it appears to be stored there in different schemata or hierarchies.

One key issue in memory is that of the retrieval of information from storage. All kinds of approaches have been used, including the use of drugs and hypnosis, in attempts to study the retrieval system or systems that humans employ. Entry to a specific bit of information can be achieved both directly and indirectly. In everyday language use we do pull all kinds of information out of long-term memory without the slightest difficulty or hesitation. But occasionally we cannot find exactly what we want. Our search procedure seems to get us close to where we want to be, but the search is not always ultimately successful. Somehow we gained access to the right schema or hierarchy, but the particular piece of information we sought still managed to escape discovery. We recognize our failure, however, as a partial failure rather than a total one.

The 'tip of the tongue' phenomenon (see Brown and McNeill, 1966) is an instance of this last kind of failure to bring an item immediately and completely out of long-term memory. Sometimes we cannot recall a name, word or phrase but know that it is on the 'tip of the tongue'. We may even be able to give a para-phrase or synonym or say of a forgotten word that it has such and such a number of syllables or some other feature. In other words, we may know certain properties of whatever it is we are searching for, but cannot immediately recall the total set of properties, i.e., the actual item itself. Eventually it may come to us: *Hartmann* may come after we reject *Hauptman, Heinemann* and *Rinehart* in turn, and the desired *Sanderson* may supersede *Ferguson* and *Richardson*.

This phenomenon argues for items, particularly words, being stored in long-term memory in a variety of ways with different properties 'filed' in different places. No particular entry would necessarily contain every bit of information in such a highly redundant system. Different search procedures would then give access to different sets of properties: associative, syntactic, seman-tic, phonological, orthographic (i.e., spelling) and so on. Success-ful resolution of a tip-of-the-tongue experience requires a search for alternative procedures to the ones initially creating the experi-ence. For example, information about how many syllables a word has, or what some of its sounds are, or what one of its syllables is, may have to be supplemented by a review of associations of mean-ings if we are to retrieve the word in its entirety.

How 'words' are stored in the mind is a particularly intriguing problem (Aitchison, 1987) because we are accustomed to think of words as discrete entities and assume that they are very much like books in a library and therefore stored in specific places. That may be the case, but it is highly unlikely and, even if it were, the problem would still be one of getting access to them. What kind of filing system must we have to allow us access and how do we use that system? Are words stored in a kind of semantic network with some kind of cross-referencing, so that *dog* finds itself related to *cat, pet, animal*, etc? Or are they stored in hierarchies, so that *dog* is found stored under *animal*? Or is *dog* stored by features, so that it is 'animal', 'canine', 'domestic', etc? And where do its phonological and 'orthographic', i.e., spelling, charac-teristics fit into this system of storage?

As native speakers of English we also have all kinds of ways of accessing words and grouping them. We can contrast words, e.g. *black* with *white, big* with *little*, etc. We know about 'synonyms', 'antonyms' and 'homonyms'. We know that *dogs* are also *animals* and that *ostriches* are also *birds*, that *apples* and *oranges* are *fruit*, that *books* have *pages* but *flowers* have *petals*, that *big* rhymes with *jig* but begins like *back*, that *go* and *went* are basically the 'same word', that in *kick the bucket* used as an idiom meaning 'die' we have no reference to kicking or to some kind of container, and that certain words do not exist at all or are clearly 'foreign'. How do we know and remember all this?

We also know what we know and what we do not know. There is more to memory that just storing, searching and retrieving. We know that we have a telephone number, which most of us can retrieve instantly. Many of us know we had another telephone number – perhaps more than one – at some earlier period in life, but may not be able to retrieve it now or can retrieve only part of it. But we also know that the Prime Minister of Japan has a telephone number and that we do not know what it is. How do we know that we do not know this? Certainly not by executing some kind of search procedure in memory and finally deciding that we have come up blank. We also know that Julius Caesar did not have a telephone number, but that again is a different kind of knowing, even from the last kind.

Sometimes we manage only to retrieve bits of words. We find a synonym rather than the exact word. We know how many syllables a word we are searching for has or how it begins or ends but cannot quite remember it exactly. It has a strong phonological presence but not an exact one. So we make those slips of the tongue or commit a 'malapropism', i.e., use a word, particularly a long word, that sounds like the one we want but is not and is hilariously inappropriate, or just hint at a word – and even have that hint suffice when the person to whom we are speaking also experiences a like experience of not quite knowing exactly the word intended but knowing enough to somehow 'recognize' it.

We understand speech as we hear it without any appreciable time delay, even though what we are listening to draws readily from the hundred thousand words or more we know and does so in all kinds of combinations. Our 'look-up' procedures must work almost instantaneously. The total system therefore must be enormously complex and flexible, certainly much better than any we can find in current computer simulations of memory.

There have been numerous investigations of memory processes, particularly investigations of the processes involved in moving information into and out of short-term memory. For a while, a major concern (see Greene, 1972) was with remembering and forgetting sentences of various degrees of grammatical complexity, e.g. 'active' sentences (*John ate the apple*), 'passive' sentences (*The apple was eaten by John*), 'active negative' sentences (*John didn't eat the apple*), 'passive negative' sentences (*The apple wasn't eaten by John*) and so on. The general conclusion of such investigations is really not surprising: less complex sentences are easier to remember than more complex sentences but no fine gradation according to some criterion of grammatical complexity is possible. Sentence length is important but so are semantic facts and real-life conditions. Consequently, the process of remembering involves a variety of factors.

Other memory experiments (Epstein, 1969; Savin and Perchonock, 1965) with quite restricted goals produced conflicting results. The assumption in this case was that sentences take up space in the memory, grammatically 'simple' sentences less space and grammatically 'complex' sentences more space. The subjects in the experiments were given a sentence followed by a string of eight unrelated words and asked to recall the sentence and the words immediately following the last of the eight words. They were then asked to repeat the task with another sentence of a different grammatical complexity and another set of eight unrelated words, and so on for 11 different sentence types. The initial results indicated that when sentences were recalled before words, the number of words recalled from each set of eight unrelated words correlated very closely with the grammatical complexity of the accompanying sentence. The more complex the sentence, the fewer the words that were recalled, so that 'active-affirmative' statements like *The boy has hit the ball* produced an average recall of 5.27 words, 'negative questions' like *Has the boy not hit the ball?* produced an average recall of 4.39 words, and 'passive-negative' questions like *Has the ball not been hit by the boy?* produced an average recall of 3.85 words. The experimenters interpreted these results to mean that grammatical 'transformations' took up storage space in memory, questions taking up more such space than longer active sentences, for example. However, recalling the words before the sentences produced no such effects. So the issue seems to be one of the relative ease of retrieval from memory rather than one of storage, with one kind of retrieval task apparently interfering with the other. While it may be easy to get things both into and out of short-term memory, the two processes are not therefore mirror images of each other.

There is some evidence (Sachs, 1967) to suggest that 'semantic' (i.e., meaning) and 'grammatical' information are not treated alike in memory. We find the meanings of sentences easier to recall than their exact grammatical shapes. If people are told that after listening to a short story, they will be asked to judge whether a particular sentence they will hear is identical to one they will hear in the story or, if changed, whether it is changed in 'meaning' or in 'form', they produce an interesting pattern of replies. Given a sentence in a story like *He sent a letter about it to Galileo, the great Italian scientist*, they will generally fail to detect changes in form like *He sent Galileo, the great Italian scientist, a letter about it*, or *A letter about it was sent to Galileo, the great Italian scientist*, as little as seven or eight seconds, or 40 or so syllables, afterwards, when those extra syllables have continued the narrative. But a meaning change to *Galileo, the great Italian scientist, sent him a letter about it* is readily detectable as long as three quarters of a minute after the original sentence. These findings suggest that the exact grammatical form of a sentence is quickly forgotten but that the information it contains is not. People remember the substance of what was said much better than they remember how exactly it was conveyed. Yet much testimony in courts is about the exact words that were spoken on occasions far remote in time and place from those same courts!

Another experiment (Bransford and Franks, 1971) offered further confirmation that memory involves a kind of imaging that goes beyond actual words. In this case the subjects in the experiment were given the following two sentences: *Three turtles rested on the floating log, and a fish swam beneath it*, and *Three turtles rested beside the floating log, and a fish swam beneath it*. The sentences differ only in that one uses *on* whereas the other uses *beside*. Three minutes later the subjects were given two more sentences: *Three turtles rested on the floating log, and a fish swam beneath them*, and *Three turtles rested beside the floating log, and a fish swam beneath them*. These sentences differ from the first pair in that *them* replaces *it*. The subjects were asked if the second pair of sentences was the same as the first pair. They agreed that the first sentence was the same but the second was different. That is, they agreed that *Three turtles rested on the floating log, and a fish swam beneath them* was the same as *Three turtles rested on the floating log, and a fish swam beneath it*, but that *Three turtles rested beside the floating log, and a fish swam beneath them* was different from *Three turtles rested beside the floating log, and a fish swam beneath it*. The judgement that the last pair of sentences are different is, of course, correct, but the first two sentences are not quite the same. They are close in meaning, however, in that if the log is beneath the three turtles and the fish is beneath the log then the fish is beneath the three turtles. One meaning 'entails' the other. But what must be stored in memory to arrive at such an understanding is some kind of image of the overall situation, not just very specific grammatical and semantic facts.

## Further investigation

1   How do you commit a new telephone number to memory? Do you group the various numbers in some way, rely on recurrent numbers, or what? How about long numbers like insurance card numbers or credit card numbers? Is seven numbers a 'magic number' for you?

2   Try to memorize four to six lines of poetry and, while doing so, keep track of exactly what you have learned at each stage. Check your memory for what you learned a day later and three days later. What can you find out about 'memory' from such an experiment?

3   In the 'derivational theory of complexity' each of the following two sentences gets progressively more difficult to 'process' because of the increase in grammatical complexity:

The dog chased the cat.
The cat was chased by the dog.
The cat wasn't chased by the dog.

The boy gave the pen to the girl.
The boy gave the girl the pen.
The girl was given the pen by the boy.
The girl wasn't given the pen by the boy.

It is possible to argue that you can maintain such a view only if you believe that listeners 'process' sentences without reference to context. How might you try to show that an appropriate context would probably make the last sentence or two in each set just as quickly comprehensible as the first?

## 4.4   Getting our words out

When we turn our attention to investigating how we plan what we say and then say it, we find a new set of problems. We understand much more than we produce, so the two processes of understanding and production are not simple mirror images of each other. The act of speaking is also for most of us much more difficult than the act of listening. Speaking involves both complex planning and the skills necessary for successful execution. This is the only way we can explain why it is that we sometimes know we must start an utterance again because the words are not coming out right. We also sometimes realize that we have made a mistake of some kind and have to 'correct' what we have just said.

Although we do produce the parts of any utterance serially there is also a 'structural depth' to that utterance. In any properly formed utterance the sounds and the words must come out correctly in order one after the other if they are to be meaningful, but there is no reason to suppose that all we must do is plan to produce this simple serial effect. We must plan to make sure that we get the right semantic, syntactic and phonological content into what we want to say and then in the process of actual execution impose the necessary serial ordering on these various bits of content. This final actual execution of our plan is not unimportant, but it is really much less interesting than what lies behind it, the plan itself and its various components.

In the preceding chapter I indicated that certain instructions to the speech organs must be extremely precise in their detail and timing, e.g. the instructions to produce the initial sounds of *den* and *ten* so that no confusion results. Similarly, the timing at the ends of *axe* and *ask* or *apt* and *act* must be extremely delicate. Timing differences of as little as one fiftieth of a second are critically important in ensuring that the right phonemes occur in the right sequences. Such evidence might seem to favour a hypothesis that, at one level at least, speech is planned and organized phoneme by phoneme and that words themselves are stored as sequences of phonemes. But still other evidence refutes that hypothesis. While there is evidence that the phoneme may be an important unit in planning and producing speech, other evidence indicates that it is not the only unit, nor even possibly the most important unit. Units both smaller and larger than phonemes appear to be involved too.

'Phonetic features' smaller than phonemes are important. We can see how important these are from the way in which particular sounds tend to 'assimilate', i.e., become more alike, to neighbouring sounds or, much less frequently, 'dissimilate', i.e., become less alike. During the production of any sound the speech organs are already moving in the direction of following sounds, so that features like 'lip-rounding' and the 'frontness' or 'backness' of vowels, 'voicing', 'nasal' quality and so on may be anticipated. The *k* at the beginning of *Kansas* is produced in a different position (more forward in what is actually the back of the mouth) than the *k* at the beginning of *Kootenay*, and the vowel in *pin* is much more likely to be nasalized (some of its sound coming out through the nose) than the vowel in *pit*. Such assimilations are a basic linguistic fact. At some stage in the production of speech, therefore, 'subphonemic' features become important and influence one another.

Evidence from pauses, hesitations, false starts and slips of the tongue (Boomer and Laver, 1968; Fromkin, 1973, 1980) shows that phonemes and units other than phonemes are involved in speech production. Slips like *Merle* for *Pearl*, *rip lounding* for *lip rounding*, *trite rack* for *right track*, *florn cakes* for *corn flakes*, *shoe snows* for *snow shoes* and Dr Spooner's famous *queer old dean* for *dear old queen* and *You have hissed my mystery lectures* for *You have missed my history lectures* illustrate that entities such as features, phonemes, permissible sequences of phonemes, grammatical endings and even categories of meaning play a part in speech production. Such slips usually do not violate the sound system of the language. That is, they do not result in the production of 'foreign' sounds or non-permissible sequences of sounds such as English words beginning with *ng-* or *lk-*. Quite often too there is a semantic similarity between the slip and

what the speaker intended, e.g. *proception* may result from trying to somehow say both *production* and *perception* at a time
when the speaker is giving less than full attention to the precise
choice of words or their careful articulation. Freudian psychology has always regarded slips of the tongue as an important
source of data, e.g. *John has just expired* instead of *John has
just retired*. However, they are at least as useful and probably
much less controversial a source of data in studies of speech
production.

Syllable units appear to be very important in planning speech
(Fromkin, 1968). We usually do not stop in the middle of a
syllable, and even babbling and stuttering show a characteristic
syllable structure. Studies (Lehiste, 1970) have also shown that syllable structure appears to control how certain sounds are pro-
longed in relation to one another. For example, a consonant that
follows an intrinsically long vowel is given a briefer pronunciation
than when it follows an intrinsically short vowel in an otherwise
identical syllable. The final consonant of *mace* is therefore slightly
shorter in duration than the final consonant in *mess* – the different spellings here are quite irrelevant to the point – because the
vowel in *mace* is intrinsically longer (but not much longer)
in duration than the vowel in *mess*. This temporal compensa-
tion suggests that whole syllables act as the organizational
units of speech production rather than individual sounds.
However, there is really no truly conclusive evidence about the
size of the organizational unit used in planning speech. Possibly
more than one such unit exists between the central thought
process responsible for an utterance and the final realization of
that utterance in sound.

The production of language seems to require an initial
'ideation' stage, in which a person, who must have 'knowledge' of
language to be able to do this, decides to say something. At this
stage the speaker must have access to certain permanent stores of
linguistic information in long-term memory. Planning processes
then allow language units of different kinds to be assembled so
that ideas can be formulated and communicated precisely. This
planning results in orders being issued to the nervous system to
do certain things which produce actual speech. Finally, during the
actual production of that speech a considerable amount of self-
monitoring occurs.

It is unlikely that in speech production we go through a series of phases one by one so that a 'correct' utterance results only when each phase is successfully navigated in a precise sequence. An alternative view is that the phases are managed concurrently. What is absolutely certain is that to produce a successful utterance a speaker must combine a grammatical structure, the right words, the right grammatical affixes, the right stress patterns for the words, the right pronunciations and so on. The evidence from slips of the tongue points to the fact that various processes are involved in the production of an utterance, but it does not tell us whether these processes occur consecutively or concurrently.

The actual self-monitoring of speech does offer us a little help in understanding what is going on. Speakers do detect errors made in the execution of a plan to speak. They sometimes know that an utterance is not working out for some reason and try to salvage it. But this self-monitoring seems to go on concurrently with speech itself, with perhaps only a momentary delay. Such delays allow us to observe, indirectly of course, some of the planning that must be going on in the mistakes that occur and through the kinds of repairs that speakers attempt.

## *Further investigation*

1   Find some instances of the 'tip of the tongue' phenomenon and try to explain them. 'Spoonerisms' are interesting too.
2   Some people criticize others for 'slurring' their speech, even for using 'contractions' like *I can't* and *he won't*. Ignore slurring caused by such things as drowsiness and drugs and consider it as a normal phenomenon. What are some of its characteristics? Why indeed might we regard 'unslurred' and 'uncontracted' speech as 'abnormal' speech?
3   Are there any useful analogies to be drawn between the process of your own editing of your written language and your self-monitoring of your speech?

## 4.5   Some general issues

Explaining the language ability that humans have would seem to be a great challenge to psychologists. However, some of the limitations of psychological interests and methods tended for a long while to curtail work on the human mind. The most important of these limitations came from a widespread refusal to try to investigate any internal characteristics of the mind. Many psychologists regarded the mind as a kind of 'black box', something quite impervious to observation, and they therefore focused their attention entirely on external and easily manipulable behaviour.

Psychologists also tend to avoid examining extremely complex behaviour; it is too 'messy' to deal with. They try to identify part of a complex problem, isolate a discrete variable or two and then work with these in the hope of resolving some issue; they prefer to use rigorous procedures in highly controlled laboratory conditions. However, there is a continuing serious doubt that many of the claims that they make about language and language behaviour as a result of this kind of methodology are valid. For example, there is a long history of studies of 'verbal learning' and an extensive literature exists on different kinds of verbal learning and forgetting, on 'interference', i.e., how learning one kind of verbal material interferes with the learning of another kind, and on patterns of 'word association'. But almost none of this work tells us anything very interesting either about how people learn a language or how they use language in everyday life.

Vast gaps exist between the findings of laboratory investigations and the everyday uses of language, between highly controlled 'learning' situations and natural learning, and between the word lists that psychologists work with and the words and combinations of words that people actually use. Yet some psychologists often do not hesitate before attempting quite bold leaps across such gaps. We should be particularly aware that in the 'soft' sciences – and psychology is one of these, as is linguistics – we must exercise considerable caution in extrapolating findings from the laboratory to real life, because we could be quite wrong when we do so.

Unfortunately too, the results of many investigations of the kind just described are either inconclusive or quite contradictory. Since the gaps between different findings and the projections of the results of these findings to natural language are so wide, it is often difficult to bridge them. An illustration may be useful. It is possible to time how long it takes a person to produce a particular response to a given stimulus, for example, to produce a 'negative' sentence corresponding to a particular 'affirmative' sentence, e.g. to produce *The cat didn't drink the milk* in response to *The cat drank the milk*. You can argue that the greater the length of time taken to produce a particular response the 'less available', or the 'more difficult', was that response because it took more processing time. If in such an experiment you can control the various stimuli in such a way that every conceivable variable is accounted for, then the different response times should indicate very directly the effects of the variables in which you are interested, e.g. sentence length or grammatical complexity. You might then make certain claims about how the different processing times required by the different pairs of sentences indicated certain workings of the mind.

As we will see shortly, many psycholinguistic investigators have used just such an experimental strategy in attempts to find out what happens when you ask people to react to or manipulate various combinations of affirmative, negative, active and passive statements and questions, and so on. The strategy is designed to test the hypothesis that when people use language they must use their grammatical knowledge rather directly, i.e., in order to understand any sentence listeners must 'unpack' its syntax. That unpacking is not a conscious activity; it is an unconscious one, which, nevertheless, can be measured. This strategy is sometimes referred to as using the 'derivational theory of complexity' in order to examine language processes in the mind.

The strategy has produced results that are not at all clear. It has proved to be impossible to account for all the variables present in the stimulus sentences, particularly as ideas about syntax have changed, or to be sure what the various response times indicate, because the latter do not vary according to syntactic properties alone but also according to the particular kind of judgement the task requires, e.g. judgements of sameness or difference of meaning, of truth or falsity and so on. Since the overall results of many of the experiments are not clear, it is therefore impossible to be certain about what bearing they have either on the 'psychological processes' claimed to be behind them or the 'correctness' of the particular grammatical theory on which they are based.

The issue of how the results of experiments of this kind are to be interpreted is a very important one. In their experiments linguists, psychologists and psycholinguists have not always been clear as to what they are actually trying to test. Are they testing how people produce speech, or how they learn new words, or how they recall sentences, or comprehend them, or make judgements as to their truth or falsity or how 'real' a particular grammatical theory is?

When we look at the recent history of psychological investigations of language, we find that before 1957 psychologists showed little interest in the kind of language behaviour that interests linguists today. Their principal interest in language lay in the area of word associations explored through various verbal-learning tasks. They tended to regard language as some kind of complex set of word associations built up through 'reinforcement', the view expressed in B. F. Skinner's *Verbal Behavior* (1957). Certain linguistic investigations, particularly those that led to the idea of the 'phoneme', did excite a few psychologists and for a while it seemed that new concepts from linguistics, together with certain concepts from 'information theory', would revolutionize psychological investigations into language. Then, in 1957, the publication of Noam Chomsky's *Syntactic Structures* completely changed the direction of linguistic work. New issues came to the fore, and old issues and findings were discarded as 'uninteresting'. One of the first psychologists to see the relevance of the 'new linguistics' for the psychology of language was George Miller and it was he who promoted some of the initial psychological investigations of Chomsky's ideas.

These investigations were based on the view of language described in *Syntactic Structures*, a view which, as we have seen, has since undergone a series of important revisions. However, the 1957 version of Chomsky's theory of language focused attention on syntax. This focus produced a drastic change in linguistic investigations in general because much of the previous focus had been on the sounds of languages and on the structure of words. One immediate result in psychological investigations was a shifting away from investigations of word associations and the information content of sentences. However, *Syntactic Structures* described only certain kinds of sentences, mainly simple one-verb sentences: statements and questions, affirmatives and negatives and actives and passives. It also proposed transformations of two kinds: 'obligatory' to manipulate certain obligatory syntactic components of sentences, and 'optional' to change a sentence of one type into a sentence of another type, e.g. an active sentence to a passive sentence or a statement to a question. Two-verb sentences were built up from combinations of one-verb sentences through 'generalized' transformations, so that *He has a red book* could be said to originate from combining *He has a book* and *The book is red*.

In 1965, with the publication of *Aspects of the Theory of Syntax*, Chomsky further developed his theory of language. The new version of the theory specified a distinction between 'deep structure' and 'surface structure' in language, required transformations that did not change meaning and established procedures for integrating the actual meanings of words into sentences. Later still, some of Chomsky's critics within linguistics demonstrated that issues of meaning were actually more important and more central to understanding how languages work than issues of syntax and proposed what they called a 'generative semantics' as a replacement for a 'generative syntax'. Some critics even went so far as to reject the 'deep–surface' distinction that Chomsky had proposed. Many psychological investigations of language have been based on one or another of these different approaches in attempts to prove that a particular approach best explains certain kinds of observed phenomena.

As I noted above, one assumption behind some of these investigations was that sentences that required fewer 'transformations' in their 'generation' should take less time to recognize, judge or manipulate than sentences requiring more transformations. Even the effects of the use of a single transformation should be measurable, e.g. the difference between an 'active' sentence and its 'passive' equivalent, or between an 'affirmative' and its corresponding 'negative'. One immediate difficulty we must confront concerns the term *generate*. A speaker produces a sentence but a grammar generates it, i.e., it offers us an account of the grammatical structure of that sentence, but whether 'production' and 'generation' are the same or in what ways they are different are much debated issues. Any measure of complexity is also fraught with difficulties. Is complexity to be measured by numbers of transformations, types of transformation, kinds of conjoining and embedding or what?

A classic investigation in this mode (Miller and McKean, 1964) measured reaction times on a sentence-matching task and found that it took subjects longer to match an 'active' sentence, such as *Jane liked the woman,* to its corresponding 'passive' sentence *The woman was liked by Jane,* than it did to match that sentence to its corresponding 'negative' sentence, *Jane didn't like the woman.* The time required to match the 'active-affirmative' sentence to its corresponding 'passive-negative' sentence *The woman wasn't liked by Jane,* was also roughly equal to the sum of the times required to match the active sentence to the passive and the affirmative to the negative. However, still another investigation (Clifton *et al.* 1965), which measured motor responses using a tachistoscope rather than the reaction times on a paper-and-pencil test, found that 'active' and 'passive' sentences were more closely related in time than were affirmative and negative sentences. In this case an additive effect was found for combinations of passives and negatives.

Other investigations (Gough, 1965; Slobin, 1966) required subjects to determine the truthfulness of different active-affirmative, passive, negative and passive-negative sentences in relation to a variety of pictures and imaginary situations. Measuring response times, the investigators found that passive sentences required more time to evaluate than active sentences, negative sentences more time than either active or passive sentences and passive-negative sentences most time of all. Once again the results appeared to support an additive effect. Again, too, actives and passives were found to be more closely linked than affirmatives and negatives, although in the particular syntactic theory the investigators were using the 'passive transformation' was more complex than the 'negative transformation'.

Sentences containing negatives, however, did not always produce such results. Negation produces semantic as well as syntactic effects. Two investigations of negation (Eifermann, 1961; Wason, 1961) showed that negative sentences are generally more difficult to understand than affirmative sentences which convey approximately the same meaning, possibly because people recast them as affirmatives to verify what the sentences mean. For example, we are likely to recast sentences like *Nine is not an even number* and *Eight is not an even number* as *Nine is an odd number* and *Eight is an odd number* before we attempt to decide whether they are true or false.

Still another study (Wason, 1965) suggested that the actual plausibility of the negation is responsible for part of the difficulty. Sentences such as *A pig isn't an insect, A spider isn't an insect* and *An ant isn't an insect* cause people to react differently. The first sentence is not a very likely sentence because such a denial seems to be rarely called for. In contrast, the second sentence is very plausible indeed in that spiders are frequently classified as insects. The third sentence is untrue rather than a denial. Consequently, real-life usefulness and truth value may well be confounding variables in accounting for how negation works.

Further investigations ( Johnson-Laird, 1969a, 1969b), which employed sentences containing quantifying words such as *some* and *all* in contexts like *All philosophers have read some books* and *Some books have been read by all philosophers* and which required subjects to explain their meanings, found that the form of a sentence tends to control the explanation that is given. Even though each of the above sentences is ambiguous in exactly the same way as the other, the first is generally understood as involving 'some books or other' and the second as involving 'some books in particular'. It is no longer surprising that investigators should have experienced difficulty in interpreting the results of experiments employing negation and 'quantifiers' such as *some, all, none* and *any*. Just as sentences containing negatives and quantifiers were producing unexpected results in psycholinguistic investigations, linguists were discovering independently through their own attempts to explain grammatical relationships among sentences that a major recasting of linguistic theory was necessary.

The most recent version of Chomsky's theory of language, called 'government and binding', very much simplifies many of the processes that were postulated in earlier versions. It adopts a 'modular' view, one in which the mind is regarded as a series of independent modules each responsible for certain types of mental activity, e.g. reasoning, visual perception and so on. Language itself is also one of the modules and is comprised of a set of subsystems or principles, themselves modular, which operate concurrently in producing and understanding sentences. It is the linguist's task to describe these principles. Furthermore, they operate independently and automatically and form an essential part of the 'mind' of every normal person.

One consequence of this shift in linguistic theory is that today investigators are much more likely than heretofore to adopt a 'weak' approach when they attempt to relate the details of grammatical descriptions to specific mental operations. No longer do they try to find close and exact correspondences between the 'derivational histories' of sentences, as a grammar might account for these histories, and 'mental operations', as these might be revealed in tests of reaction time. They rarely attempt to relate grammars to minds in this way because the latest version of the theory does not easily lend itself to postulating such relationships.

The current theory is concerned with abstract theoretical matters of language organization and its claims about mind originate from close observations of data from a variety of languages. The claims are thoroughly deductive in nature. The theory itself is the product of logic and deduction and makes no direct claims about mental processes. For example, while both the old 'deep–surface' distinction in language and the concept of 'transformation' still exist – though both in drastically modified versions – the theory denies that these are mental processes. The concepts are necessitated by the requirements of the grammar, not the mind, in that they appear to be necessary to explain how people construct the sentences they do. The mind may indeed make use of some kind of deep–surface distinction and relationships that might be regarded as transformational in nature, but there is little reason to believe that real-time processing of the 'rules' we find in a particular grammar is in any way involved.

However we account for them though and 'use' them, the actual grammatical structures of sentences seem to play an important part in how we perceive and remember those sentences, even though we may forget many of the actual details of the structures. For example, a series of experiments (Garrett *et al.* 1966) used a task that required subjects to locate where a click occurred during a spoken sentence in order to discover how they perceived units of grammar and meaning. The subjects were asked to listen to recordings in a 'dichotic listening' test. In one ear they heard sentences and in the other ear they heard a click at some point during each sentence they heard. Immediately after hearing a sentence, each subject was asked to report the point in it at which the click occurred. In one experiment sequences of words such as *George drove furiously to the station* and *hope of marrying Anna was surely impractical*, were spliced with other material to form the pair of sentences *In order to catch his train, George drove furiously to the station*, and *The reporters assigned to George drove furiously to the station*, and with still other material to form another pair of sentences, *In her hope of marrying, Anna was surely impractical* and *Your hope of marrying Anna was surely impractical*. In these pairs the syntactic and meaning break is before *George* and *Anna* in the first sentence of each pair and after *George* and *Anna* in the second sentence of each pair. The subjects heard clicks timed to occur with the vowel in *George* and the first vowel in *Anna*. However, most of them reported that the clicks occurred at the syntactic breaks, the remainder between some other pair of words, and none at all during the actual words themselves.

Working in this way, investigators can be reasonably sure that it is not the acoustic stimulus alone that produces the different responses. The observed differences result from the perceptual strategies that the subjects are using. The real controversy concerns how far such strategies predispose listeners to postulate characteristic types of grammatical structure, e.g. 'subject-verb' word order, 'subjects' as 'agents', i.e., the actual 'doers' of whatever the verb is 'doing', etc. What seems to be clear is that the grammatical structure of a sentence plays an important part in allowing listeners to make decisions about the actual physical events that occur. But at the same time we seem to be able to postulate some types of structure more easily than others and use specific strategies in making those postulations. Since speech fades so rapidly these strategies are very useful, but they also must be fairly reliable and readily available if they are not to lead us seriously astray.

Some specific strategies have been suggested (Bever, 1970). Events spoken of will be assumed to have occurred in the sequence mentioned so that the sequence of clauses will tend to mirror the sequence of events. Consequently, a sentence like *He left after I spoke* will create difficulties in comprehension that a sentence like *After I spoke he left* will not, because the sequence of clauses reverses the chronological ordering of the events described in those clauses. Passive sentences like *The woman was wounded by the man*, that allow subjects and objects to be switched and still make sense (*The man was wounded by the woman*), are also harder to verify through reference to the actual events described than sentences like *The ticket was bought by the man*, which do not allow such switching (because *The man was bought by the ticket* is not a very likely sentence).

We usually interpret noun-verb-noun sequences as actor-action-object sequences. Therefore, a sentence like *The pitcher tossed the ball tossed it* will almost certainly seem to be ungrammatical on first hearing. It is a perfectly grammatical sentence if we interpret *tossed the ball* as a participial phrase within the clause *The pitcher tossed it*, i.e., (*The pitcher [(who was) tossed the ball] tossed it*), but the most productive processing strategy we can adopt, i.e., the strategy which usually produces the correct result most quickly for a sentence that begins in such a way, requires us to interpret *pitcher* as the subject of the first *tossed* and ball as its object.

We will interpret successive nouns or noun phrases at the beginning of a sentence as co-ordinate in structure. Embedded clauses will therefore be troublesome on that account. *The girl the rat bit screamed* is less easy to grasp than *The girl that the rabbit bit screamed*, the 'complementizer' *that* effectively interposing between the two noun phrases. *The pen the author the editor liked used was new* is almost totally incomprehensible; however, the inclusion of two 'relative pronouns' *which* and *whom* radically improves comprehension, as in *The pen which the author whom the editor liked used was new*. We should note that English requires the use of a complementizer or a relative pronoun in just those cases where noun and verb phrases fall together to produce possible confusion. Consequently, *that* or *who* is mandatory in *The player who scored the goal was injured* in order to prevent *player* being interpreted as the subject of *scored* and leave *injured* without a subject. But in *The book I want is missing* a *that* or *which* between *book* and *I* is entirely optional.

We also rely on the context in which we hear something to help us out in understanding what we hear (see Bates *et al.* 1978; Keenan *et al.* 1977), and remember utterances partly because of the contexts in which they occurred. If the context is memorable, we are more likely to remember exactly what someone said; on the other hand, if the context is not particularly memorable, we are likely to retain only a general impression of the meaning of what was said. Listeners also assume that what they are hearing is in some way 'relevant' (see Sperber and Wilson, 1986) to what is going on in the immediate environment. They seek to know whether their assumptions will be confirmed or not, whether they can continue to hold them or whether they must modify or abandon them.

Today, therefore, investigators are more likely to be concerned with the strategies and heuristics that listeners appear to be using in processing sentences than with the 'reality' of grammatical processes. They are also likely to be concerned with the way in which sentences themselves are structured so as to give listeners the best chance of arriving at correct interpretations. Grammatical issues are still important (see Forster, 1979; Berwick and Weinberg, 1984; Dowty *et al.* 1985), but they are not the only relevant issues.

What seems apparent today is that when we try to describe how we use language we are able to glimpse various processes of mind at work. A basic assumption in much current work is that these processes are discrete and function concurrently. While largely independent, some must, nevertheless, interact with others to account for some of the results we find. Quite obviously then there is still much to be revealed about the human mind and language continues to offer us one of the best means of continuing our explorations.

## Further investigation

1  Read each of the following sentences and decide quickly what each means:

John said that Sally left yesterday.
He wanted to paint her in the nude.
The best bit was going to Heathrow and watching aeroplanes taking off from the roof of Terminal 4.
Fred told the girl he liked the story.
I took her soup.
He liked the idea she had shared.

Each of the above sentences is quite clearly ambiguous if you examine it closely. Now try to explain why you chose one reading rather than the other for each sentence.

2 Try to explain in as much detail as you can what you must know to understand an English sentence. For example, if you hear and understand the following sentence, specify what you 'heard' and the 'knowledge' you need to understand it: *The cat sat on the mat.* (Remember no chimpanzee has this ability!)

# 5

# Why do languages vary so?

One of the things you are soon likely to discover about languages as a child is that others do not speak the language you speak. They speak very different languages in fact. You will also notice quite soon that those who do speak the language you speak do so with noticeable differences. As you get older you may note more and more such differences. For example, one speaker may use only a little aspiration at the beginning of *pin* as the initial *p* is pronounced, but another quite a lot; *stickin'* and *sticking* may alternate as pronunciations of the same word; the vowel in *man* may be considerably 'nasalized', i.e., pronounced through the nose as well as the mouth, or not nasalized at all; *Did you eat yet?* may be slowly and carefully articulated or be pronounced something like *Jeechet?*; one person's *I don't have any* may be equivalent to another person's *I haven't got any* and to still another person's *I ain't got none*; and someone's *truck* may be another's *lorry*. Such variability is an important characteristic of any language; however, linguists find it extremely difficult to describe in writing their grammars (see Milroy, 1987). This variability seems to be associated with such factors as the regional origin of speakers, their social class and age and gender differences.

It is partly for such reasons that some linguists often choose to describe the language of an individual speaker – an 'idiolect' – through the careful elicitation of language data in well controlled circumstances, while others attempt to describe an idealized linguistic 'competence' in a language rather than the complexities of actual linguistic 'performance'. In both cases the result is a statement of the invariant units and processes that apparently underlie what are generally acknowledged to be in fact quite variable data. The kind of grammar of a language that results in either case is also likely to be an account of that language as it is used by a small proportion of its speakers, usually better educated people using the language on formal occasions.

Variability has still a further consequence for the statements that linguists make about languages. Inevitably, it would seem, such statements can never be quite complete, because even the most carefully wrought statement fails to cover all the data, i.e., there is a gap here, an exception there or something left over. The linguist Edward Sapir once declared that all grammars 'leak'. When he said this, Sapir was actually talking about the intrinsic structures of all languages rather than about particular grammars that linguists had proposed for one or more languages. Such leakage seems to be important in explaining not only why linguists themselves suffer some of the frustrations they do over variability, but also why it is that any language is like it is at any time and possibly too why it changes. A language is not a perfectly wrought system complete unto itself and existing in some kind of splendid isolation from everything else. It has no independent existence. To rephrase John Donne's words, no more than a man is a language an island.

Linguists, however, often find a certain usefulness in treating languages as though they existed or could exist in splendid isolation from speakers and speaking. In a sense this is the basic approach adopted in Chomskyan linguistics. They are able thereby to produce descriptions that focus on sets of invariant relationships among fixed and well-defined units. Impressive results have been achieved, and continue to be achieved, in this way, but they cannot possibly exhaust all that we might want to say about language.

Variability also creates problems of another kind for linguists. Speakers of a language are aware of variation within the language and their everyday linguistic behaviour demonstrates that awareness. They know that people speak differently on different occasions. However, it is an awareness that they usually cannot describe consciously in any very precise way. Individuals are well able to make the subtle adjustments in pronunciation, word choice and grammatical structure that the different situations they find themselves in require. They seem to know the correct percentages of occurrence of particular linguistic forms and to be able to realize just the right percentages according to the situation. They know just how often they must alternate between the final *-in'* and *-ing* in participle forms (*fishin'* versus *fishing*), 'slur' words together (*Jeechet?*), omit syllables (*'bout*) and use words like *ain't*. Recently, some linguists have tried to take such variability into account in writing grammatical descriptions of languages, but the resulting statements about the probabilities of occurrence of linguistic forms do not fit easily into currently established ways of writing grammars. These ways require the writing of 'categorical' rules which state that X becomes Y in certain circumstances, e.g. 'cat' plus 'plural' always becomes *cats*. They do not state that X becomes Y sixty per cent of the time and becomes Z forty per cent of the time with the actual conditions that bring about those realizations not clearly understood. This last kind of statement, or 'variable' rule, would tell us that nearly all native speakers of English use both the *-in'* and *-ing* participle forms without allowing us to predict with absolute reliability when one form occurs rather than the other.

Statements of probability create still other problems. A grammar of a language is in one sense a claim about the 'knowledge' that speakers of that language have acquired. If some of that knowledge is subtle statistical knowledge about probabilities, how do speakers acquire such knowledge? It is difficult enough to attempt to explain how they acquire abstract linguistic knowledge. How do they also acquire sensitivity to subtle differences in probability? What is an organism like that not only acquires 'abstract categorical knowledge', i.e., knowledge that something is or is not in a definite category (something is a *p* not a *b*, is *man* not *men*), but also acquires 'variable probabilistic knowledge', i.e., knowledge that some variant is more appropriate than another depending on certain environmental characteristics which are themselves extremely complex and also highly variable, e.g. use *stickin'* not *sticking* this or that percentage of the time in this or that situation?

We will look at some of the above issues within investigations of single languages. Then we will turn our attention to the phenomenon I mentioned initially, the fact that languages themselves are different from one another. We will try to discover what are some of the interesting observations we can make about that kind of difference and find that it appears to open up for us a way – possibly more than one – of exploring the past.

## 5.1 Speaking a language differently

When we look closely at any language we are almost certain to find that there will be considerable variation not only in how people use sounds, words and grammatical structures, but also in the actual choices they make on different occasions. Of interest will be the extent of such variation and the possibility that discrete, identifiable sub-varieties of the language exist. The existence of the term *dialect* in addition to the term *language* suggests that recognizable discrete varieties of some kind do exist within languages.

A 'dialect' is often considered to be a regional – less often a social – variety of a language and an 'idiolect' to be a variety that a specific individual uses. A dialect is also sometimes distinguished from a 'standard' variety of the language, when one exists, with the standard being the variety that is favoured by the 'establishment' – social, political, religious or whatever – and supported by major social institutions. However, attempts to give more exact definitions to *dialect* and *idiolect* and even to *language* itself have proved to be rather unsuccessful.

It has been said that not too long ago a person could travel from the north of France to the south of Italy and, if the journey were slow enough, the traveller would never be conscious of crossing a language boundary and hardly be conscious at all that the language was changing during the course of that journey. Yet speakers living in some of the different regions through which the traveller passed would be quite incomprehensible to one another. They could not be said to speak either the same language or even very different dialects of the same language. But how many languages and how many different dialects of these languages did the traveller come into contact with during the course of the journey? The last question can be answered only if there exist clear definitions of the terms *language* and *dialect*.

Linguists generally agree that a language is a linguistic system which a number of speakers share when different, but mutually intelligible, varieties of that system exist; these varieties themselves are the dialects of that language. Sometimes too, one dialect may have more prestige than the others as a result of the prestige of the particular group of people who use it. People may then come to regard this dialect as the standard form of the language or even regard it as the language itself. In that case the other dialects may appear to be inferior variants of this standard form, and *dialect*, as a term, then assumes certain pejorative associations.

However, such definitions do not help us a great deal in making decisions as to where to place the boundaries for each language and dialect traversed by our fictitious traveller. They are much too broad and inexact to be very helpful in that task. Even today, there are parts of the world, e.g. India, with characteristics not unlike those just mentioned for the France and Italy of a recent era. There are also areas in the world in which speakers can communicate reasonably easily with one another even though they claim to speak 'different languages', e.g. Norway, Denmark and Sweden, or Serbia and Croatia, or Ukraine and Russia, and other areas in which they fail to communicate even though they claim to speak 'dialects of the same language', e.g. China.

Today, what is or is not regarded as a language is often related to what is or is not regarded as a nation (see Haugen, 1966). As a trenchant commentator once observed: 'A language is a dialect with an army and a navy.' We live in an era of national languages, and we quite often regard dialects as merely sub-varieties of these languages. Numerous anomalies result. Norway, Denmark and Sweden are three nations but Norwegian, Danish and Swedish are not really three different languages (or four if you give full language status to both varieties of Norwegian) in the same way that English, French and German are three different languages. They are much closer, even closer than certain dialects of a single language are in many other cases, e.g. some of the dialects of Hindi or Arabic. Spanish and Portuguese blend into each other in the Spanish province of Galicia (north of Portugal), and Dutch and German blend in the same way along the Dutch–German border. Hindi and Urdu are basically the same language with different written forms, different ways of coining new words and different religious associations, being rather like Serbian and Croatian in these respects. Chinese is not one language but about half a dozen mutually unintelligible languages that find unity in a common writing system. English, the most widely distributed language in the world, exists in very different dialects. A Scot from Glasgow may find it difficult to communicate with a Texas oil worker from Houston and both may find a student from Calcutta to be almost incomprehensible. However, each of the above speakers will claim to be a speaker of English, but at the same time acknowledge some kind of pre-eminence for the varieties of English heard on the World Service of the BBC or on the Voice of America.

Linguists (see Chambers and Trudgill, 1980; Davis, 1983; Francis, 1983; Petyt, 1980) have generally assumed that it is worthwhile to examine the geographic, i.e., regional, distribution of anything they consider to be a language. They have also considered regional differences to have been brought about by the kinds of processes that we will consider in the next section of this chapter. Linguists are also concerned with the social varieties of language and much effort in recent years has been expended on refining techniques in this area. However, all such work, whether it is regional or social in orientation, is based on the assumption that languages do vary and such variation is to be regarded as the norm. Some linguists would go even further and point out that attempts to limit or even in some cases to eliminate variation are doomed and that those who deplore the fact that language variation exists are quite ill-informed about the very nature of language. Languages are inherently variable.

The easiest way to describe the regional characteristics of a language would be to conduct some kind of geographical survey. In practice, however, there are considerable difficulties. Even commonly-held, national, ten-yearly censuses that seek only the simplest demographic information in a population take considerable organization. Sampling of some kind is nearly always necessary when a large population is to be surveyed. But, as everyone who has engaged in survey work knows, finding a representative sample and then eliciting from that sample the information that you seek can be troublesome tasks. In a language survey, who are truly representative speakers or informants? What are the truly representative linguistic items that must be surveyed? And what, when you have finally collected them, are you to make of the data? As we will see, the history of dialect study is also a history of attempts to answer questions such as these.

In the late nineteenth and early twentieth century, investigators such as Wenker and Wrede for German, Gilliéron for French and Jaberg and Jud for Italian developed a variety of sampling techniques. In the study of German, the principal technique was a questionnaire that Georg Wenker sent to every German-speaking village in Europe. The local schoolteacher was asked to complete and return the questionnaire, which consisted of 44 sentences that were to be translated from standard German into the local dialect. Since comprehensiveness was the goal of the survey, it covered over 40 thousand villages. However, there was no guarantee about the quality of the individual responses. What there was, however, was a kind of safety in numbers that allowed the investigators to recognize truly aberrant responses.

In his study of French, Jules Gilliéron employed a single field-worker, Edmond Edmont, to collect the data he wanted. Edmont travelled to over six hundred villages in France and neighbouring countries in order to collect a rather narrow range of phonological data on French. The Italian study, which covered the Italian-speaking area of Switzerland as well as Italy, saw further refinements in the selection of informants, the training of fieldworkers and the addition of towns and cities to the survey. The investigators also followed up parts of the general survey with studies of particular regions and particular linguistic items.

One of the more sophisticated approaches to dialect study was initiated by the American Council of Learned Societies in the 1920s, as the first part of a projected 'linguistic atlas' of the United States and Canada. The initial investigation, conducted under the direction of Hans Kurath between 1931 and 1933, covered the regional distribution of speech forms in New England. It required the systematic selection of those New England speech communities that were likely to produce the kinds of information the survey sought, a selection that was carried out with the help of historians and anthropologists. Three or four speakers of certain kinds were chosen in each of the selected communities so as to provide the information sought through use of a relatively short, well-organized questionnaire. The survey also used only very highly skilled fieldworkers. More recent surveys, e.g. those conducted in Great Britain, have been concerned with further refining these techniques rather than with questioning the major underlying assumptions of this approach to dialect study.

The basic outcome in each case is an atlas containing a series of maps of one kind or another, e.g. the *Sprachatlas des Deutschen*

*Reichs*, the *Atlas Linguistique de la France*, the *Sprach-und Sachatlas Italiens und der Südschweiz* and the *Linguistic Atlas of New England*. The maps record the data so that it is possible to see which words are actually used, how these words are pronounced and so on, in the various regions shown on the map. Because the map making itself has proved to be extremely expensive, the investigators sometimes provide lists of linguistic forms by place and informant instead of actual maps. Numerous derivative studies often follow from the information which the maps and various lists provide, and the distribution of the forms on the maps also allows investigators to make hypotheses about possible 'dialect areas'.

A dialect area is an area that possesses unique linguistic characteristics; no other area has quite the same distribution of linguistic forms. The actual distribution of forms can be determined by inspection of the data recorded on the maps. Sometimes a particular form is found only in a specific geographical area. We can then draw a line, called an 'isogloss', around this area. This isogloss marks the geographical boundary of the distribution of that form. When we find the isoglosses for several different forms running together, i.e., when we find a 'bundle of isoglosses', we might want to claim that the resulting boundary is a 'dialect boundary'.

One famous set of isoglosses in Europe is the 'Rhenish Fan', the boundary between High German to the south and Low German to the north. When the Rhenish Fan was first described, the *ich-ik* isogloss crossed the Rhine at Ürdingen, the *machen-maken* isogloss crossed it between Düsseldorf and Cologne, the *Dorf-Dorp* isogloss south of Bonn and the *das-dat* isogloss south of Coblenz. As I have just noted, when several isoglosses for different forms converge, we can interpret the information to indicate the border between two dialect areas, in this case between High German to the south and Low German to the north. Since these isoglosses converge more to the east, the break there between High German and Low German is more abrupt than it is to the west, where the convergence is not so great. The characteristics of the 'fan' have also shifted somewhat since it was first described.

The conclusions drawn from this method of collecting, processing and presenting data are, not surprisingly, determined in large part by the underlying assumptions. One assumption is that distinctive regional varieties of a language do exist and that it is possible to distinguish among them through plotting the distributions of a fairly small set of linguistic forms. Moreover, the linguistic differences in the forms can be accounted for through well-known processes of language change. Exceptions will result from inter-dialect or inter-language borrowing. A second major assumption is that fieldworkers can uncover the different forms by gathering data from a very restricted, carefully chosen sample of informants, these data being responses elicited in interviews of predetermined form and content. A third assumption is that the best source of data lies in 'folk speech', although 'cultured' and 'educated' speech is of some interest too. A final assumption is that the results of any investigation are most revealing when they are presented on maps that allow the distribution of linguistic forms to be related to such factors as geographical features, trade routes, settlement patterns, political and religious boundaries and so on.

The result is that a linguist can talk about different dialects of a language by reference to specific linguistic forms and can also give some account of the origin of each of those different forms. A dialect will have unique characteristics. It may be characterized by a unique set of sounds, or a particular set of words, or certain kinds of grammatical forms or some combination of these. It is the uniqueness of its content that defines it as a dialect. Other unique contents define other dialects. The term *dialect* itself is also used entirely without prejudice. In this view of language the Queen of England speaks a dialect of English, the President of the United States another dialect and the Prime Minister of Canada still a third dialect. Admittedly, all these are prestige dialects and each has a status far beyond, respectively, the Liverpool dialect, the Ozark dialect or the Newfoundland dialect.

More is involved in dialect differentiation than the kinds of factors accounted for in atlas-type studies. Dialect differences are really more subtle and pervasive than such studies indicate. The studies suggest that fairly sharp boundaries occur between dialects and that speakers in the different dialect areas all make the same kinds of distinctions. However, these distinctions are not always apparent in the dialect areas in which they are supposed to occur. The sampling and mapping techniques, the use of restricted questionnaires and sometimes the selection of older, untravelled and poorly educated informants also all guarantee that only certain kinds of data will be recorded.

Although there may well be certain characteristics of speech that do have an exclusive regional distribution, the majority of the characteristics that mark off Bostonians, New Yorkers and Virginians from one another are too subtle to describe merely by using the techniques employed in linguistic atlas work. Whether *r*s after vowels are or are not pronounced and the quality of the vowels in *aunt* and *half*, *law* and *order* and *down* and *out* may be very noticeable perhaps, but alone they make up only a small part of the total set of differences among the speakers. (They are, nevertheless, highly indicative of such differences.) An emphasis on gross differences really offers us little more than stereotyped descriptions.

One way of assessing the results that emerge from dialect studies is to ask what help they provide in understanding what happens when speakers of different dialects of a language talk to one another. How do they understand one another? The atlas-type approach might suggest that in such circumstances speakers communicate by means of a 'matching' process of some kind, i.e., they match individual sounds, linguistic forms and classes of forms in the speech of others to equivalents in their own speech. So *skillet* would be matched with *frying pan*, or *lorry* with *truck*, *r*-less words with *r*-ful words and so on. Such a model for inter-dialect communication is a very improbable one because a language is more than an inventory or collection of items, no matter how systematically arranged, and such a matching process, either item by item or class by class, is just too cumbersome to account for what happens when people who speak the language 'differently' still succeed in communicating with one another.

An alternative approach requires us to postulate shifts of a different kind. It requires the listener to make very general shifts to accommodate what is heard. The listener uses a set of general rules to equate the language system the speaker employs to the one the listener possesses. This equation or conversion process is similar to the one that people use even when gross dialect differences are not involved. For example, we continually adjust to the personal characteristics of other speakers' voices without being aware of the fact. In this view the kind of shift in listening to another dialect has nothing special about it. The process is also a lot easier to understand if language ability is assumed to be an abstract or principled ability that requires some use of 'rules' to allow us to express ourselves and to process what others say to us. There may, of course, be individual differences in the ability to use some of these rules, because such abilities as being able to mimic other speakers and of even being able to understand speakers of other dialects do not seem to be equally distributed to all.

I have mentioned only a few of the problems that arise in the study of regional dialects, but these problems do not in any way undermine the claim that there is usually considerable variation within a language. They merely serve to show the kinds of difficulties we face in trying to describe that variation. However, the concept of a 'dialect area' does have built into it the notion of invariance, because in this view a dialect area is an area in which speakers are alike in their linguistic behaviour. The linguist must therefore assume that the linguistic forms within the area are essentially uniform, fixed and invariant. The sampling techniques used to gather data for the various atlases embody such an assumption and the static representations on maps further reinforce it. Moreover, the exclusion of urban speech communities, younger, better-educated informants and complex social distinctions does nothing to undermine its apparent validity. However, so far as language is concerned, heterogeneity is more typical than homogeneity and variation than uniformity, and other distributions than regional ones may also be of interest. Such possibilities were not seriously considered until quite recently, and it is to these I will now turn.

Social variation is as much a fact of human life as regional variation. No society is without it and only the extent appears to be different. The variation may show itself in any number of ways, some of them largely symbolic but no less real for that, e.g. 'blue blood' or descent from ancestors who came over the Atlantic on the *Mayflower* or across the world in 1788 to Botany Bay. But usually the manifestations are more overt. They are things like money, houses, possessions, clothes, manners, i.e., artefacts and other characteristics associated with a particular job, way of earning money, gender, age or some other social grouping. Almost any artefact or characteristic can be used as an indicator of social difference, e.g. possession of a specific kind of car, a huge piece of stone 'money', a membership in a particular club, a medal of some kind, an 'Oxford' accent and so on.

In every society people must learn which characteristics go with which social distinctions. They must also learn how particular characteristics can or cannot be acquired and can or cannot be lost, i.e., what freedom exists to change their position. Sometimes there is little or no such freedom, so change occurs only through some kind of revolutionary upheaval; sometimes there may be a great deal of freedom and social distinctions may be blurred and confused. Sometimes the change is bestowed, e.g. a knighthood or an earldom or an appointment to an ambassadorship or a judgeship; and sometimes it is mandated, e.g. the loss of certain rights on conviction for a crime. The important point in all these examples is the pervasiveness – often very subtle – of social variation.

This subtlety itself is very important. The indicators of social variation are often below conscious awareness, and they are all the more powerful for that reason. But just because they are below conscious awareness does not mean that people are insensitive to them. As we will see, people are quite sensitive to language indicators of social differences, even though they may be quite unable to explain exactly what it is they are sensitive to.

Each individual exists in a variety of social settings and relationships; hermits and prisoners kept in solitary confinement may be some of the rare exceptions. There is not just a single social system in a society; rather there is an overall social system composed of myriads of interrelated subsystems. Each person must learn to adjust to the demands of that variety and to seek fulfilment through mastery of the intricacies of the individual subsystems. Each language community exhibits complex patterns of social organization and is composed of numerous subsystems. It is not, therefore, homogeneous in this one important respect at least.

There is no reason either to assume that any one individual consistently uses exactly the same language forms in every situation. There appear to be few, if any, 'single-style' speakers, i.e., people whose language never varies no matter what the circumstances in which they find themselves. A person's speech usually varies according to the social context in which it occurs.

Some contexts demand certain styles of speaking because of their physical characteristics, e.g. speech-making in a large auditorium without a microphone, but the most usual cause of variation is the social relationships that exist among the participants in any exchange. These relationships account for the degree of formality each speaker adopts and for the amount of conscious attention that is devoted to the act of speaking itself. A speaker can also speak differently on the same occasion, e.g. to make an informal aside during an otherwise formal presentation or to clarify a point that was made during that presentation in a discussion that follows it. Moreover, a speaker can repeat the same kinds of behaviour on other similar occasions, thus indicating that the language shifts are systematic and part of the language user's total repertoire of language knowledge and behaviour.

It is this systematic ability to shift from one kind of speech to another that is at the centre of any study of social variation in language use (see Labov, 1972b; Trudgill, 1983; Wolfram and Fasold, 1974). Two questions arise immediately. What kinds of shift occur? What brings about the shifts? To answer the first question we must isolate a particular linguistic phenomenon in order to see what happens in a variety of circumstances. Such a phenomenon is called a 'linguistic variable'. It may be the exact pronunciation of the ends of words like *hunting* and *going* (alternatively *huntin'* and *goin'*), or the pronunciation of the middle consonant in *water, better* and *sitting*, or whether a word such as *bath* is pronounced as though it were spelled *baff* or *then* as though it were spelled *den*, or the quality of a particular vowel, as in *now* or *bag*, or the distribution of a particular 'tense' or 'aspectual' form of verb, as in *He is here, He here* and *He be here*, or a negation system, as in *He doesn't have any, He hasn't any* and *He ain't got none*. The linguist looks for instances of the use of the variable and for the particular realizations that people use. These different realizations are then related to the quantifiable characteristics of the social contexts in which they occur.

The linguist answers the second question concerning what brings about the shifts in use by attempting to relate the distri-bution of the variants of the variable to identifiable parameters in these social contexts, e.g. regional origin, social class, age, ethnicity, gender, occupation and so on. The linguist's conclusion is a statement of the distribution of the variants of the variable within a population rather than an account of the actual language behaviour of a specific individual.

Let us look closely at two variables to see what kinds of things we find when we investigate language behaviour in this way. We will look at the final *-ing* of verbs as in *going, hanging, singing* and so on, and at words pronounced with a final *t* sound (which may be spelled *-ed*). The *-ing* ending of verbs may be given varied pronunciations. In informal speech *-in'* often replaces *-ing*, and boys are more apt to behave in this way than girls (and men more apt to behave in this way than women). Cutting across this distribution, however, is the fact that 'common' verbs like *chew, punch* and *swim*, are more likely to be given the *-in'* endings than 'learned' verbs like *correct, criticize* and *read* in otherwise identical situations. Once again the sexes behave alike in this regard. However, place names like *Cushing* and *Flushing* are nearly always pronounced with *-ing* in any circumstance.

So far as the final *t* is concerned, it is least likely to be dropped when it represents the 'past tense' in front of a word beginning with a vowel, as in *He passed Ann*, and most likely to be dropped when it is part of a word and is not an indicator of past tense and the following word begins with a consonant, as in *the past week*. *Passed* followed by a consonant, as in *He passed Vera*, and *past* followed by a vowel, as in *the past era*, show intermediate degrees of loss of the final *t*. Again, the amount of loss correlates closely with the degree of formality of the occasion with less formal situations showing a greater incidence of loss in all four forms than more formal situations.

Considerable difficulty arises in trying to define situation or context with any degree of precision. Social class is notoriously difficult to define, as are levels of formality. Data collection procedures that depend on sampling are both laborious and expensive. Even so, considerable success has been achieved in each area. Linguists and psychologists have also been able to relate certain styles of speaking to people's perceptions of social relationships, and the actual techniques for eliciting data have been continuously refined. It is now generally agreed, for example, that reading a passage aloud produces a very careful, formal type of speech because it puts people on their 'best' linguistic behaviour. Reading word lists aloud, answering a fixed set of questions, participating in informal talk with a stranger, talking casually with associates and friends in the presence of a stranger, and, finally, but extremely difficult to observe, talking casually without any awareness of being observed at all successively take people further and further away from this best behaviour toward 'most casual' behaviour. William Labov, the linguist who has done considerable work on variation, has even argued that this last kind of talk, this casual, very difficult to observe language behaviour – what he has called the 'vernacular style' – cannot be ignored if we are to understand how languages vary and also how they change.

## *Further investigation*

1  What is the popular understanding of 'dialect' and 'vernacular'?
2  'Dialect' and 'accent' are not the same things. Try to clarify the distinction (and the relationship).
3  Regional dialect differences are revealed through such things as the different pronunciations of words, different names for objects and different ways of using certain aspects of grammar. Find examples of all of these in comparing your use of English to some other person's use of English. Each 'dialect' also has a history. Now try to account historically for the differences, i.e., for the existence of these pronunciations, words and grammatical structures.
4  Try to identify exactly how you think you identify someone as coming from a particular part of the English-speaking world, e.g. as an American, a Scot, an Australian, a Cockney, a Texan, a New Yorker, etc. What characteristics are you using? Check these against the facts you find in good accounts of dialect differences in English, e.g. Trudgill (1990) for the dialects of England.
5  Studies of social dialects have focused on a number of 'linguistic variables'. Some have proved to be very useful in widely different places. For example, we can try to find out who uses or does not use the sounds indicated in brackets in words like (h)ot, ca(r) and shoppin(g), and on what occasions. Try to find out what you can about the use of these variables.

## 5.2 Relating different languages

I have just alluded to the issue of trying to understand how languages change. With a language like English it is easy to see that it has changed over the centuries. We have only to try to read Shakespeare in the original Folios, Chaucer and the *Anglo-Saxon Chronicle* to find ample evidence of change. Furthermore, contact with certain other languages sometimes reveals interesting cross-language correspondences, e.g. between English and French and English and German, and so on. We might well ask then why we find these and what they tell us about the particular languages in which we find them and language in general.

There are several plausible reasons why different languages might appear to be alike in some way. One would be pure coincidence: the resemblances may occur entirely by chance. For example, since languages make use of so few 'sounds' and they need so many 'words' we might not be surprised to find that certain languages have the same sounds to represent the same meanings. Resemblances of this kind are statistically predictable and it is only when appropriate statistical tests show us that chance alone cannot explain the resemblances that we need to seek some other explanation. Such an explanation might involve 'borrowing': one language has borrowed items from another. We know that borrowing does happen – English, for example, has borrowed heavily from a wide variety of languages – but borrowing tells us only about how people who speak different languages have had significant contact with one another and little about the actual languages themselves. A third explanation is that there might be a 'genetic' relationship between the languages: at some point the languages were 'related' in some very intimate way, a relationship that continues to be manifested in some of their essential characteristics. It is this last explanation that interests us.

That languages are related to one another in certain ways that we can clearly demonstrate is an idea we can trace back for a couple of centuries. Before that, for the most part, languages appeared to be very different unrelatable entities, the result for many of the confusion visited upon humanity after the dispersion following the attempt to build the Tower of Babel. We do know that some people did perceive relationships among languages. For example, in the fourteenth century Dante, while seeking to develop Italian as a language of literature, recognized the affinity of Greek, Latin and Germanic, and in the seventeenth century Leibniz recognized the affinity of Hebrew and Arabic and of Finnish and Hungarian. By the eighteenth century many people had also come to believe that Sanskrit was the common ancestor of a number of contemporary languages even though this view conflicted with another, that Hebrew was the ancestor of all languages, in fact was the 'pre-Babel' and 'original' language. Modern explanations of language relationships of the kind that interest us, however, are said to date from 1786, when Sir William Jones, a judge in India, in a paper read before the Royal Asiatic Society of Bengal, declared that Sanskrit, Latin, Greek, Germanic and Celtic had 'sprung from some common source, which, perhaps, no longer exists'.

Sir William Jones had observed that languages had correspondences that could not be attributed to chance or to borrowing. They must, therefore, be evidence of a relationship that went back, possibly far back, in time. Perhaps there was an ancestor common to all, the ancestral language had changed and varied in different locations, and only the descendant languages provided evidence for both its existence and those changes. Jones was interested in the kinds of evidence we find today. We find that corresponding to English *three* we have *tri* in Irish and Welsh, *treis* in Greek, *tres* in Latin, *tre* in Italian, Danish and Swedish, *tres* in Spanish, *trois* in French, *drei* in German, *drie* in Dutch, *trzy* in Polish, *tri* in Russian and *se* in Persian. However, we find *üc* in Turkish, *tiga* in Malay and *san* in Chinese. Such evidence would suggest that the languages in the first group are related in some way but that those in the second are neither related to those in the first group nor even to one another.

The nineteenth century saw the development of principles for making sense of this kind of evidence. 'Historical linguistics' (see Hock, 1986, for a good introduction) developed rapidly as the result of work by investigators such as Rasmus Rask, Franz Bopp, Jakob Grimm (one of the two Grimm brothers noted for their work in Germanic folklore) and August Schleicher. In the latter part of that century Arthur Leskien and Karl Brugmann became famous for their attempt to state these principles in rigorous fashion, and they and their followers became known as the

*Junggrammatiker* ('neo-grammarians'). By that time investigators had decided that change in language was 'lawful', i.e., it could be stated in somewhat general rules or laws expressed as 'if *x*, then *y*'. The *Junggrammatiker* were prepared to go one stage further than this, rejecting rules and laws that allowed for a certain imprecision in their application and declaring instead that sound laws, or *Lautgesetz*, operate without exception and that no exception operates without a rule.

This 'comparative method' relies heavily on procedures that allow the investigator to formulate laws of the appropriate kind. In Indo-European studies one of the most famous of such laws is 'Grimm's Law'. This law accounts for certain sound changes that occurred between the original language, Proto-Indo-European, and its Germanic descendants. In these Germanic descendants the original Proto-Indo-European voiceless stops became voiceless fricatives, e.g. *\*p* (the asterisk denotes a hypothetical original form) became *f*, original voiced stops became voiceless stops, e.g. *b* became *p*, and original voiced aspirated stops became voiced unaspirated stops, e.g. *bh* became *b*. Consequently, corresponding to Proto-Indo-European *\*trei* we find English *three*, to Proto-Indo-European *\*ped-* we find English *foot* and to Proto-Indo-European *\*bher-* we find English *bear*. There are well-known exceptions to Grimm's Law, exceptions brought about by the placement of accent. 'Verner's Law' accounts for these. There are still other 'laws' needed to account fully for Indo-European (see Collinge, 1985).

Linguists believe that the comparative method can be applied universally to all languages. They have no reason to believe that it is applicable only to the languages on which it has so far been 'proved'. Many believe that it has definite limitations, allowing us to go back in reconstructing ancestral languages – or significant parts of them at least – no more than 10,000 years, although some would halve that period and others would double it.

The comparative method is complemented to some extent by the method of 'internal reconstruction'. This second method allows the investigator to use evidence internal to a language to make useful hypotheses about previous states of the language. Once again the investigator must eliminate 'borrowings', but this time internal ones. For example, we know that in English *vixen* comes from a different dialect than *fox* and that *great, break* and *steak* are also anomalous pronunciations almost certainly due to the same cause, although a little harder to explain in this case. The previously mentioned sound laws tend to create disorder with the 'morphology', i.e. word structure, of a language. Speakers may then proceed to try to undo some of that disorder by 'analogizing', i.e., 'correcting' in some principled way. However, this process too creates its own disorder. The method of internal reconstruction allows us to sort out the various effects of the resultant disorders so that we can make useful hypotheses about previous conditions in a language. It requires us to look at inconsistencies and irregularities and see them as 'relics' of some previously 'ordered' state.

This kind of historical linguistics leads to the postulation of 'proto-languages'. A proto-language is the postulated ancestor of a group of descendant languages. The whole group is sometimes referred to as a language 'family' with a 'parent' language, i.e., the proto-language itself, and the various 'daughter' languages, the descendants. Of course, this model uses 'parent' and 'daughter' in a way that is different from real life: in real life parents do not turn into daughters as they do in the language metaphor. For example, English is the version of Proto-Indo-European that is spoken now by one group of speakers, Russian another version, Albanian still another and so on. We owe this 'family-tree' model mainly to Schleicher. The 'family' of resultant languages is also given a name. English belongs to the Indo-European family, one that also includes other Germanic languages such as German and Danish, Celtic languages, Balto-Slavic languages, Romance languages, Indo-Iranian languages, Greek, Albanian, Armenian and the defunct Tocharian and Anatolian languages. The latter are different from Latin and Sanskrit, which are also Indo-European, in that they provide us with no modern reflexes; Latin continues through the Romance languages and Sanskrit, less directly so perhaps, through languages like Hindi.

A proto-language is also a hypothesis about an actual language that we presume to have existed at some time in the past, although the famous Russian linguist Trubetskoy denied any such existence to proto-languages. It is therefore a kind of theory about what the original language must have been like. When we 'reconstruct' a proto-language we must also propose for that language a structure that meets the kinds of conditions we see in actual languages around us. A proto-language must look like a real language. Consequently, if we reconstructed a proto-language that required 125 phonemes we would probably rule it out and almost certainly ascribe our results to a gross mistake in using the methods of historical linguistics. Similarly, we would be tempted to reject a reconstructed proto-language that had no vowels at all.

The proto-languages that linguists do reconstruct turn out to be limited in certain obvious ways. They are very much limited in the vocabulary that we can reconstruct because there is never enough evidence to reconstruct every word that must have existed. We also know that living languages tend to have a 'substratum' of items from languages that preceded them. Our methods do not allow us to have much access to the substrata of proto-languages. For example, while we can recognize certain substratum items in Ancient Greek, e.g. the words for vine, fig, olive, tin, bronze, king, slave, etc., we cannot easily identify a similar substratum in Proto-Indo-European. Any 'borrowings' the proto-language must have contained are also excluded because the methods allow you to make statements only about 'native' words, since the comparative method is limited to the heritable characteristics of 'native' sound systems. Finally, a proto-language is a language without any kind of internal variation in use, but such internal variation seems to be a basic fact about all languages.

One of the best proofs of the effectiveness of the methodology described above and of its results is found in the reconstruction of Proto-Romance. Proto-Romance is the historical ancestor of the modern Romance languages, principally French, Spanish, Italian, Portuguese and Romanian. However, we also know that these languages are the modern descendants of Latin, so we might expect that the reconstructed Proto-Romance would be just like the Latin we encounter in school. It is not; the differences are not great but they are nevertheless significant. However, the explanation is really quite simple. The Latin we encounter in school is the Latin of a particular kind: the literary Latin of a specific time and place, i.e., it is only one variety of the whole language that existed over a considerable time and distance. Proto-Romance is a theory about that latter kind of Latin, about the spoken language of soldiers, merchants and common people. It was from such people's language that French and the other languages have come, not from the writings of Virgil and Cicero.

We can, of course, get somewhat carried away about our ability to reconstruct a proto-language. August Shleicher, for example, tried to write a simple folk tale in Proto-Indo-European – he called it *Urindogermanisch*. In 1868 he published his version of what he thought a tale entitled 'The sheep and the horses' might have been like in Proto-Indo-European, giving it the title *Avis akvāsas ka*. In 1979 Winfred Lehmann and Ladislav Zgusta, drawing on a century of work since Schleicher's time, rewrote the tale under the revised title *Owis ek'woses-k$^w$e*. In similar vein Robert Hall offered a short retelling of George Orwell's *Animal Farm* in Proto-Romance in which 'All animals are equal' became *Omnes béstie súnt ekuáles*.

The reconstruction of proto-languages has led some investigators to pursue two other related issues: the location in which a particular proto-language was spoken and the date at which it was spoken. Trying to find the location is sometimes described as 'linguistic paleontology', a term that originated with Adolphe Pictet in 1859 in a book on the possible place of origin of the Indo-Europeans. Such a place is sometimes also called the *Urheimat*, the 'primordial home', of the *Ursprache*, the 'primordial language'. Such an endeavour looks at what the reconstructed language can tell us about the kind of place in which its speakers lived and about the kind of culture they appear to have enjoyed.

So far as Proto-Indo-European is concerned we find words for mountains, rivers, lakes, winter (and snow), spring and summer, for copper, possibly even bronze tools, for wheeled vehicles and for various types of trees and animals (including the horse and dog). However, there are serious problems with absence of an equivalent for *beech* and there is controversy over equivalents of *salmon*. There are also numerous cultural indicators. But how does one interpret the evidence (see Diebold, 1987; Gamkrelidze and Ivanov, 1990; Jamieson, 1988; Lehmann, 1990; Mallory, 1989)? One widely accepted original location for speakers of Proto-Indo-European is the area to the north of the Black and Caspian Seas, but other suggestions include such places as Lithuania, Turkey, Armenia and various parts of northwestern Europe. A date of about 5000 years ago is also usually given and the dispersion of the language associated with the activities of a nomadic culture, the Bronze Age Kurgan culture. However, another theory (Renfrew, 1987) adds 3000 years and puts the Proto-Indo-Europeans back about 8000 years ago into an original homeland in what is now Turkey and accounts for dispersion through the diffusion of agricultural practices. The central issue in all such accounts appears to be the reconciliation of all the evidence we have: the linguistic reconstructions, the archeological evidence and a plausible model of the diffusions of languages, peoples and cultures, diffusions which cannot easily be correlated.

There are other ways than those mentioned above of looking at the pasts of languages. One method that was in vogue for a while assumed that the key vocabulary of languages was replaced at a fixed rate. This 'lexicostatistical' idea was then applied to comparisons between languages known to be related, in order to try to indicate how long ago they separated. This technique became known as 'glottochronology'. Morris Swadesh (1971), with whom this technique is most clearly associated (but see also Dyen, 1975), actually developed two diagnostic word lists that investigators could use in their work of comparing pairs of languages for a possible relationship. The first list had two hundred words, which were reduced in a second list to half that number. (The first 20 of these words are *I, you, we, this, that, who, what, not, all, many, one, two, big, long, small, woman, man, person, fish* and *bird*.) Investigators were to seek the equivalents of these words in languages they considered to be related and then use a replacement formula – something like a carbon-dating technique – to calculate a time of separation for the languages. This technique has always been highly controversial and although some who have used it claim that it shows that Spanish and Portuguese split apart in 1586, Romanian and Italian in 1130 and English and German in 590, most investigators find it to be far too subjective to use and therefore not scientifically reliable.

The use of the comparative method alone has actually been severely criticized by those who believe in what has come to be called the 'wave theory', proposed by such linguists as Georg Curtius, Johannes Schmidt and Hugo Schuchardt. This theory rejects the idea that changes in languages occur as sharp breaks. The comparative method and the view of change that must

accompany it require sudden changes and breaks: these are artefacts of the method. Those who subscribe to the wave theory
claim that changes proceed through languages in waves and
that such changes also often do not respect language boundaries.
A modern version of this view is sometimes called 'diffusion
theory', which attempts to show how specific changes percolate
either through a language or across several languages. For
example, diffusion theory might help to explain the earlier
mentioned residual pronunciation we find in words like *great,*
*break* and *steak* in English – they should have the same vowel
sound we find in *meat*. A particular sound change that affected a
certain group of English words containing a vowel often spelled
*ea* began slowly, capturing only a very few words with the vowel
at first, then later a lot of the rest, and still later all but the residue
we now have.

The comparative method also confronts the issue that languages spoken in a particular geographical area may influence
one another whether or not they are related. The result is what
has been called a *Sprachbund*. In the Balkans, for example, there
is mutual borrowing of linguistic features among four different sub-groupings of Indo-European: Slavic (i.e., Bulgarian,
Macedonian and Serbo-Croatian), Romance (i.e., Romanian),
Albanian and Modern Greek. On the Indian subcontinent Indo-
European, Dravidian and Austro-Asiatic languages show clear
signs of the same phenomenon (Masica, 1978), and there is also a
similar area of sharing stretching from southern Mexico to Costa
Rica (Campbell *et al.* 1986), in which some 70 or so languages
show the occurrence of five widespread features: 'possession'
marked like 'his dog the man', the use of 'relational nouns'
equivalent to English forms like 'with-me' and 'below-him', a
counting system based on 20, non-verb-final word order and
some widespread 'loan translations' such as 'door' becoming
'mouth of house', 'cedar' becoming 'god-tree' and 'thumb' becoming 'mother of hand'.

We have seen that languages change and vary and we might
ask why they do so (see Aitchison, 1991). We can hazard a few
possible explanations. Languages contain internal variety of
various kinds: they are not completely consistent, i.e., they 'leak'
in Sapir's words. They have substrata. They – or at least their
speakers – are likely to be in contact with speakers of other

languages. Their speakers 'interfere' with the language they speak, mainly through trying to undo the effects of sound change but also to try to 'correct' and possibly even 'improve' the language. Sometimes they also try to improve themselves and attempt to change their language in such attempts. That success-ive generations have to learn each language anew may also be a contributory factor, but it is not at all easy to demonstrate.

That each language is a kind of abstract target that its speakers must somehow aim at but never quite hit is also another idea, particularly if the actual target is not absolutely fixed. We might even ascribe to each language a kind of life of its own, independ-ent of those who use it, and claim that it is the dynamics of that life which bring about change. In this view a process like 'vowel raising' and 'diphthongization' in a language like English some-how becomes an inherent part of the very nature of the English language. The 'language' has certain internal forces which either 'push' or 'drag' certain parts in definite directions. Finally, we may ask ourselves whether or not change proceeds at the same speed at all times in all languages. Or do individual languages undergo periods of rapid change and slow change in either the language as a whole or in its various parts? Then, how would we know this? Or can we see change only after it has actually occurred and not during the actual process?

The various issues I have discussed above are all well known within linguistic investigations. Recently, several new issues have drawn some attention. One major issue concerns how far we can go back in time in saying anything useful about language. Traditional methods have led to the postulation of a number of language families and proto-languages. Can we do anything more with these? And are there any additional methods not discussed above that will provide us with a still greater 'time depth' in historical work?

Joseph Greenberg is one linguist who has answered such questions affirmatively. After the widely acknowledged success of his work on the classification of the 1500 or more African lan-guages (Greenberg, 1962), Greenberg turned his attention to the problem of classifying the thousand or so indigenous languages of the Americas (Greenberg, 1987). His method required what he has referred to as the 'multilateral comparison' of a fairly small number of what he believes to be related words – actually word etymologies – in these languages. From this work, and it has been extremely extensive, Greenberg concluded that there are three basic groups of indigenous American languages: Amerind, Na-Dene and Eskimo-Aleut. He claims too that this hypothesis is confirmed both by settlement history, i.e., that the settlement of the Americas began some 12,000 years ago and there were three great migrations, and by genetic work, principally of Luigi Luca Cavalli-Sforza, and dental studies.

Greenberg's conclusions are highly controversial and have met with much criticism. However, Greenberg believes that his work is valid and that the kind of genetic classification that he is interested in is a necessary prerequisite to the rigorous 'comparative' work discussed above. In his view the comparative method cannot be used as a way of arriving at a classification of languages; rather it is a method of proving a classification that has already been hypothesized. He points out that this is exactly what happened in Indo-European studies.

However, Greenberg goes still further. He also believes that various 'families' of languages can be shown to be related in a kind of 'super' 'Eurasiatic' family: Indo-European, Uralic, Altaic, Eskimo-Aleut and individual languages like Japanese, Korean and Ainu (although the last three may actually be a sub-group in Greenberg's opinion). This kind of claim puts Greenberg among another group of investigators who try to relate language families using methods that are also extremely controversial. These are the 'Nostraticists'.

The Nostraticists believe that it is possible to develop methods that will allow linguists to postulate super families of languages, possibly even characteristics of the 'original language' of mankind. We owe the term itself to the Danish linguist Holger Pedersen, who placed the Indo-European, Semito-Hamitic, Uralic and Altaic families, and some other individual languages, into a Nostratic family. Modern Nostraticists (see Ross, 1991; Wright, 1991), such as Vitaly Shevoroshkin and Aharon Dolgopolsky, inspired by the earlier work of Vladislav Illich-Svitych, who died quite young in 1966, have used what they refer to as 'broad comparison and deep reconstructions' in order to relate their Indo-European, Afro-Asiatic and South Caucasian families into a west branch of Nostratic and their Uralic, Dravidian and Altaic families into an east branch.

Some of the work has even more grandiose claims. There has been some attempt to reconstruct 'Proto-World', the original language, spoken perhaps 100,000 years ago (see Shevoroshkin, 1990). Shevoroshkin himself has postulated that 'I' was *\*ngai* in Proto-World and some other suggestions from the same line of research are for Proto-World *\*waru* 'burn, be hot, fire', *\*pari* 'fingernail' and *wina* 'ear, hear'.

This line of investigation meets with considerable scepticism. In some quarters it merits little more attention than a claim that language (and the world and all that is in it) originated in one week in 4004 BC or another claim that all the languages of the world descend from the dispersal of the three sons of Noah: Japhet, Shem and Ham. But it is a claim that is likely to be around for a while and cause some rethinking about how we should go about 'deep' historical work in linguistics.

Work in genetics (see Brown, 1990) has now led to the 'Eve hypothesis', i.e., that every human alive today has a common female ancestor who lived in East Africa somewhere between 100,000 and 200,000 years ago. Such a claim comes from work done with tracing the distribution of mitochondrial DNA in the world population. That common female ancestor may actually not have been a *homo sapiens sapiens* and may therefore not have had the language capability we enjoy today. But sometime between 5,000 years ago, the time we can safely reconstruct languages to, and possibly 100,000 or more years ago, language as we know it must have come into existence. Most linguists also assume that this process happened once only.

Finally, that language is *not* continuing to evolve is an assumption that most linguists share in their work. Within the time span with which we are familiar there are no signs of evolution, only signs of change. No language can be demonstrated to be either more or less evolved than any other, nor is there any evidence in the past for the existence of any language that was less evolved. Hence the fundamental dilemma of trying to explain the 'evolution' of language: just what would be appropriate evidence? It is not really surprising, therefore, that the second bylaw of the Linguistic Society of Paris, founded in 1865, should read (in translation): 'The Society will accept no communication dealing with either the origin of language or the creation of a universal language'.

## Further investigation

1  Most languages of the world can be grouped with some other language or languages into a 'family'. A few are complete 'isolates' with no known 'relatives', e.g. Basque (in Spain and France), Gilyak (in Russia), Nahali and Burushaski (in India), Ainu (in Japan) and the extinct Iberian, Etruscan, Sumerian, Elamite and Beothuk. Can you see any reason why some linguists find language isolates to be an intriguing problem?

2  Some Nostraticists believe that in making 'deep' comparisons among languages you should look at how each language expresses certain basic 'concepts'. They suggest concepts like 'I/me', 'two', 'who/what', 'tongue', 'name', 'eye', 'heart', 'tooth', '(finger/toe)nail', 'louse', 'water' and 'dead'. What would be their rationale? How likely is it that the particular sounds used to express such concepts should show fewer changes over many thousands of years than those used to express other concepts?

3  Historical linguists have used metaphors like 'push chains' and 'drag chains' to talk about sound changes in languages. They have also discussed such things as 'rule conspiracies' when two or more 'rules' in a language seem to be 'working together' to bring about a particular change. Such metaphors seem to suggest that languages have 'lives' of their own, independent of those who use them. How useful (or dangerous) is such a notion?

4  It has been said that in the development of individual humans 'ontogeny recapitulates phylogeny', i.e., that individual human development from conception to adulthood recapitulates the history of the species from the creation of the first cell to final *homo sapiens sapiens*. Try to reverse the idea. Can we learn anything about the possible ontogeny of language by using our knowledge of the development of the various species that have inhabited the earth and, in particular, by looking into human ancestry?

5  Linguists believe that there is no evidence at all for the idea that language is continuing to evolve. What would you consider to be evidence of the continuing evolution of language?

6  'Pidgin' and 'creole' languages are sometimes cited as examples of less-than-full languages. Linguists, however, prefer to regard the former as forms of communication developed for highly restricted purposes and the latter as no different from any other languages, except for their known recent historical development. How tenable is this view (see Mühlhaüsler, 1986; Romaine, 1988)?

## 5.3  Other types of variation

When we investigate the language of individuals, we find that speech varies not only with region and social class, but also with the age of the speaker and listener (see Hudson, 1980; Montgomery, 1986; Scherer and Giles, 1979; Wardhaugh, 1992). For example, as we will see in the final chapter, children acquire language in such a way that their speech differs at different stages in their lives: they babble for a while during the first year, speak in single-word utterances at some time early in the second year and gradually build up command of the language until they are using extremely complicated utterances by the end of their third year. Parents and older children also often speak to very young children using language forms specially tailored to the occasion, i.e., 'baby talk' or 'motherese'. But we must remember that baby talk is the talk that others use to babies, not the talk of babies. Some of the forms used in both baby talk and motherese may actually be helpful to very young children, e.g. 'reduplications' like *bow wow, bye bye* and *choo choo*, simplifications like *tummy* for *stomach*, marking nouns with a final -*y*, as in *kitty* and *doggy* and referring to oneself as *Daddy* or *Mummy*. However, some may not be at all helpful, particularly the numerous phonological distortions such as pronouncing *rabbit* like *wabbit* or some of those that completely distort the normal 'pitch' level of speech and the quality of individual vowels.

We also assume that children of five or six have learned enough language to be able to begin some kind of formal education. However, their speech continues to change. In particular, school-age children continue to develop their grammatical abilities and the influence of peers becomes very important. The language of early adolescence is particularly likely to show such peer-group influence. The whole of the childhood–early adolescent period is also the period during which children acquire much of the folk-lore of their culture (Opie and Opie, 1959) and become aware of, and eventually master, many of the rituals on which successful human relationships depend. The later part of the period may be characterized by the adoption of special vocabularies of 'slang' terms, whose principal function is to identify the members of particular groups. Specific slang words rarely find their way into regular use in the language, but slang as a phenomenon has persisted over the centuries. Early adulthood sees the elimination, or fossilization, of much of this slang as more emphasis is given to acquiring the language necessary for work and leisure-time activities.

Because language use varies quite predictably with the age of the user we can say that certain language uses are 'age-graded'; each individual seems to pass through a sequence of age grades. Violations of age-grading are readily noticeable when they occur, e.g. a 50-year-old talking like a teenager, a ten-year-old talking like an old man, a six-year-old talking like a baby, a 13-year-old attempting to talk like a 19-year-old and so on. Sometimes the result is embarrassment or discomfort to listeners because of the false notes that are struck as a consequence, but sometimes it is one of amusement. However, since the grades in age-grading are not absolutely discrete, the possibility for variation does occur. It may not always be possible to know exactly what is required to 'be your age' so far as language is concerned, and part of being a 13-year-old might actually be sounding like a nine-year-old on one occasion and like a 19-year-old on another!

Gender differences in language also exist (see Baron, 1986; Coates, 1986; Lakoff, 1975; Smith, 1985). Differences associated with gender should be easier to detect than those associated with region, social class and age because there are only two genders in contrast to the continua involved there. Certain differences have been observed between the characteristic language uses of men and women. Women tend to have higher-pitched voices than men because of fairly basic anatomical differences, but they are also likely to be more precise and 'careful' in speaking in general and this fact has nothing to do with anatomy. For example, they are more likely than men to pronounce the final *-ing* forms discussed earlier, with *-ing* rather than with *-in'*, preferring *fighting* to *fightin'*. In general, they take more 'care' in articulation. This behaviour accords with certain other findings, e.g. that women tend to be more conscious than men of socially preferred usages, are more likely than men to use 'appeal tags' such as *isn't it?* or *don't you think?* and employ a wider range of intonation patterns.

Women also use some words that men do not use or use somewhat differently. (This sentence could just as well read that men use some words differently from women; I intend no value judgement in stating the comparison one way rather than the other.) Women have more colour names than men, e.g. *mauve, lavender, turquoise, lilac* and *beige*. Men either do not use these colour words or, if they do, use them with great caution or because they are engaged in particular trades such as interior decorating. Intensifiers such as *so, such* and *quite*, as in *He's so cute, She's such a dear* and *We had a quite marvellous time* comprise still another set of words not available to most men, who also avoid adjectives like *adorable, lovely* and *divine*.

It has recently been asserted that a language can have a gender bias built right into it (Spender, 1980; Penelope, 1990). In this view a language can actually favour one gender over the other. English has been cited as an example of such a language. English speakers refer to *mankind*, not *womankind* or *personkind*, and use *him* to refer back to *person* in utterances, thus, it is said, giving a preference to men rather than to women in the species as a whole. It has been pointed out too that *He's a professional* and *She's a professional* have very different meanings, as have *master* and *mistress*.

Differences such as these are said to indicate quite clearly that language is used to downgrade women in society, both who they are and what they do. Words like *lady* and *girl* are also said to demean their referents in many of the usages in which they occur, e.g. *lady doctor* and *She's out with the girls*. On the other hand, there is usually nothing pejorative about *man* and *boy*, e.g. *He's quite a little man* and *He's out with the boys*. Men may sometimes be addressed by last name alone (*Smith* or *Jones*) but this practice is hardly known at all with women, who instead tend to be addressed by a term that refers to their marital status (*Miss Jones* or *Mrs Smith*) or patronizingly employs a first name (*Mary* or *Jane*), even when such first-name use is not reciprocated, i.e., Mary replies using *Mr Smith*. The adoption of *Ms* in writing has been a deliberate attempt to right a perceived imbalance in the writing system.

English does have a system of gender classification, as do many other languages. It is also clear that many speakers of English, both men and women, exhibit gender biases in their behaviour. We can also acknowledge that people do react to different linguistic usages in predictable ways and that many such reactions are related to gender. We might feel it unfortunate that a male worker on an assembly line cannot easily say *What a marvellous idea!* to a male co-worker without perhaps having his masculinity called into question, or that profanity from a woman is sometimes very differently viewed from identical profanity from a man. The important issue so far as language is concerned is how particular linguistic forms are regarded on different occasions and why they are so regarded. To say that they should be differently regarded is to adopt the role of the social engineer not that of the linguistic scientist. It may be a very important role, but it is almost certainly a different one, nevertheless.

Ethnicity also plays some part in language variation: we can identify certain styles of speaking with certain ethnic groups. In particular, the Pennsylvania Dutch and the Jewish groups in the United States have provided popularizers with numerous examples of ethnic pronunciations, grammatical structures, morphological patterns and vocabulary items. Yiddish, for example, has provided a particularly fruitful source, e.g. *You should live so long, Beautiful she isn't, I need it like a hole in the head, He asked me for it yet, Jerk schmerk!* and so on.

More recently black Americans have occasioned the same interest in ethnicity and language, as a search has been undertaken to find any special characteristics that might be distinctive of the English spoken by many members of this group. Various characteristics have been proposed (Burling, 1973; Dillard, 1972; Labov, 1972a) as defining examples of 'Black English' or 'Vernacular Black English', two of the most frequently used labels for this variety. For example, in words like *pin* and *pen* the vowels will usually be nasalized and the final consonants dropped. These two words will also become 'homophones', i.e., they will be pronounced alike, through the resulting 'neutralization' (i.e., loss) of the vowel contrast. Such neutralization of vowels also frequently occurs before *r* or *l*, which themselves may 'vocalize', i.e., become vowels, in addition. Final consonant groups often simplify so that *test* comes to sound like *Tess* and *mask* like *mass*. *Then* and *den* may seem to be interchangeable pronunciations of *then*, and *three* and *tree* of *three*. Final *-ing* is pronounced as *-in*; unstressed syllables are often lost, giving us *'bout* and *'cept* for *about* and *except*, and stress is often shifted forward to produce *Détroit, pólice* and *hótel.*

In syntax the use of *do* is somewhat different from the use of *do* in Standard English, as in *I done told him about it*. Similarly, the use, or sometimes non-use, of *be* is different, as *He be waitin' for me every night* and *He waitin' for me right now*. The *be* in the first example shows a customary, recurring activity, i.e., marks a 'durative aspect', whereas the absence of *be* in the second example shows a momentary, non-recurring state. William Labov (1969) has pointed out, however, that *be* can be deleted only in those places in which contraction of the verb is possible, i.e., *I don't care what you are* resists deletion because *I don't care what you're* is not possible. The agreement of subject and verb may also be different, as in *He have done it* and *He walk there every day*, multiple negation may be frequent, as in *She don't say nothin'*, *ain't* abounds and quite different forms from Standard English are sometimes found, e.g. *I asked Tom do he want to do it* and *Didn't nobody see it?*

Rhetorical, i.e., stylistic, usages are also likely to be somewhat different. Black English employs considerable exaggeration and hyperbole, a wide intonation range, use of the falsetto voice on occasion and in certain circumstances audience or listener participation and encouragement, e.g. *Amen, Right on*. Many different kinds of verbal displays are also found, in which an emphasis is placed on the very quality of the linguistic performance, e.g. 'roasting', 'rapping', 'signifying', 'playing the dozens', etc. Good performances are 'cool', and to be unable to participate is to mark oneself as a 'lame'.

There has been considerable discussion concerning whether Black English originated as a variety of southern states English, therefore is just another dialect of American English, or is a 'creolized' variety of English – like some Caribbean varieties that exist – and therefore really a different language from English. (A creole is a separate language, and even though one may speak of it as being a creolized variety of X, it is still a different language from X.) No matter how Black English began, today the differences between it and other varieties of American English are quite superficial. For example, William Labov's point about the impossibility of deleting *be* in certain circumstances, i.e., when contraction is not possible, appears to be an argument which strongly suggests that Black English is really quite close to Standard English, and that any differences are no more than minor differences in the application of a few rules, the consequences of which are superficial rather than profound. However, the creolist view is that the differences are profound rather than superficial and cannot be accounted for by rules of this kind. Creolists insist that only if we are prepared to recognize the languages as being quite different will we be able to appreciate the true nature of the communication problems that sometimes appear to exist between speakers of Black English and English.

There is no question that we do associate certain types of speech with certain ethnic backgrounds. Various experiments have shown that in parts of the United States people are able to distinguish between blacks and whites on the telephone with about an eighty per cent reliability and in general fail to pick out only atypical individuals. Studies that deny this fact have always used a disproportionate number of such individuals. The results are therefore useless for making generalizations to the total population. 'Stereotyping', i.e., using only one or two or a very few features for the purpose of classification, is clearly demonstrable in black–white relationships in general and in speech in particular. However, it is not unidirectional, it involves other ethnic groups too, and it is not confined merely to North America. This is one area in life in which language co-varies with social grouping. It is also one area where we might predict that if this kind of social grouping were to become less important in society we might find a reduction in language variation. However, the resurgence in the late twentieth century of 'ethnicity' as a factor in social organization seems to suggest that this kind of variation will persist.

Occupational and role differences can also be associated with language differences. Occupations tend to have their own 'jargons', i.e., technical linguistic usages, including their own ways of using otherwise familiar words. Linguistics is full of special words, e.g. *phoneme, morpheme, uvular* and *creole*. It also uses familiar words in unfamiliar ways, e.g. *generate, transformation, government* and *binding*. Doctors, preachers and pimps obviously use different words, and they use them in different ways for different purposes. Successful doctoring, preaching and pimping require mastery of the different kinds of language of each vocation, and the professional fairly readily distinguishes the imposter through failures of usage.

An individual, of course, must choose jargons according to circumstances. Language must be varied according to the role that you are playing, e.g. father, son, consultant, drinking companion, etc. Speaking requires a choice of 'register'. A physician discussing a medical problem with colleagues will use one register, discussing roses with a fellow gardening enthusiast another, discussing bicycles with a daughter a third and discussing car insurance with an insurance agent a fourth. But if a register offers choices that depend on topic and listener, it also offers 'stylistic' choice too, because one can discuss a medical problem at various levels of style.

The anthropologist Clifford Geertz (1960) has pointed out that Javanese – Java is the main island of Indonesia – provides its speakers with a very rich system for making choices in both register and style. Considerations of gender, kinship, occupation, wealth, education, religion and family are among those that determine what form a particular linguistic act will take, even a simple statement or question. On the other hand, Indonesian is a neutral 'democratic' language in that it does not have this elaborate system. Consequently, people often use Indonesian in Java when uncertainty exists as to what Javanese forms would be appropriate on a specific occasion. As issues of appropriateness become more and more important as Javanese society undergoes social change, the use of Indonesian allows them to be set safely off to one side while communication goes on.

Following his investigation of 'style' differences in language use, the linguist Martin Joos (1962) proposed that there are five distinctive styles, what he called the 'frozen', 'formal', 'consultative', 'casual' and 'intimate' styles. We can look at these as they apply to the spoken language but should note that they can also be applied to the written language. Frozen style uses highly formalized and ritualistic language. It is the language of high ceremony and ritual. In a sense this kind of style completely ignores the listener because the listener is merely one of the actors in a kind of performance. Pledges are pledged, vows are exchanged, prayers are intoned, proclamations are proclaimed and set pieces of prose and poetry are delivered. Interruptions rarely occur and, when they do, they stop or violate the ritual rather than change it, and the speaker or speakers merely start again from where they left off, as though nothing had happened, if they have not just simply ignored the interruption. In frozen style the 'performance' is often as important, sometimes more important, than any 'message'. In fact we might even say that the actual performance comprises most of the message itself.

Formal style also allows for little participation from the listener. It is speech that is carefully planned and deliberately delivered, sometimes to a large audience. Between individuals, formal style indicates social distance, reproof or deference. It is the mother's *John Smith, what are you doing?* to her misbehaving son. Consultative style, on the other hand, does involve the listener. Information gets communicated and feedback occurs. Ellipses, contractions and interruptions are possible. This was obviously the style that Queen Victoria expected from her prime ministers. Unfortunately William Gladstone, one of the most long-serving of these, seems not to have used it, preferring a formal style which led the queen to observe that 'He speaks to Me as if I was a public meeting'.

Casual style is the style which friends use with each other, or which people who are intimately acquainted with a topic usually adopt for discussion of that topic. Casual style indicates a sharing of considerable background information and many assumptions. Ellipses, contractions, interruptions, jargon and slang occur frequently. The sharing of so much background understanding enables many comments and decisions to be made quickly, e.g. *'s good movie, Can't go – homework, OK.*

Intimate style is even more terse, often just consisting of rather frequent single-word utterances and non-verbal communication. Its function also tends to be different from the functions of the other styles. It is used to express feelings rather than to make statements or to work through to decisions. It is therefore the language of people who know each other extremely well and is often very private. It is the language of the long-married, of lovers and sometimes of people engaged in very intricate and well-practised work, e.g. a team playing basketball, performing surgery or drilling an oil well.

Register and style are intimately related, if only for the fact that they cannot clearly be separated because both address themselves to many of the same issues. People do have a wide range of choices available to them when they speak: they can be technical or non-technical; they can be formal or informal; they can be extremely conscious of their roles or quite unconscious of them; they can be familiar with the listener or unfamiliar; and so on. The consequences will show in the way they use the language: in the amount of technical terminology they employ; the care they take in articulation; the speed with which they speak; the kinds of omissions they make and others are prepared to tolerate; the types and complexity of grammatical constructions they choose; the standards of grammatical 'accuracy' they observe; the use they make of phrases like *You know* and *You see*; and even how they use the pronoun *I*.

## Further investigation

1  One of the main defining features of 'slang' appears to be its ephemeral nature. How might you go about documenting this fact? (Note that there is a problem here in the idea of 'documenting' because slang is quintessentially a phenomenon of speech rather than of writing.)
2  'Jargon' is the technical language of a particular group. I have tried to keep the jargon of linguistics to a minimum in this book, but have found some use of linguistic jargon to be quite unavoidable. Look at the words I have used. Could I have avoided some of them? Look at some other group's 'jargon' in the same way. Note that sometimes people develop a jargon deliberately in order to give the appearance of learning, expertise, exclusiveness and so on.
3  Look into the debate about 'sexism' in language. What are the issues? What counts as 'evidence'?

## 5.4　Is variety useful?

Language variation may seem to be as regrettable a fact about language as language change. A single language used by speakers throughout the world with no variation may appear to many people to be a perfect state of affairs. Indeed, artificial languages like Esperanto are promoted largely to serve such a purpose; at the very least they appear to offer people everywhere a fixed and invariant second language! The development and spread of major world languages, particularly English, the rise of literacy, the use of computer technology for storing and processing information and the potency of the mass media might be interpreted as indicating that the fulfilment of such a wish may not be too far distant without having recourse to artificial means. And certainly much of public education everywhere in the world is predicated on the assumption that variation within existing languages should be eradicated and, if possible, the natural processes of language change should be resisted. Given a fixed and invariant language, people would not have to worry either about being quite unable to talk to people from other parts of the world or about their speech 'giving them away' in their personal relationships closer to home. Language would then be a unifying force in human organization, not a divisive one. But how realistic is such a view?

The question about the desirability of such an occurrence is obviously not a linguistic one alone. Language change and variation are associated with cultural change and variation, and possibly more fundamentally with human change and variation. It is even possible to argue that this kind of variation – biological, cultural and language – is a necessity for the very survival of the human species. Such diversity encourages types of evolutionary development that sustain the viability of the species. A species which cannot change and adapt becomes at best a living fossil, out of place in the times it finds itself in, and at worst extinct.

Fernando Nottebohm's (1970) investigations of the songs of chaffinches and white-crowned sparrows led him to speculate that the 'dialect' differences he found in such songs have a survival value for the birds. The differences create just enough distance to keep groups of birds apart but not enough to stop cross-breeding. The result is a healthy, varied gene pool. A single catastrophic blow would not wipe out a whole species because the variation in the gene pool ensures the survival of some members. Adaptation is also possible when circumstances change.

There is good reason to believe that language change and variation are inevitable and that we can do very little about it. From time to time we can try to apply a brake here or give a little push there, but change itself goes on. Similarly, with language variation: we may deplore this or that bit of variation, but at the same time we are not even aware of considerable variation elsewhere and even participate – generally unconsciously but sometimes quite consciously – in actually promoting variation. However, if, as many linguists believe, languages inevitably change and vary by their very nature, what else can we do? Dealing with language change and variation may be part of the price we must pay to remain viable as a species. That price may seem excessive on some occasions when misunderstanding and conflict arise as a result, but when we realize the advantages that the ability to use language confers on us as a species it is probably a very small price to pay for benefits unknown to any other species on earth.

## Further investigation

1   Does the development of 'standard languages' and the spread of 'literacy' encourage or discourage linguistic variation in the world?
2   'Languages' like Esperanto have been promoted for their usefulness as universal 'auxiliary' languages. Do you see any problems such languages would face if they did become established in very different places and among very different peoples?
3   There is a scientific concept known as 'entropy' i.e., the idea that all systems have a natural tendency toward disorder. If languages are 'systematic' they would have the same tendency. What countervailing forces appear to be at work?

# 6

# *Of what use is language?*

Language is both an individual and a group possession. However, as I have observed, linguists generally prefer to investigate those aspects of language to which all the members of a group have access rather than the idiosyncrasies of the speech of individuals. The general rather than the particular has claimed their attention. One consequence is a kind of paradox: linguists usually attempt to describe the language system all speakers of a language presumably share by using data they gather from very few speakers – sometimes even only a single individual – and they do not attempt to describe individual variation unless they have access to data from many individuals. Since, as we have discovered, these last kinds of data are also extremely difficult to acquire, linguists have made relatively few such attempts.

Linguistic investigations and theorizing instead tend to be concentrated on attempts to specify the formal characteristics of 'language', i.e., its overall design and its various component units and processes, rather than on the uses that language might have in our lives. Attempts to deal with the 'communicative uses' of language, i.e., with how any group or individual makes use of language, have seemed to be far less important than attempts to make statements about phonemes, morphemes, rules, transformations, principles and so on, and how these may relate to one another. Some linguists even believe that issues of this last kind are at the heart of linguistic investigation and that they should devote most of their attention to them. In this view, only when linguists know what language is can they usefully turn their attention to what people use it for.

Consequently, while linguists readily acknowledge that language is speech, in practice most actually tend to ignore or downplay the various acts of speaking. It almost seems at times that an agreement exists to deny that we use language to communicate with one another. Of course, we communicate in a wide variety of ways, through our clothing, where we live, how we stand, how we gesture, our manners and so on. But, above all, we communicate through language and no other such system that we use has the potential for communication that language has. It seems therefore quite remiss to ignore this aspect of language.

A number of issues come immediately to mind. What functions does language serve in the total system of human communication? What relationships, if any, are there between the linguistic forms of a language and the various functions these forms serve? How do particular bits of communication work, e.g. how does a particular conversation succeed or fail? Answers to questions such as these can be sought only in a linguistics that is concerned with both linguistic form and linguistic function, with both speech and speaking, and with both language and language use. Fortunately, some linguists are concerned with how people use the languages they possess and with some of the consequences for them of having languages to use.

A well-justified initial assumption in investigations that result from such a concern is that every language is a system that allows its users to interact with one another. The system not only allows individual 'minds' to function, but also provides a means for sharing the results of that functioning with others. We can understand and appreciate the system in its entirety only if we are also prepared to consider this transactional aspect of language, i.e., only if we complement a study of the formal properties of language with a study of its functional uses.

A second assumption is that language use is systematic. Just as individual speech is not haphazard, neither is collective speech. Monologues, dialogues, conversations, narratives and language used for thinking, imagining, speculating, ordering, questioning and answering all reveal certain systematic features. A simple illustration of the validity of this assumption is that people quite consistently recognize failures to use language properly, e.g. a word that is inappropriate, a story that is incoherent, a joke that falls flat and many other kinds of 'aberrant' language use.

People make systematic use of language to identify themselves with others and also to differentiate themselves from still others.

Language performs an important social function in that it allows people to express their identities, to show their solidarity with others and, of course, on occasion, to achieve some distancing too. No other species has anything like language that members of that species can use to do these kinds of things. Such uses are therefore well worth investigating.

## 6.1   Language as action

One of the simplest yet most essential uses of language is that of social bonding and maintenance; a language helps to define and perpetuate a particular community. People who share the same language are able to communicate with one another. Without a common language they would experience a host of difficulties in conveying any but the simplest messages. A shared language or variety of a language provides a channel for communication which allows people to bond to one another in a variety of ways, e.g. by language group itself, ethnic origin, religious persuasion, social class, occupation, gender, age and so on.

The availability of a shared language or variety does not necessarily mean that only new and original things are said, i.e., that people use that language or variety only to pass genuine information among themselves. Language also serves the purpose of 'phatic communion' (see Malinowski, 1923). The presence of language allows people to feel that they are in touch with others and that a channel of communication is open should they really need to use it. Exchanges of *How do you do*s and *Hi*s function in this way, as do many comments about the weather, health, feelings, relatives and recent or current events such as ball games. Requests for matches or the time, and sometimes even exchanges of easily accessible information, e.g. directions, also fall into this category. 'Idle gossip' too is another manifestation, e.g. the 'small talk' of the workplace, which though often 'job talk' is not usually serious job talk. In all of the above, little or no real information is exchanged, but shared knowledge and understandings are rehearsed while essential social contacts are maintained. People indulge in a kind of continual 'checking' to see that the channel of communication remains open, and the same rituals occur time after time.

Phatic communion has an additional function in that it establishes the worth of the participants by acknowledging that they could talk to one another about more important matters if that were necessary. They are not complete strangers. They have not been excluded from sharing. They do not threaten one another with their silences or by their failure to indulge in meaningless exchanges and small talk. They participate in a communion of words and achieve a sense of group solidarity through that communion. In some ways, therefore, this use of language serves humans much like 'grooming behaviour' serves many animals. Grooming behaviour brings animals together and helps them maintain social relationships. An ungroomed animal, one that for some reason does not participate in this important group activity, is a rejected animal. Who can talk to whom and how easy or not it is to talk to another are important in human society in much the same way. As we well know, a word of approval can have a powerful effect on a person's self-esteem and exclusion from a group can be quite damaging.

Investigations have shown that voice quality, posture, distance and other kinds of behaviour are also important in communication. Glancing, looking, staring and complete eye avoidance all produce different effects. Both looking at someone and returning a look are social acts. English has numerous expressions indicating the importance of eye contact, among them *to stand eyeball to eyeball, to recognize a speaker, to catch someone's eye* and *to be downcast.* Speakers also relate to each other in very subtle ways. In conversation they may vary their rates of speech, their loudness, their speech rhythms, their habits of pausing, their amounts of talking and even their accents in relation to other participants. In doing so, they demonstrate that there is more to speaking than just using words, and more to a conversation than what a transcript of that conversation records.

Watching people talk to each other is in some ways like watching a dance. In performing that dance, the participants show whether they are in harmony or conflict with one another, and they may also show who is leading and who is following. The amount of eye contact, the quality of the voices, the gestures and the conversational rhythms will reflect the participants' feelings about what is happening during the conversation. A conversation which all participants feel is 'good' or 'useful' will be

accompanied by a different kind of dance from one they feel to
be 'bad' or 'destructive'. There will be a harmony of words and
gestures among the participants – a symmetry of behaviours.
An effective communicator is one who is capable of getting
others to dance to the communicator's tune, not to some other
tune. And not to get anyone to dance at all indicates complete
failure!

This function of language, then, is a socially supportive one.
The claim is a very different one from that advanced by Benjamin
Lee Whorf (see Carroll, 1956) that the way a language is structured determines certain kinds of intellectual and social behaviour.
As we will see soon, that claim arose from a somewhat superficial examination of languages and from drawing unwarrant-
ed conclusions from literal translations of certain words and
expressions. The claim being advanced here is that many words
and expressions we use in everyday speech are so fixed, ritualistic
and conventional as to be virtually 'meaningless'. It is their ritualistic value, the dance of speaking itself, and the place of that
dance in social organization and maintenance that is important.

Language also allows for communication of another kind. It
allows for memory, particularly the collective memory called
history, in contrast to instinct, or genetic memory. Language
allows people to build communities not bounded by either the
recent past or the immediate circumstances, but on the basis of
abstractions and speculations about past, present and future, and
of ideas and ideals that all members of the community share. In
this view language provides the cornerstone of all 'higher' behaviour and whatever freedom humans enjoy to move beyond genetic
constraints. It gives humans new powers of adapting to the
environment and of adapting that environment to them for good
or ill. Therefore, language provides our species with the opportunity to bring about cultural change. Animal 'culture' cannot be
changed in the same way.

Any attempt, therefore, to discuss how language functions in
communication requires you to make a clear distinction between
'language forms' and 'language functions'. Language forms are
the phonological, syntactic and semantic properties of language;
language functions, in the sense used here, are the uses speakers
make of language forms in communication, i.e., the 'pragmatic'
uses of language (see Leech, 1983; Levinson, 1983). Certain

language forms are often quite closely related to certain language functions. For example, forms like *Let's go* and *Please sit down* generally function as requests, forms like *What would you like?* and *Are you ready?* generally function as questions and forms like *He scored a goal* and *She didn't come this morning* generally function as statements. The important word here is *generally*. In actual language use, language forms do not correlate quite so neatly with language functions on many occasions.

A sign that says *Dangerous dog* is a warning, not just a simple statement that a particular kind of dog is somewhere nearby. *I like that one* may be a request for someone to buy the object that occasioned the remark. *I would like that dress* said to a sales assistant is a request to buy the dress, but, said to a companion during a window-shopping outing, may indicate no more than a bit of wishful thinking. *You've changed!* said about someone changing clothes may be a request for a reason for an unexpected action. *Your room's a mess!* said by a mother to her child is usually not meant to be taken as a simple statement of fact about the condition of the room but as a command to tidy it up. *I can't find my glasses* may well be an indirect request for assistance, just as a teacher's comment that *It's warm in here* may lead a student to open a window. *Will you send me your trial offer?* in a letter to a mail-order house is a request, although the form is that of a question. *Can you do it for me?* may get either one of two responses: *Yes* or the doing of the requested action. *Don't tell me that he's gone and done it!* will usually lead to an act of telling that he has indeed gone and done it, in spite of both the form and content of what was said. The question *Are we going to stand for that kind of treatment?* cannot appropriately be answered *Yes*; it is a rhetorical question requiring *No* for an answer and not a genuine *yes-no* question, which would have allowed either answer. A child who asks another child *Why is a Volkswagen like an elephant?* expects not an answer to that question, but a response such as *I don't know* followed by *Why is a Volkswagen like an elephant?* Moreover, the second child knows that this answer is expected and is actually the best possible answer in the circumstances.

Any attempt to classify language forms that disregards the function of those forms must miss a good deal that can and should be said about language. It must certainly miss the fact that listeners know that they interpret particular forms used in certain contexts in different ways from the same forms used in other contexts. Data such as those just cited are therefore not in dispute and must be accommodated in any truly comprehensive account of how we use English. The key issue is one of deciding on some principled basis which language functions are important within communication and then of relating, so far as it is possible, language forms to these functions. Some interesting investigative work has been done on this issue, particularly by philosophers.

A basic assumption behind any attempt to understand language functioning is that most utterances have a purpose, i.e., they are spoken with an 'intent' to communicate something. We must ask what a speaker intended by an utterance before we can fully understand what the utterance really meant. The speaker's intention, therefore, is part of the meaning of any utterance. But it is necessary to make hypotheses about what is going on inside the blackboxes that are people's minds in order to decide on intentions. In contrast, we do not usually inquire about the intentions of the sun, rainbows, rivers and trees. We also may well experience some intermediate degree of difficulty in trying to decide whether animals 'intend' certain things. Just what are we implying about intent when we say *The cat wants out?*

We can consider speaking to be a series of 'acts' of a particular kind rather than a series of 'events', the difference between an act and an event being that an act has an element of purposefulness or intent to it, whereas an event is just something that happens. If speaking did not consist of acts but only of events then it would be empty because communication would cease. Speech would be a set of artefacts rather than a set of utterances. An undeciphered writing system offers just such a set of artefacts in the absence of any knowledge of the meaning and intent of the writing. Speech must also use acts systematically; otherwise communication would break down through sheer unpredictability.

According to the philosopher of 'speech acts', John Austin (1962), there are three different kinds of such acts: 'locutionary' acts, 'illocutionary' acts and 'perlocutionary' acts. A locutionary act is an utterance with a certain sense and reference, i.e., the utterance is meaningful. All meaningful utterances are locutionary acts. But a speech act may also be an illocutionary act in that it may do one of a number of different things, e.g. announce, state, assert, describe, admit, warn, command, congratulate, comment, request, reprove, apologize, criticize, approve, welcome, thank, promise, regret and so on. It may also be a perlocutionary act, one that brings about or achieves some other condition or effect by its utterance, e.g. an act that convinces, amuses, deceives, encourages, bores, embarrasses, inspires, irritates, persuades, deters, surprises or misleads someone. Any properly formed utterance is therefore a locutionary act. The difference between an illocutionary act and a perlocutionary act is that the second requires the first to be successful.

The words *Stop that!* comprise a locutionary act because the utterance is well formed. *Stop that!* may also be an illocutionary act in the right circumstances, e.g. if said by one person to another who is doing something that should not be done, and the person uttering *Stop that!* has the right to insist that it be not done, and the person to whom the command is being given is in a position, and under some obligation, to desist. If the illocutionary act is successful in bringing an end to the activity, then we have a perlocutionary act. Illocutionary acts are locutionary acts, but perlocutionary acts do not necessarily require locutionary acts as a base; non-linguistic acts can amuse, deceive, embarrass, irritate and so on, but only words can be used to state, admit, request and promise – or some conventional substitute for words.

Within the category of illocutionary acts there is an important division to be made between 'constative' utterances and 'performative' utterances. Constatives are propositions that can be stated positively or negatively, e.g. *The sun will rise at seven tomorrow morning, I don't like cabbage, He's Fred's cousin, Sally denied the story, Angels look over my bed at night* and so on. They are statements of 'fact', sometimes of generally agreed fact (*The sun will rise at seven tomorrow morning*) and other times of disputed fact (*Angels look over my bed at night*). At the centre of any argument is the question of either the truth or falsity of the statement (*No, the sun will rise at seven fifteen tomorrow morning*) or the impossibility of verification (*There are no such things as angels*). On the other hand, performative utterances do not report on anything and cannot be said to be either true or false. It is the very uttering of a performative in the right circumstances that is the action or some part of the action, e.g. *I bet you a pound* or *I promise I will stop smoking.* The speaker does something in the act of saying something. A later report of that doing or saying is, of course, a constative utterance, i.e., it is either a true report or a false one and not an act of the same kind (unless it is considered an act of reporting).

Austin distinguished five different kinds of performatives, each kind relying on certain characteristic verbs. The first kind, 'verdictives', give verdicts, findings or judgements, e.g. the umpire's *Out!* or *Safe!*, the jury's *Guilty* or *Not guilty* and the appraiser's *I estimate £400.* The second kind, 'exercitives', show the exercise of powers, rights or influence, e.g. the lawyer's *I advise you to say nothing*, the judge's *I sentence you to four years in jail*, the police officer's *Stop*, the employer's *You're fired* and the voter's *Aye* or *Nay*. The third kind, 'commissives', indicate commitments or promises of different kinds, or the taking on of an obligation, or states an intention, e.g. *I promise you my loyalty, I swear I saw her do it, I guarantee it for six months* or *I bet you a pound.* The fourth kind, 'behavatives', comprise a miscellaneous group to do with expressions of attitudes and social behaviour; it covers the use of verbs like *congratulate, compliment, welcome* and *apologize*, statements like *I'm sorry*, expressions of approval like *Thank you* and terms of abuse. The final kind, 'expositives', keep discussion and argument going by providing different kinds of clarification, e.g. *I assume you will have an explanation to give, I concede that point* or *I hypothesize that at least half will fail.* The kinds are not clear-cut since there is some overlap, but the performative nature of an individual utterance is usually quite clear.

So far as the use of such verbs and expressions is concerned, while the subject *I* and the object *you* are often present in a performative utterance, they do not have to be. However, most performatives can be recast to include *I* and *you* if one or both are absent. Similarly, the performative verb is in the present tense and the word *hereby* can be included: (*I hereby judge you to be*) *out!*; *I* (*hereby*) *bet you £5* and even (*I hereby say to you*) *I'm sorry.* Of course, the performative utterance must occur in suitable circumstances, what John Searle (1969, 1972) has called the necessary 'felicity conditions'. In the first case I must be in a position to judge whether or not you are out. In the second case there must be a point in dispute on which a wager is possible, my wager must not be outrageous, not *I bet you ten million pounds*, and you must accept it for the bet to be 'on'. And, in the last case, I must be aware that you have been injured in some way. That the utterance itself occurred in the proper circumstances is also sufficient to establish that a particular act occurred, e.g. that a certain decision was made in a game, that a bet was actually made or that either an apology or an expression of sympathy was offered.

As I have just mentioned, so far as the various speech acts themselves are concerned, certain conditions must prevail if they are to be used correctly. For example, requests or commands must be reasonable, in that the speaker must genuinely want something done. It must also be possible for the person to whom the request is made to do that something, a condition that rules out *Be seven feet tall* and *Bring me all heaven for a throne* as genuine requests. That person would also not otherwise do what is requested because being asked to do something you are going to do without asking may well cause some ill-will. Finally, the person making the request must be in a position to make the request of the person or persons to whom it is made. If the request is reasonable, i.e., if it meets these conditions, it must be honoured. Of course, you may dispute a request in different ways, but if the above conditions have been met, failure to honour the request and any such dispute will be construed to be an act of defiance of one kind or another.

In like manner, statements must give an appearance of being true if they are to be believed to be true. Certain conventions actually serve to mark particular classes of statements as not to be believed from the very start, e.g. *Once upon a time, Have you heard the one about. . .?* and *Let's suppose that. . .* Questions must be answerable or follow fixed patterns, as in riddles (*Why is a Volkswagen like an elephant?*) or in rhetorical usages (*Are we going to stand for this?*). *Why aren't you going to wash the dishes?* said to someone who was going to wash the dishes is a challenge not a question, and *Why don't you love me anymore?* said to a spouse whose love is unchanged is hardly likely to produce anything but marital discord. Answers also must be truthful, not evasive, and promises must be sincere. Sincerity or genuineness of intent is frequently a matter of concern in conversations of all kinds.

This approach to language function through an attempt to understand speech acts is a useful one. Utterances are usually intended to be understood in certain ways. Sometimes that intent is quite clear from the form of the utterance itself, sometimes not. Generally, both form and intent find support too in the physical and social context of the utterance. Lack of clarity in the relationships among form, intent and context leads to ambiguity and possible misunderstanding. A superior's use of the verb *wish* may be intended as a command, understood as a command, but later denied to be a command. When, in addition, each party to a particular language transaction brings different assumptions about what others know and do not know, different views of events that are under discussion, different perceptions of social relationships and different agendas about the purposes of the transaction itself, still further complications are likely to arise. What is perhaps surprising is that so much understanding seems to occur in such unlikely circumstances. Of course, the survival of the species requires no less.

People who know each other well are often quite sure about each other's intent. Strangers do not have those same assurances, particularly strangers who do not share a similar background. The less background that is shared the more explicit everything must be, even what is to be judged as this kind of act or that kind of act. Ceremonies that draw strangers together on an irregular basis must make every act explicit, e.g. weddings, trials, funerals and initiations. This is one purpose of ritual. At the other extreme, over-familiarity can have its dangers. In eliminating many of the customary overt markers of the different kinds of acts, it can produce some uncertainty about the exact status of a particular utterance, its form alone being insufficient to establish the kind of act it is. Again, a speech act does not occur in isolation but within a series of acts that are chained together. What was said, therefore, in any exchange is not just the few words that were exchanged – though why these exact words were used is of very great interest – but the totality of meaning that the individual speech acts communicated in the context. Impressions of conversations also usually last longer and are stronger than memories of the actual words that were used – or all but a very few of these.

### *Further investigation*

1 'Phatic communion' is very important. Try to list a number of instances of it during your day. How might your day have been different without such a use of language? Would the world be a more welcoming or a more threatening place in the absence of phatic communion?

2 How do you make 'requests' to others? Look at the exact grammatical form of a number of requests. Is it correct to say that most such requests are quite 'indirect', i.e., that their language is more like *Would you mind leaving the room for a minute or two!* than like *Get out!*?

3 It is possible to claim that part of learning to speak is learning when to be silent. Try to work out what you know about 'knowing when not to speak'.

## 6.2   Language in action

When we examine the actual words used in any verbal exchange, we must be prepared to view them within the wider physical, mental and social context (see Wardhaugh, 1985). Actual communication can take place only in situations in which the participants share much in common, e.g. a physical location (or some substitute for this), a common goal, a mutual interest, etc. In most cases such communication does not involve ideas that are brand new, the conveyance of large quantities of entirely new information or attempts to bring about complete changes of view or behaviour. Such events are really quite rare. The goals of communication are generally much more limited, and achieving them depends mainly on processes of adjustment and accommodation. The participants assume that they share a body of knowledge and understanding that will provide the basis for the exchange. What they must do is co-ordinate their activities to ensure that sharing occurs. One of the most important things shared is knowledge of language and its uses in communication.

When the participants have long shared much in common, an 'ordinary' event may occasion very little verbal interaction. Even an extraordinary event may arouse little discussion. When there is a great commonality in background, assumptions and interests, few words are needed, and what words that are used may not be very explicit. A heavy dependency will be placed on knowledge that is shared, and everything will be viewed and commented on from a shared perspective. People who have enjoyed a long and intimate relationship with one another often need very few words to communicate effectively and sometimes even none at all. However, in the presence of an outsider they must expand what they say if they wish to include that outsider, because the outsider is not privy to their common perspective. At any time though that outsider may be excluded through resort to the privately shared perspective. All of us at one time or another have had the experience of being excluded quite suddenly in this way by others; what was said and how it was said drew on resources beyond our knowledge and did so knowingly. Of course, after two people become attuned in this way and one has reason to distrust the other or the relationship changes, such inexplicitness is potentially dangerous. No longer are assumptions shared, so utterances may become ambiguous, speech acts not clearly defined and effective communication jeopardized.

When we begin to analyse what goes on in particular conversations, we may find that certain things not mentioned directly are actually being talked about or talked around. We sometimes find that a particular word or sentence quickly opens up or even closes down a whole topic or indicates how issues related to the topic are to be resolved or to be left unresolved. But this process does not go on in a logical way. We must tolerate ambiguities, unclarities and gaps in information in the expectation that there will be some later resolution if uncertainty remains. So we must fit the different pieces together and check and re-check as the conversation continues. We assume that only really new information is important and that only the smallest quantity of old information necessary to set the scene needs to be supplied. We also do not state what is obvious to all because we know that those who insist on stating what everyone knows are likely to be exhorted 'to get on with it'.

The actual record of any sequence of utterances in a conversation will almost certainly provide an outsider with a poor record of what happened. The outsider will encounter a collection of utterances that are difficult to comprehend if nothing is known about the participants, their biographies, the nature of their relationships, the events talked about, the agendas, i.e., intents, of the participants and so on. He or she may be able to draw a few conclusions about these from the sequence, because it will have its own internal orderings, its own patterns of action and reaction, and it is about something, and the outsider is likely to know at least a little bit about that something. But verbatim recordings of conversations can be very misleading and leave open a variety of interpretations. Personal recollections of conversations are weak enough, and explanations of why something was said and what was meant by it may be no more accurate.

Participants must agree about a number of things if a conversation is to be effective and such agreement is implicit rather than explicit. They must agree that certain kinds of knowledge are shared and do not have to be mentioned. Similarly, they must agree that certain rules of conduct apply during the course of a conversation because a conversation is a social event with its own conventions. There must be some kind of agenda, i.e., some sharing of perspective on what the conversation is about. There must also be some recognition of who is or who is not party to the exchange, hence the abhorrence, on the one hand, of 'bugging' and 'eavesdropping' and the need, on the other, to speak 'off the record', i.e., to conceal a source to some extent.

So far as what is said is concerned, each participant must tolerate a considerable amount of inexplicitness on the part of the other. Vagueness rather than precision will prevail and words will be understood metaphorically as well as literally. Exhaustiveness will neither be sought nor required and there will be appeals to the obvious and to what 'everyone knows'. Items may not be sequenced logically or chronologically, some may not be mentioned at all and others never explained. Constant extrapolation, filling in and checking out will all be necessary. All these will occur too within a context which assumes that the conversation has a legitimacy of its own. Interruptions must therefore be excused and clearly marked as such, and someone's 'hanging up' on someone else on the telephone or a negotiator's 'breaking off talks' may have serious consequences because of the severity of the violation of this convention.

Communication requires co-operative endeavour. According to Paul Grice (1975), participants in a conversation recognize that they should say only what they need to say, and that their contributions should be informative, relevant and truthful. They should also not say too little or too much. A question requires an answer. *Where are you going?* can be answered *Home, None of your business, I'm not telling, Why do you want to know?* or *Ask him,* depending on the circumstances. Answers like *Apples are red* or *Because it is raining* are quite unlikely. An answer like *It's noon* may be appropriate, but only if the listener can relate this answer to the question through some understanding that both speaker and listener share, e.g. that the person who responds in this way goes out for lunch each day at noon. If they are strangers to each other and have no such mutual understanding, then the answer is almost certainly just as inappropriate as the others. Disruption is the antithesis of communication as well as a form of communication in its own right.

There is an element of 'trust' in a conversation. In order for any conversation to work the participants must take much of what is said to them at its face value. The participants must assume that they are being given relevant, necessary, full and truthful information. Someone who says *John tried to hit Fred,* when John did indeed hit Fred, has not told an untruth but only a partial truth. However, that partial truth will be regarded as an untruth in a conversation once it is discovered, because it will have misled listeners. If three people are invited to a party and none comes, but, in reporting this fact to someone who knows the circumstances of the invitation, a speaker says *Sally didn't come,* then the listener will assume that the other two did come. We can note that the utterance implies something different from or something in addition to what it asserts. If we inquire over the telephone for someone and are told *He's not in,* only to find out later that the person has been dismissed, we are justifiably aggrieved in our belief that *He doesn't work here anymore* would have been a more appropriate response. Children sometimes produce partial responses of this kind. In an answer to the question *Why is John crying?* a child may answer *Because he fell down,* which in fact he did, rather than *Because I pushed him down,* which was actually what happened. They may be telling the truth and nothing but the truth; however, the assumption on which conversation proceeds

is that they are telling the whole truth. It is not surprising therefore that we have a term *half truth* for failure to observe this
requirement.

Grice calls these other meanings that are not asserted
'conversational implicatures'. Participants in a conversation must
watch not only their words but also what their words imply.
What is implied is sometimes quite different from what is
asserted. It is sometimes the stuff of the 'big lie' or the dirty insin-
uation rather than of the slanderable action, as in *I am not aware
of any wrongdoing on the part of my opponent for this office.* It
has been pointed out that if two acquaintances are talking about a
mutual friend now working in a bank and one asks the other how
that friend is getting on and is told *Oh, quite well I think. He likes
his colleagues, and he hasn't been to prison yet,* the final clause
violates the maxims of not saying more than is required and of
not offering gratuitous information. Because of these violations,
the utterance may well be taken to assert that the mutual friend is
a dishonest person. He has been victimized without actually being
slandered. In like vein, a remark like *Oh, your wife is faithful!*
introduced by one male haphazardly into a conversation with
another, is likely to prove to be far more unsettling than reassur-
ing. At the very best the conversation is likely to undergo a
profound change in topic and the agenda of the husband, if not of
both parties, may be considerably rearranged.

Some of the assumptions in conversations are actually built into
the language forms themselves. For example, *I saw John leave*
can be true only if someone called John exists, he did leave and
the speaker saw it happen. Sentences have 'presuppositions' (see
Keenan, 1971), e.g. *I reported the burglary* presupposes that a
burglary took place, *I bought another car* that the speaker had a
car at some time, *John stopped shouting* that John was shouting
(hence the unfairness of *Have you stopped beating your wife?* as a
question if you have never beaten her), *Jones has been here before*
that Jones is alive (and in the word *before* asserting that he is
expected to return), and *Our cat had kittens* that the cat is
female. These presuppositions are not all of the same kind, nor
are the examples intended to be exhaustive. However, the range
illustrated shows how various kinds of linguistic information
are also involved in the interpretation of sentences used in
conversation.

Language transactions require that their participants agree not only on certain assumptions about what can and should be said, but also on how specific encounters are to be regulated. Every encounter occurs in a social setting and there are rules to regulate what goes on, whether the occasion is a commencement address, a sales meeting, a seminar, a cocktail party or a late-night snack. There may also be sudden shifts of participants and settings, and changes in those rules will accompany each shift. A complex setting such as a courtroom will see many shifts and changes, e.g. a dispute between counsel, a remark to the jury, the questioning and cross-examination of witnesses, a ruling by the presiding judge and so on. An elaborate system regulates 'turn-taking' in a courtroom and determines who gets to speak, how topics are introduced, how questions are asked and how they must be answered, and how certain things must be left unsaid and still others not even hinted at.

A physician–patient consultation may be far less elaborate but it too must have its own rituals involving careful elicitation of symptoms, systems for checking and cross-checking information, typically uni-directional questioning with nearly all the questions coming from the physician and nearly all the answers and offers coming from the patient, and cautious diagnosis and prognosis. The physician–patient relationship (see West, 1984), as it reveals itself through turn-taking and questioning, is a particularly interesting one as the medical profession undergoes change. Good doctoring depends in part on good exchanges, but ideas about what a 'good exchange' is differ widely among physicians and patients. One group of physicians, psychiatrists, even make a professional specialty of exchanges (see Labov and Fanshel, 1977). A peculiar characteristic of certain psychiatrist–patient exchanges is that at any time the psychiatrist may bring up any remark made by the patient during the course of the exchange and place it on the agenda for discussion. Similar 'dredging up' in ordinary conversations is not expected and is scarcely tolerated when it does occur.

We must not forget that usually only one person speaks at a time and that silence is required of the other or others during that speaking. Talk is also orchestrated in such a way that a speaker tends to give up the floor voluntarily, and not allowing someone else to talk is a deliberate act. In fact, to be commanded to be silent is sometimes too unnatural a command to obey. But silence can also be used effectively when the rules require speech. Silence itself can even be construed to be a kind of speech act, a deliberate act not to speak. It may indicate agreement with the speaker or be understood as indicating assent, as it was used in the phrase *the silent majority*; it may be regarded as a device for insuring that someone eventually gets heard, as in *We haven't heard from Gabrielle. What do you have to say?*; and it may be required as a sign of respect of some kind, as in *Children should be seen and not heard, Remember, no talking in church, Don't speak until you are spoken to* and *Who asked you?*

Self-imposed silence can have many uses, e.g. a sign of disrespect, reinforced perhaps by asides or side exchanges, a calculated snub bringing about a comment such as *He didn't even speak to me*, a refusal to venture an opinion when asked, as in *No comment*, or a refusal to answer a question in court. Knowing when to keep silent or refusing to talk is part of knowing when to talk, because the consequences are the same. Each act reflects a person's knowledge of what is or is not acceptable in society and contributes to that person's success or failure in communicating.

As soon as we attempt to give a full and systematic account of how language is used in actual speaking, the complexity of such a task becomes apparent. The number of variables is considerable. Language exchanges can vary in so many different ways. Characterizing what is going on in a particular exchange requires an understanding of the context in which the exchange occurs and of the relationship of the participants to one another and to that context. We know that strangers interact differently from familiars and that familiar contexts bring about different reactions than do strange ones. An exchange between close friends in a familiar setting is likely to be very different in form and content from one between two strangers meeting in a setting unfamiliar to both.

The agenda of an exchange is also important, i.e., what each participant hopes to achieve through it. Similarly, situational constraints will regulate what occurs: a job interview is different from a blind date, and both are different from a legal inquiry. It is also possible for the participants to vary the degree of formality they will adopt, make subtle alterations in the tone of what they do say or play with the usually accepted norms of language behaviour. They may also vary what they do because of certain constraints in the environment. For example, a radio commentary on a sporting event is different from a television commentary on the same event, as anyone who has merely listened to – not both listened to and watched – such a commentary on television can testify. And, finally, there are the actual language devices that are used, such as the particular kinds of speech act, the specific word choices that are made, the pauses, the devices that allow one to be heard, the sequencing signals between utterances and between speakers and the specific techniques by which we signal beginnings, endings and the introduction of new topics.

Investigators (see Button and Lee, 1987; Coulthard, 1977; McLaughlin, 1984; Wardhaugh, 1985) who have actually attempted to state what happens in conversations, a large amorphous subset of exchanges, have necessarily limited themselves to very specific topics. They have investigated such topics as how certain conversations begin and end, e.g. telephone calls and psychiatric interviews, how topics are introduced and followed up in conversation, how other people are addressed, how successive utterances are sequenced in relation to one another, how speakers claim their rights to be heard, how individual utterances are understood in context, how refusals are made, how particular places are referred to, e.g. the layout of rooms within a house or apartment, and how we give directions to strangers. They have also been concerned with the ways in which certain kinds of individuals use language to attain their ends, e.g. teachers and students, physicians and patients and mothers and children. Imparting knowledge, diagnosing illnesses and treating them and bringing up children lead to different kinds of language behaviour.

It is possible to pick out some kinds of linguistic signals that often correlate closely with what a speaker intends in a particular exchange. For example, expressions like *Yes, Uh huh, I see* and *That's right!* usually signal some kind of agreement or attentiveness while another is speaking. Those like *Oh!, Really!* and *Is that so?* serve to comment on what is being said. There are prefacing expressions such as *anyway, say, well, why* and *now* which serve to introduce a comment, offer or reservation: *Well, I'll have to think about it*; *Say, what could she have meant by that?*; *Anyway, I have to be going.* Expressions like *I believe, I guess* and *I think* used during a conversation or presentation serve to meliorate what is being said, making it less positive so that the speaker appears to be less assertive. Certain situations seem to require this lack of assertiveness even though everyone present regards such qualifying expressions as empty, e.g. situations in which one person is clearly in a position of authority and the others subordinate, but in which the leadership must be exercised covertly rather than overtly.

Taking one particular kind of exchange as an example, telephone calls, we can quickly discover a few typical characteristics of the language used in such calls. Telephone summonses have specific rules. In North America the person picking up the telephone answers with *Hello* or, in business use, with a name. In the United Kingdom the answer is quite often the number you are calling. However, in some other cultures, Norway for example, the person calling must speak first as soon as the connection has been established. In North America a ringing telephone is interpreted as a summons to be acknowledged by a verbal response, not just merely by picking up the telephone. Once that initial response is made the caller must acknowledge it and initiate the substance of the conversation or emphasize that a call is being returned. In cases when the call is purely social it must rather quickly be acknowledged to be so (*Oh, I just thought I'd give you a call*) if the person called is not to say something like *Well, what's on your mind?* In this respect telephone calls are like telegrams in being about something and unlike casual greetings in the street, which are really about nothing. (However, if at the beginning of a casual greeting in the street, one party to the exchange breaks the bond of casualness, that person takes on an obligation to initiate some kind of follow-up by introducing a topic.) When telephone companies began to encourage family members and friends to call one another long distance just to 'keep in touch' rather than to convey messages, one of the immediate difficulties they had to confront directly was the non-use of the telephone for this kind of phatic communion. Consequently, in the telephone companies' promotion of this use of the telephone, a mother's inquiry of her son *Why are you calling, son? Are you in trouble?* was answered by the son protesting he was all right and was just calling to say *Hello*.

The telephone has another unusual characteristic for many people in that it gives summonses which they generally feel unable to ignore. There appears to be a strong social obligation to answer the telephone. If there is no answer when the telephone rings, the caller generally assumes that nobody was there to answer, not that the summons was ignored. There is also often a feeling of considerable dissatisfaction if a telephone call is not later returned when a message is left asking someone who turns out not to be present to return the call. Of course, since summonses are a sub-class of greetings, therefore of offerings, ignoring a particular summons is a snub, threat or rebuke involving primal feelings. It is understandable, therefore, that there should be rituals which cover this class of events even in the special circumstances of telephoning. Another ritual is the pretense that you do not listen in on another's telephone conversation when that person must answer the telephone in your presence. You can make a comment on the conversation only if you are invited to do so. Otherwise, it is bad manners even to pretend a conversation occurred. This rule accounts for some of the reprehensibility felt for the practice of 'bugging', because telephone conversations are held to be as private as letters.

If we approach exchanges from the point of view of asking how a particular kind of activity – the use of questions – is involved, we can look at the example of the classroom to show some issues. Questioning in the classroom (see Sinclair and Coulthard, 1975) is very different from questioning in most other circumstances. For example, most of the questions go in one direction, from the teacher to the students. Students are allowed to ask questions, but the teacher may choose to answer them or not or to delay answering them. On the other hand, students must answer the questions asked of them without delay. The teacher's questions are quite often addressed to a group of students with an instruction that a student who is prepared to answer should indicate that preparedness in some way, generally through some kind of gesture such as raising a hand. The teacher usually then chooses one student among the various bidders to answer and a typical pattern of interaction is that the teacher then confirms or disconfirms the answer which that student provides.

The teacher also decides the overall agenda of the class, those things that are to be talked about and how they are to be talked about. Any questions the students ask must fall within that agenda or be classified as diversionary acts. The teacher is also assumed to know the answer to any question he or she asks and it is the students' task to find out what that answer is. In other circumstances questions of this kind are regarded as insincere. If the person asking a question knows, or is discovered to know, the answer already, protests such as *You know, so don't ask me* and *Why, you knew all the time!* are legitimate. However, the first of these is socially unacceptable in a classroom and the second is redundant because everyone knows that the teacher knows the answer. When children go to school they must learn how questions are used in classrooms. If they do not learn or if they refuse to go along with this questioning convention, their behaviour will be regarded as disruptive in one respect or another as they provide inappropriate answers, refuse to wait until an answerer is designated, ask too many questions, thereby usurping the teacher's function, or reject the answers the teacher provides.

The examples in the preceding paragraphs show how difficult it is to make statements about language exchanges. Extended examples of language use, e.g. long conversations, discussions, lectures and texts, both formal and informal, serve to compound the difficulties. Not only must we examine every individual locution closely but we must also examine it for its illocutionary and perlocutionary force in the context in which it occurs. The locutions are also parts of exchanges and sequences that are themselves often parts of some still more general exchange or sequence. Finally, each exchange takes place against a background of all that the participants know, or believe they know, about the world, themselves and others, and about the place of that particular exchange in the further development of that knowledge and of their relationship to one another. Language itself, of course, is the key component in all the above.

## Further investigation

1  Look at conversations as they are represented in novels and plays. Then record one or two informal conversations, e.g. at the dinner table. Compare the two kinds; they will almost certainly be quite different. What are 'real' conversations like?
2  What can you learn about the uses of language by comparing a lecture with a seminar, a sermon with a sales talk and a formal

job interview with a casual conversation between strangers seated together on an aeroplane? Consider such matters as the 'rules' for who speaks, topic selection, interruptions, use of questions, shared information, etc.

3   It has been said that the upper bound of linguistic investigation is properly the 'sentence'. In this view it is doubtful that language can be shown to be 'structured' above the level of the sentence. You might examine such a claim with regard to such entities as conversations, paragraphs, folk tales, poems, jokes, stories and so on. Can any of the 'structures' we posit for these usefully be considered as 'linguistic' in nature, or are they 'aesthetic', conceptual', 'narrative', etc?

## 6.3   The functions of language

Still another way of investigating how language is used in social relationships is to attempt some kind of broad classification of the basic functions of language. Roman Jakobson, a linguist thoroughly familiar with just about every aspect of modern linguistics, both European and North American, offered a six-fold classification of language functions. According to Jakobson (1960), language must serve the following functions: 'cognitive' or 'referential' to convey messages and information; 'conative' to persuade and influence others through commands and entreaties; 'emotive' to express attitudes, feelings and emotions; 'phatic' to establish communion with others; 'metalingual' to clear up difficulties about intentions, words and meanings; and 'poetic' to indulge in language for its own sake.

Another classification, proposed by the British linguist Michael Halliday, refers to seven different categories of language function: 'instrumental', 'regulatory', 'representational', 'interactional', 'personal', 'heuristic' and 'imaginative'. Still other classifications employ different categories and use different terms, but all cover essentially the same data. I will therefore use Halliday's (1973) classification in the comments that follow.

The instrumental function of language refers to the fact that language allows speakers to get things done. It allows them to manipulate the things in the environment. People can cause things to be done and happen through the use of words alone. An immediate contrast here is with the animal world in which sounds are hardly ever used in this way, and, when they are, they are used in an extremely limited fashion. The instrumental function can be 'primitive' too in human interaction; quite often the intent of a speaker is judged on the basis of an intrinsically deficient utterance, one possibly complemented by gesture, but the intent is nevertheless unequivocal. Performative utterances clearly have instrumental functions of their own if the right circumstances exist; they *are* acts, e.g. *I name this ship **Liberty Bell**, I pronounce you husband and wife* and *I bet you a pound*. But the instrumental function may be served by other utterances than performatives, e.g. by suggestion and persuasion as well as by direction, as in *I suggest you stop, It's going to rain* (so take your umbrella) and *You'll get hurt* (so stop).

The regulatory function refers to language used in an attempt to control events once they happen. Those events may involve the self as well as others. People do try to control themselves through language, e.g. *Why did I say that?, Steady!* and *Let me think about that again*. But more conspicuous is the fact that we use language to regulate encounters among people. Language helps to mark roles, provides devices for regulating specific kinds of encounters and contains a vocabulary for approving or disapproving and for controlling or disrupting the behaviour of others. It allows us to establish complex patterns of organization in order to try to regulate behaviour, from game playing to political organization, from answering the telephone to addressing the nation on television. It is this function of language that allows people some measure of control over the events that occur in their lives.

The representational function refers to the use of language to communicate knowledge about the world, to report events, to make statements, to give accounts, to explain relationships, to relay messages and so on. Sometimes misinformation is given, because telling lies is an example of this same function. As I mentioned earlier, certain rules exist to regulate language behaviour when an exchange of information is involved. For example, the truth must be whole not partial, assumptions must be made about what the listener knows, the information supplied must be neither inadequate nor gratuitous, and, if the intent is honest, any kind of misrepresentation and ambiguity must be avoided. In circumstances in which a speaker has a highly idiosyncratic view of what the world is like, utterances which claim to represent that world will be treated as peculiar by others. Certain types of peculiarity will lead to the speaker being classified as either a fool or a genius, a lunatic or a visionary, a sinner or a saint. The precise designation of an individual may also shift from time to time as the consensus which forms the basis for judging various representations of the world shifts, e.g. the earth as flat, atoms as particles, God as dead, sex as dirty, language as words and so on.

The interactional function refers to language used to ensure social maintenance. Phatic communion is part of it, those small 'meaningless' exchanges which indicate that a channel of communication is open should it be needed. In a wider sense this function refers to all uses of language that help to define and maintain groups, e.g. teenage slang, family jokes, professional jargon, ritualistic exchanges, social and regional dialects and so on. People must learn a wide variety of such different language usages if they are to interact comfortably with many others. Successful interaction requires good 'manners', i.e., saying things appropriately whatever they are, and using language in the socially prescribed way. Breaches of manners are easily observed, whether they are 'dirty' words in the wrong setting or refusal to stand on certain occasions. They may sometimes also be punished far out of proportion to any misdemeanour that was actually committed.

The personal function refers to language used to express the individual's personality. Each individual is conscious of the fact that language comprises part of that individuality. Individuals have a 'voice' in what happens to them. They are also free to speak or not to speak, to say as much or as little as they please, and to choose how to say what they say. Language also provides the individual with a means to express feelings, whether outright in the form of exclamations, endorsements or curses, or much more subtly through a careful choice of words. There may even be a cathartic effect to *letting it all hang out* or *getting it off your chest*.

The heuristic function refers to language used in order to acquire knowledge and understanding of the world. Language may be used for learning. Questions can lead to answers, argumentation to conclusions and hypothesis-testing to new discoveries.

The heuristic functioning provides a basis for the structure of knowledge in the different disciplines. Language allows people to ask questions about the nature of the world they live in and to construct possible answers. Formal education is partly a means for introducing those who participate in such education into this function. The product is often the acquisition of some familiarity with a set of abstract systems that claim to offer explanations of one kind or another. Insofar as the inquiry is into language itself, a necessary result is the creation of a 'metalanguage', i.e., a language used to refer to language, containing terms such as *sound, syllable, word, structure, sentence, transformation* and so on.

Finally, the imaginative function refers to language used to create imaginary systems, whether these are literary works, philosophical systems or utopian visions on the one hand, or daydreams and idle musings on the other. It is also language used for the sheer joy of using language, such as a baby's babbling, a chanter's chanting, a crooner's crooning and sometimes a poet's pleasuring. Pig Latin, punning, verbal games, playing the dozens and telling tall stories are just a few of the instances of language used imaginatively in order to entertain yourself or others. The imaginative function also allows people to consider not just the real world but all possible worlds – and many impossible ones too! It enables life to be lived vicariously and helps satisfy numerous deep aesthetic and artistic urges.

Much of the everyday use of language has a representational function, but instrumental and interactional functions are also well represented. Channels are also constantly being tested to ensure that they remain open. The imaginative function is prized when it leads to artistic creation, but for most people it seems to be more of a safety valve than anything else in the opportunities for creativity and escapism that it allows. The heuristic function has tended to become institutionalized in educational settings and the knowledge industries. The possible ways of knowing through language and without language still continue to fascinate different investigators, and how knowledge is structured, reordered and developed is also a matter of concern. Language itself also plays an important role in the changes that occur in the rhetoric of the various disciplines.

The personal function undoubtedly exists, but it is possibly the most difficult of all the functions to describe with any exactness.

In that function, language, thought, culture and personality come together to interact in ways that are still quite mysterious to us. The various functions are also not discrete but overlap. Speaking is a complex activity which proceeds on more than one plane at a time and a single brief exchange can be made to serve a variety of functions.

Language has many different functions and is put to many different uses in society. An important part of the knowledge that every speaker has of that speaker's language is how to use it in different circumstances. Speakers must learn not only the sounds, grammatical forms and words of that language, but they must also learn how to use these sounds, grammatical forms and words appropriately. They must learn who speaks when to whom for what reason about what things and in what ways (see Saville-Troike, 1989). Children acquiring a language must learn the complexities of this 'ethnography of speaking'; they must learn how to use sentences appropriately concurrently with how to form them correctly.

The sociolinguist Dell Hymes (1974) has proposed a useful acronym, SPEAKING, to cover all the factors that we must take into account when we try to describe what happens when people use language. Hymes says that the 'Setting and Scene' (S) of speech are important. The setting refers to the concrete physical circumstances in which speech takes place, whereas the scene refers to the psychological and cultural circumstances. Settings vary widely; courtrooms, classrooms, telephone conversations, passing acquaintances in the street and poetry readings are all settings. Scenes are also extremely varied and involve such matters as consulting, warning, pleading, conferring, confessing, etc. Settings and scenes do not necessarily stay constant throughout a particular language exchange, although it is generally easier to shift scenes than it is to shift settings; for example, to tell a joke in an attempt to change a serious scene into one that is less serious.

The 'Participants' (P) may be of various kinds. They may be referred to as speakers and listeners, addressors and addressees or senders and receivers. Participants generally have fixed roles in exchanges, e.g. physicians and patients, teachers and students, conversants over the telephone, husbands and wives, parents and children, etc. In any exchange you must try to define your participant status in order to be comfortable. To misjudge that status or to mishandle it may result in inappropriate language behaviour, e.g. saying the wrong thing or saying something at the wrong time.

The (E) in SPEAKING stands for 'Ends', the conventionally recognized and expected outcomes of an exchange as well as the personal goals that each of the participants seeks to accomplish through that exchange. There are definite ends to the activities that go on in courtrooms and classrooms, but within these settings the different participants have widely varying goals. In a courtroom, for example, during a criminal trial, the goals of the judge, prosecuting counsel, defence counsel, members of the jury and members of the press are quite different.

The (A) in the acronym refers to 'Act Sequences', the actual language forms that are used, how these are used and the relationship of what is said to the actual topic at hand. The 'Key' (K) refers to the tone, manner or spirit in which a particular message is conveyed, i.e., whether it is light-hearted, serious, precise, pedantic, sarcastic, mocking, pompous, etc. Gesture, posture and bodily movements are also important here. Sometimes there is a good fit between what a person says and how he or she says it – its key – and sometimes there is not. It is, of course, even possible to burlesque an otherwise serious ritual by just altering the key a little.

The 'Instrumentalities' (I) refer to the choice of channel one makes. Is it oral or written, a language or a dialect, a code or a register and so on? Do you telephone or write? Should you be formal or informal? Should you use the local dialect or the standard language? Is a story to be narrated in the first person or in the third person? Should I in writing a book use *I* or *we* to express my views?

The 'Norms of Interaction and Interpretation' (N) refer to the specific behaviours and proprieties that attach to speaking and also to how these are viewed by someone who does not share them. Who usually talks in this situation and for how long? Who asks questions and who answers them in a courtroom? How loudly should you speak in a church or in a library? Who initiates telephone calls? How far do we stand apart when we talk to each other at a cocktail party?

Finally, (G) refers to the 'Genres' that we must recognize in certain kinds of exchange. There are novels, poems, riddles,

jokes, prayers, confessions, wills, editorials, operating instructions, summonses, etc. To function adequately in any society
you must be familiar with the basic genres that the society uses.

We can easily recognize that such an ethnography of speaking
does exist because we are able to recognize various violations
of normal linguistic behaviour. Contradictions, half-truths,
inadequacies, disruptions and irrelevancies are usually easy to
detect. We are also likely to be sensitive to linguistic discourtesy
and rudeness, as when there is a failure to observe customary
patterns of exchange or when a particular language encounter is
wrenched out of shape. We may even know people with whom
any kind of language encounter is scarcely possible or extremely
painful because they have apparently never learned the rules that
may be said to govern such encounters, or they deliberately
choose to violate these rules, or they fail to observe them because
of some psychological impairment. People may be considered
'smooth', 'brilliant', 'crazy' or 'disruptive', partly on the basis of
their control of such rules or their lack of control. And such
control seems to be quite independent of control of the rules of
syntax and phonology or of the control of the written form of
language. As the actor David Garrick remarked of the poet Oliver
Goldsmith, he 'wrote like an angel, but talk'd like poor Poll'.

Language, of course, is just one of the 'codes' that we must
learn to use in general social interaction. There are also behavioural codes and moral codes to be observed, the products
of law or custom. There is a code that regulates interpersonal
distance and one that regulates permissible physical contact. And
there is a general code that regulates the trust each person places
in others to observe all the other codes. Violations of this last
code apparently produce the gravest kinds of psychological
damage, as when, for example, captives who undergo 'brainwash-
ing' procedures can never be sure what is going to happen to
them next. In such circumstances this fundamental trust that
certain types of behaviour will regularly prevail is broken, a break
often considered to be quite necessary before any kind of 're-
education' can begin, such re-education being mainly concerned
with building an alternative system of trust. The particular trust
that people place in words is also, unfortunately, the source of
considerable harm because effective lying and deception depend
on that trust for their success.

In dealing with others, we must assume a great deal of shared understanding about the world. We must assume that the stage on which we are to perform the particular dance of a language encounter is set very much alike in the minds of all the participants in that encounter. We must then proceed to choreograph or direct the action and events on that stage jointly with the other participants so that at any time all can agree where everything is and what everyone is doing. But the language we use and the rules for using that language require that at any one time only certain things can be said and usually that only one participant can speak at a time. There are numerous ways in which a participant can quickly get out of step in the dance. Consequently, constant checking back, reviewing the present moment and projecting forward are necessary. The total pace of the dance must also be controlled, as must its relationship to the dances which preceded and those which are to follow. Any knowledgeable choreographer or director will assure us that this is not the best way to put together a successful show. But it is the best we can do with language, and the results are often surprisingly good.

## *Further investigation*

1  One particularly interesting type of speech is 'glossolalia' or 'talking in tongues' within certain religious groups. What is its function?
2  Language can be used to express 'power' or to show 'solidarity' with others. How would you go about finding evidence to support or refute such a claim?
3  Bodies are set up to control and regulate languages or parts of a language, e.g. the French Academy. Others are less formally constituted, e.g. the organizations that produce dictionaries, publishing houses, etc. How effective are such practices? Are they any more effective than King Canute's famous attempt to hold back the advancing tide by royal fiat?

## 6.4   Can language use us?

A very different point of view about language use – and one that has attracted a lot of attention and numerous investigators over the years – is associated with the linguist Edward Sapir (1921) and his student Benjamin Lee Whorf (see Carroll, 1956). This view is that language structure more or less determines human thought processes. It is actually not easy to be quite sure where Sapir himself stood on this issue. He said both that human beings are very much at the mercy of the particular languages they speak, their language habits predisposing them to certain kinds of behaviour, and also that it is difficult to see what causal relationships could be expected to exist between particular experiences and the way in which a society expresses those experiences. Like his eighteenth-century and nineteenth-century predecessors Herder and Humboldt, Sapir was obviously intrigued with the connection that might exist between language structure and thought processes, but he was somewhat equivocal in describing that connection.

His student Whorf, however, had little such hesitancy. A professional chemical engineer by training and an insurance adjuster by vocation, Whorf lacked Sapir's considerable caution in linguistic matters. As a result of comparing what he called 'Standard Average European' (languages like English, French and German) with Amerindian languages, particularly Hopi, Whorf proposed that the structure of language determines thought and that speakers of different languages experience the world differently. This proposal is now sometimes known as the 'Whorfian hypothesis' about language and thought.

For some of his examples Whorf used English and drew on his own experiences in looking for the causes of fires. For example, he noted that 'empty' oil drums were often treated quite haphazardly, whereas 'full' ones were not; people working around them often completely ignored the fact that they were sometimes full of fumes and, therefore, dangerous fire hazards. The word *empty* was the culprit, according to Whorf, because it gave people entirely the wrong idea about the situation.

The strongest statement of the Whorfian hypothesis is that language structure determines thought completely and controls the way a speaker views the world; consequently, different languages produce different 'world views' in their speakers and, so far as viewing the world is concerned, we are at the mercy of the particular language we speak and of the categories and distinctions within it. A weaker position is that the structure of a language makes certain kinds of perception easy and others difficult, but does not make anything impossible. Each language acts as a kind of filter for reality. It makes certain kinds of situations in the 'real world' more likely to be commented on than others, but it does not necessarily leave the latter unnoticed. In this second view language structure predisposes rather than determines certain kinds of behaviour.

In attempting to confirm or refute any version of this hypothesis, an investigator can draw on a variety of evidence. However, that evidence cannot consist merely of casual observations about how strange an exotic language sounds or how peculiar are its words and their arrangements. The words and grammatical structures may be important evidence, but the key issues have to do with the interpretation of that evidence. What conclusions can you really draw from the fact that in one language a certain distinction, e.g. a 'singular-plural' distinction, must be made in all 'meaning' words, i.e., nouns, but in another language such a distinction is not required? Or from the fact that adjectives must precede nouns in one language but follow nouns in another? Or from the fact that one language has a word for a particular concept but another must use a phrase if it uses anything at all? The interpretation is all.

German has words like *Gemütlichkeit, Weltanschauung* and *Weihnachsbaum*; English has no exact equivalent of any of them, *Christmas tree* being fairly close in the last case but still lacking the 'magical' German connotations. Both people and bulls have *legs* in English, but Spanish requires people to have *piernas* and bulls to have *patas*. Arabic has many words for types of camels; English does not. But speakers of English have many words for different kinds of cars and the Trobriand Islanders of the South Seas many words for different kinds of yams.

The Navaho of the Southwest United States, the Shona of Zimbabwe and the Hanunoo of the Philippines divide the colour spectrum differently from one another in the distinctions they make, and English speakers divide it differently again. English has a general cover term *animal* for various kinds of creatures, but it lacks a term to cover both fruit and nuts; however, Chinese languages have such a cover term *guo*. English has a word *fruit* to cover both apples and strawberries but Russian does not because *frukty* cannot include berries. French *conscience* is both English *conscience* and *consciousness*.

German, French and other languages have two pronouns corresponding to English *you* and Japanese has an extensive system of honorifics which is quite outside the experience of English speakers. The equivalent of English *stone* has a 'gender' in French and German, and the various words in the three languages must always be either singular or plural in number. However, in Chinese number is expressed only if it is relevant, which turns out to be surprisingly rare for anyone who comes to Chinese from English. In reporting on something involving a stone, Kwakiutl speakers in British Columbia must indicate whether the stone is visible or not to the speaker at the time of speaking, as well as its position relative to one or another of the speaker, the listener or possible third party.

Given such a wide range of evidence, an investigator is faced with the task of assimilating it and drawing defensible conclusions from both it and any experiments that seem to bare on the issues. The conclusions are generally different from those that Whorf drew. For example, the words *fist, wave, spark* and *flame* are nouns in English, so we tend to see the events or actions they name as having some kind of objective existence, some kind of 'thingness'. But we also know that this existence is of a quite different kind than that of houses, rocks, cats and trees. We can, therefore, understand that words for the same events or actions can appear as verbs in Hopi because we know that houses and rocks comprise a different order of 'things' from fists and waves. One language refers to certain characteristics of the real world in terms of one possible subset of characteristics, whereas another favours a different subset. Speakers of both languages may still be aware of all the characteristics; however, they are not required to refer to all of them.

Syntactic evidence can also mislead investigators. Literal translation provides much of the evidence, as though we understand *breakfast* as 'break in a fast', or *cats* as 'cat' plus 'plural' (as though we see several cats together by observing the 'cat' quality first and then a 'quantity' quality next), or *It's raining* as involving some 'animate' bringer of rain. Over-literal translation is very dangerous and misleading, particularly of metaphoric language. English, for example, is full of metaphors: *I see what you mean, He grasped the idea, You're behind the times* and so on. At best, the syntactic evidence suggests that languages allow their speakers to make certain observations more easily in some cases than in others. An obligatory grammatical category, e.g. 'tense-marking' in English verbs, will lead to certain things being said in English that need not be said, for example, in Chinese; an available vocabulary, e.g. the various words for yams among the Trobriand Islanders, will have the same result.

It may be the case that recognition, recall, problem solving and concept formation are influenced by the particular language that is used. One experiment (Carmichael *et al.* 1932) showed that different names given to 12 briefly presented figures resulted in these figures being reproduced differently on a later occasion. A line drawing that resembled both a bottle and a stirrup would be reproduced to resemble a bottle when a person heard it referred to as a bottle. However, another person hearing it referred to as a stirrup would reproduce it as a stirrup. The word labels guided the participants in remembering the original drawings but not in remembering them absolutely correctly. Just what effect the labels had on the actual perception of the drawings is much less clear.

Experiments (Berlin and Kay, 1969) with the perception of the colour spectrum show that speakers of various languages do favour referring to certain parts of the spectrum, but that they can also make distinctions they do not usually make if they are required to do so. Different languages have also been examined for the basic colour terms they use in dividing the colour spectrum. A basic colour term must be a single word (not *light blue*), not be a subdivision of another term (like *crimson*), and not be highly restricted in use (like *puce*).

Although different languages contain different numbers of basic colour terms a natural hierarchy appears to exist for referring to the parts of the spectrum. An analysis of the basic colour terms of nearly a hundred languages revealed that if a language has only two colour terms, these are for 'black' (or dark) and 'white' (or light); if it has three, these are for 'black', 'white' and 'red'; if it has four, the additional term is for either 'green' or 'yellow'; and if it has five, the additional term is the remaining one of green or yellow. Then the terms for 'blue', 'brown', 'purple', 'pink', 'orange' and 'grey' are added, although not necessarily in that order.

There is apparently a connection between the first few terms used and the colours in nature that are most noticeable, colours

like black, white, red, green, yellow and blue. These may therefore be called the 'prototypical' colours. Languages differ in
where they place colours in such a hierarchy, with the languages
of more technologically-oriented and complex societies having
more such colour terms. The different placements therefore might
account for the different colour-naming practices of speakers.

The most valid conclusion to all such studies is that it appears
possible to talk about anything in any language provided the
speaker is willing to coin new words and tolerate some degree
of circumlocution. Some concepts are also more 'codable', i.e.,
easier to express, than others. A speaker, of course, may not be at
all aware of the circumlocution in the absence of familiarity with
another language that uses a more succinct means of expression.
Every natural language provides both a language for talking about
language and every other language, i.e., a 'metalanguage', and an
entirely adequate apparatus for making any kinds of observations
that need to be made about the world. If such is the case, every
natural language must be an extremely rich system that readily
allows its speakers to overcome any structural peculiarities.

So far we have looked at the issue of linguistic determinism and
relativity largely from the perspective of the individual speaker,
i.e., how far a particular language constrains a speaker of that
language to a certain view of the world. The Whorfian hypothesis, however, has been extended to cover whole cultures. For
example, one writer – best left nameless – has gone so far as to
argue that some of what he identified as the 'worst traits' of
German character could be blamed on what Mark Twain called
the 'awful German language', particularly its extensive use of
nominalizations and its capitalization of nouns! More recently,
others – again to be nameless – have argued that the post-
positioning of French adjectives, as in *les plumes rouges*, reflects
'deductive habits of thought', whereas the preposing of English
adjectives, as in *the red pens*, reflects 'inductive habits', and that
Navaho grammatical structure, which does not clearly separate
actors, actions and objects in the way English does, reflects the
'underlying passivity and fatefulness' of the Navaho. In each case
a close causal relationship is postulated to exist between certain
linguistic forms or structures and certain cultural characteristics.

If language does not control thought but merely inhibits
thought processes, it should not control any aspect of culture

either. All the evidence we have tends to show that there is no such control. There is no evidence that language type correlates with cultural type. Speakers of different 'agglutinative' languages, i.e., languages like Turkish and many Amerindian languages, which build up very complex words rather than complex sentences to express ideas, can be associated with very different cultures. The same is true of 'inflectional' and 'isolating' languages. Speakers of very different language types can also share much the same culture, and a single language – English is a good example – can be spoken by members of very different cultures. While it is a truism that each language is different from every other just as is each culture, singling out a few isolated forms or structures where this difference is most obvious – as in the examples in the previous paragraph, or in attempts to show how different Japanese is from English by exploiting the Japanese system of honorifics – results in highlighting the peculiar at the expense of illuminating the usual. The result is a collection of language curiosities rather than a set of linguistic insights.

Two important experiments (Carroll and Casagrande, 1958) have cast serious doubts on the proposition that the language people speak binds them to a particular world view. In one, speakers of English and Hopi were presented with 12 sets of three pictures of actions or events. From each set they were asked to select the two pictures that went best together. For example, one set consisted of a picture of peaches being poured from a box, another of coins being spilled from a pocket and the third of water being spilled from a pitcher. English uses the words *spill* and *pour*, the first for an accidental action and the second for a deliberate one. Hopi uses the words *wehekna* and *wa:hokna*, the first for an action involving liquids and the second for one involving solids. The twelve sets of pictures dealt with situations which could be described differently in English and Hopi. Fourteen Hopi-speaking adults, many of whom also spoke English well, 12 rural New England English-speaking adults of an educational level comparable to the speakers of Hopi and 15 English-speaking graduate students sorted the sets of pictures.

The results showed only a rather small non-significant difference in the expected direction between the speakers of Hopi and English. The Hopi actually favoured the unexpected English groupings more often than they did the expected Hopi groupings by a ratio of not quite three to two. In contrast, the ratio for speakers of English was three to one. The fact that most of the Hopi were also speakers of English might have accounted for the lack of a significant difference. Of course, it did not account for the fact that approximately twenty per cent of the responses by the speakers of English supported Hopi categorizations of the pictured actions or events.

The second experiment investigated grammatical categories that must be expressed in Navaho. Navaho verbs of handling require an obligatory grammatical marker that indicates certain characteristics of the shape of the object handled. A request to be handed a long and flexible object such as a piece of string requires the verb to have one marker, *sanleh*, and a request to be handed a long and rigid object such as a pencil requires another, *santiih*. A request for a flat and flexible object such as a piece of paper requires a third, *sanilcoos*. Would Navaho children therefore tend to classify objects they handled on the basis of their shape rather than on some other basis, e.g. their size or colour?

Navaho children between the ages of three and ten were used in the experiment. Since the children were bilingual, they were tested for language dominance and grouped as either Navaho-dominant or English-dominant. White middle-class children from Boston, who spoke only English, were also given the same task to perform and served as the control group. The task itself was quite simple. Each child was shown pairs of objects differing in both colour and shape, e.g. a blue stick and a yellow rope. Then the child was shown a third object, either a blue rope or a yellow stick, and asked to match it with one of the previously shown objects. The Navaho-dominant and English-dominant children performed significantly differently in the predicted direction; however, the control group from Boston out-Navahoed the Navaho-dominant group. When a further group of black children from Harlem was tested in the same way, these children resembled the English-dominant Navaho children in their performance.

All the children who participated in the experiment, regardless of language and ethnic background, relied more and more on the shape of the objects than on their colour as they increased in age. If a reliance on shape rather than on colour is interpreted to be a sign of cognitive development, then such development seems aided both by having a necessary grammatical category in the language which requires reference to shape and by factors in a middle-class environment. It appears to be hindered when both are absent. The correct conclusion from this experiment seems to be that the grammatical structure of a language is but one of the variables that influence cognitive development. Culture itself and the experiences provided by the culture are at least as potent in the development of thought and cognition.

There is still a further corollary of the hypothesis that language and culture are intimately related, with language structure determining cultural patterns to some extent. It is that individuals are constrained in their cultural behaviour and opportunities by the language of their subculture. Very young children are obviously constrained by the language they speak, but these constraints seem to be of a different kind, developmental rather than behavioural. The constraints that are at issue here are those that are said to arise from the gender, class, regional and racial biases that have been built into language subvarieties. The claim is that a language can be 'sexist', 'classist', 'racist', etc., within itself and predispose speakers to have certain attitudes to others within society. Just as the main thesis has never been proved, neither has this corollary. Both thesis and corollary have been asserted to be true, both are provocative, both seem to offer explanations for phenomena in the outside world, but conclusive data to support either do not exist.

Finally, there is no justification for the existence of beliefs in either 'primitive languages' or primitive patterns of thought. The former do not exist in the sense that *primitive* is always intended, i.e., in the sense of 'inferior', and the evidence cited for the latter generally ignores the complexity of the linguistic issues and short-changes the culture which is being considered. When the linguistic evidence has been assessed, it has generally been so within a very superficial Whorfian perspective. For example, since there are few or no grammatical markings for tense, time must be of little or no importance to the speakers of the language, or since there are no obvious words for logical relationships, reasoning and problem-solving must be minimal and complex scientific thought an impossibility. Such conclusions are quite invalid, betraying as they do preconceptions about how time relationships must be expressed or what forms argumentation must take. They also fail to take into account the complexity that any language must have if it is to function as a cohesive bond in a group that lasts for any length of time in even the starkest living conditions. We know today how difficult it is to provide anything like an adequate account of the language and culture of any group, no matter how small. Explaining the relationship that is presumed to exist between language and culture is a task of still another magnitude entirely.

It is not unreasonable to say that an individual's language acts as a guide in thinking about the world in certain ways and in thinking about it in much the same way as others who speak the same language. But the structure of that language does not determine either thought or behaviour. New ways of thinking and behaving remain possible. The history of Western science is a particularly good example of individuals and groups developing new patterns of thought. 'Western' science is also exportable, though not without some inconvenience at times, to 'non-Western' languages and cultures. While language is intimately related to thought and culture in subtle and pervasive ways, at the same time every language has resources that allow its speakers to talk about language, thought and culture. It is this capacity above all that must make any belief in linguistic determinism highly suspect. Once again we see how 'liberating' language is for the only species to possess it.

## Further investigation

1  Write out as many English words as you know beginning with *sl-*. Do you find any common element of 'meaning' within the list? Now do the same for words beginning with *sn-* and *fl-*. The claim exists that each of these beginnings of English words has its own 'sound symbolism', i.e., a meaning that attaches to the specific combination of sounds. Do you agree?
2  What would a 'primitive language' be like? Is this an answerable question?
3  There have been, and continue to be, many attempts made to associate particular languages with particular 'races' (see Montagu, 1974, and Poliakov, 1974). You might look into the reasons behind such attempts and into the various claims that are made. Note that a milder form of the same phenomenon

would be a claim that one language is 'better' than another because it allows this or that not allowed by the other (and so by extrapolation its speakers are 'better' too).

# 7

# How do we 'learn' a language?

There is a very long history of interest concerning the development of language in children and much has been said and written on the topic. Some of what has been said is quite speculative, but much is sound – though often seriously limited – reporting of the results of conscientious observation. The Roman historian Herodotus tells us of a simple early experiment conducted by Psammetichus, a pharaoh of ancient Egypt, that involved bringing up two children in complete isolation to see what language they would speak 'naturally'. We do not know much about his results – we are told only that the first word they used was *bekos*, 'bread' in Phrygian! – but can be sure that the experiment could not be repeated today nor would we want to repeat it.

In the last half century or so much of the investigative work has been 'taxonomic' and 'normative' in nature, e.g. diary-like records of the appearance of 'first words', lists showing the order in which children 'acquire' specific 'sounds', inventories displaying the growth of grammatical control, catalogues of the utterance and sentence types used at different ages and so on. Some of this work can be criticized for being naive linguistically and somewhat unreliable in its methodology, and it became considerably more revealing following the development of modern linguistics. That development led researchers to pose a succession of interesting questions about such matters as the course of 'phonemic' development, the progressive differentiation and control of grammatical categories, the increasing awareness of semantic relationships and the acquisition of complex grammatical skills. Issues to be resolved rather than inventories to be compiled became central to investigations of language development as these became less 'data-driven' and more 'theory-driven'.

At the same time investigators were forced to confront the issue of what language itself is and how that something – whatever it is – could be acquired so uniformly, so easily and so quickly by naive children. Is language development some kind of 'natural' development like physical growth itself? Are humans endowed with a specific 'capacity for language'? Is language 'innate' in some sense? Or is language an entirely 'learned' behaviour, acquired in much the same way as many skills are learned? What, therefore, are the relative influences of 'nature' and 'nurture' on language acquisition? One aspect or another of this last issue is behind just about every controversy in language acquisition today.

Investigators were also forced to consider the actual process of language acquisition. As we saw earlier, linguists have never felt very comfortable trying to work with dynamic, changing systems and the variability that exists in large quantities of data. One consequence is that there still continues to be an emphasis in studies of language acquisition on 'stages of development' and a noticeable tendency to draw evidence not from large numbers of children but usually from one, two or three children studied periodically at fixed intervals. Of course, this concept of stages of development fits quite well with the usual linguistic emphasis on 'categorical differences', i.e., on whether or not two linguistic features are 'contrastive' and whether or not a particular distinction can be shown to exist in a specific body of data.

Another consideration that has come to the fore from time to time has been the need to make explicit the assumptions behind any theory of acquisition. Something must be innate if language is to be acquired. It could be a specific ability to acquire language, but it could also be an ability to do certain kinds of things with phenomena that the developing organism encounters, i.e., an innate general ability to respond to the environment and then to learn in carefully regulated ways through 'conditioning' or through a general 'cognitive' ability that also develops through experience.

There are other issues too that are much more specifically related to the acquisition of language. Language is 'doubly articulated' in that it employs two systems, one of sounds and the other of meanings. Do children 'know' this fact about language in advance of learning, or must they 'discover' it for themselves? What kind of knowledge would such knowledge be or what kind of discovery? Where do the primitive concepts of 'sense' and 'sentencehood' come from? Sentences make sense but how do children know this? Does such knowledge arise from inside the minds of children because they know – instinctively as it were – that the world must somehow 'make sense', or does it come through 'reinforcement' because people make sense of the world for children? If the latter, how do the processes of 'reinforcement' and 'generalization' work with essentially the abstract set of relationships that any language is? And, finally, why should very young children even talk at all, since almost every need they have is met and met almost immediately? Yet all children do learn to talk unless they are sorely deprived or afflicted.

As we will see, as soon as researchers begin to delve into issues related to language acquisition in children, they must confront just about every important issue in linguistics. Partly for this reason language acquisition has become one of the most interesting and controversial topics in linguistics in recent years. It is impossible to proceed very far in such research without asking questions whose answers have important consequences for linguistic theory. Any proposal that an investigator makes concerning how children learn or acquire an aspect of some language must not only cover the known facts for that language but also related facts in all other languages. It must also account for the learning or acquisition in a way that recognizes what we know about language itself, about children's cognitive capacities, about the sources of data that children have available to them and about the 'real time' that is involved in the actual learning or acquisition. A serious confrontation of issues such as these drastically limits the possible accounts we find we can give of language acquisition and indicates clearly some of its unique characteristics.

## 7.1   'Facts' to be explained

Most studies of language acquisition have concentrated on the first half-dozen years of life with the preponderance of emphasis directed to the second to fourth years, these appearing to be the most interesting years, those considered to be the most critical in the total acquisition process. Most studies have involved careful observation and recording of how children use language, but not a few have employed subtle kinds of testing to probe specific abilities (see Ingram, 1989, for an excellent survey).

Children, even children of mute parents, 'babble' for a considerable time during their first year. This babbling apparently ranges over the whole inventory of possible human sounds, but in at least one view gradually 'drifts' toward the phonetic characteristics of the language spoken in the environment of the child, possibly as a result of reinforcement. According to this view, there is adequate evidence that children have begun to acquire the sound system of the particular language spoken around them well before the period of babbling ends. I have already noted that the vocal tract of a very young child is different from that of an older child or mature adult and this difference alone would impose severe constraints on articulation.

An alternative view of the development of sound systems in children maintains that such development proceeds according to a set of universal principles. Babbling actually ceases altogether near the end of the first year of life and children learn to make certain basic phonological distinctions in a fixed order. They first of all learn to make a consonant–vowel distinction, with a *p* or *b* the first consonant and an *a* the first vowel; they also use an open syllable of the *pa* kind. In this view *p* is the 'optimal consonant' because it requires closure of the vocal tract at its furthest point and has a very low energy level. In contrast, *a* is the 'optimal vowel', the one that is widest at the front of the mouth and narrowest at the back. It is also a continuant with a very high energy level. In *pa*, therefore, a basic and very obvious labial closure comes to contrast with the simplest of all vowels. Children then learn to differentiate labial nasals from stops, i.e., *m* from *p* or *b*. (In this view then *papa* or *baba* occurs before *mama* in a child's speech.) Afterwards children come to differentiate 'labials' from 'dentals' (or 'alveolars'), i.e., *p*, *b* and *m* from *t*, *d* and *n*, they learn to contrast *i* with *a*, and *u* with *i*, they add 'velars' such as *k* and *g* and so on.

According to Roman Jakobson (1968, 1971), the linguist who proposed this theory, the operative principle is one of the achievement of 'maximal contrast' at each successive differentiation and it applies in a variety of ways to every language through laws of 'irreversible solidarity'. In this view no language can have 'back' consonants unless it also has 'front' consonants, i.e., it cannot have sounds like $k$ without those like $p$, or have 'fricatives' unless it has 'stops', i.e., it cannot have sounds like $f$ without those like $p$, because front consonants are more 'basic' to a language than back consonants and stops more basic than fricatives. They are more basic to the way all languages work, to the way children acquire language and to language impairment in certain kinds of aphasia in which more basic contrasts are retained and less basic ones lost. Although Jakobson's theory has not been thoroughly tested, it continues to intrigue many investigators because of its widespread implications. Although there may be controversy about the driving force behind it, the actual process of phonological acquisition seems to be just about complete in children by the age of six, with most of the major characteristics acquired much earlier.

So far as control of the system of meaning is concerned, the first unit that excites most parents is the appearance of a child's 'first word', an occurrence usually put somewhere near the end of the first year of life. But it is really quite difficult to specify exactly when a child begins to 'talk', i.e., to be sure that what you are saying to a very young child is being understood in the way you intended, or even understood in any way at all, or that what you are hearing from a child are words being used meaningfully. This difficulty is further compounded by the fact that, just as in adults, young children's comprehension abilities outstrip their productive ones. Finding out what a child 'knows' then is not an easy task.

Children's initial utterances are sometimes considered to be 'holophrastic' in nature, i.e., to be whole words possessing some kind of 'sentencehood' of their own. Such holophrases are found late in the first year of life or early in the second year. They appear to express commands to others or to self, as in *go, sit* or *down*, to describe actions, or to refer to objects in the environment, as in *mama* or *milk*, or to express emotions, sometimes in highly idiosyncratic ways. They may also refer to locations, name objects, assert properties of these objects and indicate agents. They show unequivocally that children are interacting in a meaningful way with their environment even though the kinds of meaning are clearly constrained.

Single-word utterances are heavily context-dependent for their success in communication. If we ignore the 'performative' intent behind any word, we may regard it as expressing only a single concept. Therefore, if we define 'sentencehood' as the overt expression of a relationship between two or more concepts, single words do not qualify as sentences. But such words could be considered to be the building blocks out of which children then proceed to form actual sentences in the language in the next stage of their development (see Gleitman, 1982).

Two-word utterances are characteristic of the last half of the second year of life, e.g. *Allgone milk, Allgone shoe, There chair, More juice, More cookie, More read, No baby*, etc. Such utterances are sometimes said (Brown and Bellugi, 1964) to be 'telegraphic' in nature. They consist almost entirely of 'content' words such as nouns and verbs, together with a small set of 'function' words like *there, more* and *no* in the above examples. The verb *be* and inflections on words such as plural marking on nouns and past tense marking on verbs have no place in such utterances. However, the utterances themselves are usually readily comprehensible to those who hear them.

Adults readily react to such utterances and even 'expand' them in ways which the children who utter them apparently find quite acceptable. The words in the utterances often seem to fall into fixed patterns. For example, in the above utterances *allgone, there, more* and *no* appear to operate as a small set of 'pivot' words which are always used before members of a much larger set of 'open' words like *milk, shoe, chair, juice, cookie, read* and *baby*. Some definite organizational principle appears to be at work.

The word-order patterns also seem to be fairly fixed, even though the actual language that is being acquired may have a rather free word order, as have languages such as Finnish, Russian and Korean. The patterns express such relationships as 'agent and action' (*Doggie sit*), 'agent and location' (*Daddy chair*), 'agent and object' (*Mummy water*), 'action and object' (*Take chair*), 'possessor and possession' (*Christy room*) and so on (see Brown, 1973). Since words are uninflected in their speech, children appear to gravitate naturally to fixed word order as an organizational principle for utterances. It is of no small interest too that the uninflected word itself is quite distinguishable in children's speech at this stage; it does, therefore, seem to possess some kind of 'reality' for children.

At this stage, too, the words which children use are 'perceptually salient' in that they are words which carry the heaviest stress in language as well as the most meaning. Function words, unstressed and contracted *be* and inflections lack perceptual salience; consequently, they are almost always absent from children's utterances. When children repeat long adult words, they generally say only the stressed parts, e.g. *'raff* for *giraffe* or *'pression* for *expression*. But children at this stage are quite capable of using stress and intonation for effect, e.g. to distinguish *Christy room* ('Christy's room') from *Christy room* ('Christy is in the room').

After the two-word stage children slowly begin to develop control of the 'inflections' on words, i.e., differences in word endings, and to use 'function words', i.e., words like *a, the, very, in, can*, etc. There is good evidence that three-year-olds are quite able to distinguish among the major word classes in their language, i.e., to distinguish among nouns, verbs, adjectives, pronouns, etc. Children learn irregular forms along with the regular ones and some exhibit a pattern of use in which the learning of a general rule for dealing with regularities leads to the elimination for a while of some previously learned irregular forms, e.g. *goed* may replace *went* for a while. When this happens, the child must later relearn the irregular forms. Other children will use both forms for a while. Six-year-olds will have mastered most of the inflectional system of even an extremely complexly inflected language.

Syntactic development proceeds concurrently with the learning of inflections. A three-word stage appears briefly after the two-word stage, e.g. *Mummy take cup*. Three-word utterances seem to be hierarchically ordered rather than linearly ordered, i.e., to be combinations of two two-word patterns rather than to be entirely new three-word patterns. However, the pace of development is so fast, with the ability to construct noun phrases, verb phrases and systems of modification all developing such complexity, that some organizing principle other than that of hierarchical arrangement alone must be operative in the acquisition process, because we soon observe utterances like *Chair all broke* and *Where baby chair?*

Using negation as an example (Klima and Bellugi, 1966), we can observe the emergence of different kinds of complexity. First of all, the negative element is attached (in the form of *no* or *don't*) to some kind of nuclear sentence to produce utterances like *No flag, No go back* and *Don't wear shirt*. Then at a later stage negation appears in still more varieties, e.g. *not* and *can't*, and is found internally in utterances, as in *Why not he go?* and *He can't go*. In the next stage the negation appears much as it appears in adult usage but on occasion without a complete mastery of all the details, as in *You don't want some supper* and *That not go in there*. Finally, the child achieves complete mastery of all the complexities.

As I have indicated, utterance length and syntactic complexity increase quickly and some of the actual limits in use may appear to be 'cognitive' in nature rather than 'linguistic', i.e., to be limits associated with general intellectual development, available memory span and increasing knowledge of the world. One view of what happens in language acquisition is that all the groundwork has effectively been laid by the time children complete their fourth year of life. A lot of details remain to be filled in and these may take a considerable time to master, but the major task is over quite soon in life.

Carol Chomsky's research (1969) showed that between the ages of five and ten English-speaking children learn to use a sentence like *The doll is easy to see* later than a sentence like *The doll is eager to see* because the first sentence is syntactically more complex than the second. In *The doll is easy to see*, while *the doll* is the 'grammatical subject' of the sentence as a whole, it is actually the 'logical subject' of neither *easy* nor *see*. However, in *The doll is eager to see*, *the doll* is both the 'grammatical subject' of the sentence as a whole and also the 'logical subject' of both *eager* and *see*. Such children also find *ask* more difficult to use properly than *tell*, because it can take different kinds of objects. *Promise* is difficult too, in much the same way as *ask*, but since it is consistently difficult, it causes children fewer problems than *ask*. Chomsky also found that pronominal reference created difficulties at this age level in that a sentence like *He knew that John was going to win the race* is often interpreted as though it were equivalent to *John knew that he* (i.e., John) *was going to win the race*.

Language acquisition is undoubtedly a life-long process for most of us. It does not stop at four or ten or any other age. But at the same time it is never so intense as it is before the age of four. It is also quite clear too that formal schooling for most children begins well after the most significant part of the acquisition process is complete. Never again will children – or even adults – acquire anything that even approaches language in its complexity so quickly, so uniformly and so effortlessly. We must therefore ask a fundamental question: why should this be so?

## Further investigation

1  What would you regard as conclusive evidence that a child had uttered his or her 'first word'?
2  Observe a two-year-old. Write down everything he or she says in an hour or so. Attempt to write a brief 'grammar' of the child's ability/knowledge. What problems confront you?
3  Find several accounts of the 'developmental norms' of children's language. What do they tell you and what terms do they use? What do they not tell you?
4  By the time children come to school they 'know' their language. All we do in school is teach them about it (often badly) and teach them some special forms and uses. How valid is this view?

## 7.2  What does 'learning theory' tell us?

Why do children all learn to speak, and why do they all follow much the same pattern of language development? Several different answers have been proposed to these questions, at least two of which are diametrically opposed to each other. The first is a 'behaviourist' or 'empiricist' answer, which holds that a language is learned in much the same way as many other things are learned, and it is the essential similarities among environments in which general laws of learning operate that account for the sameness. The second is a 'nativist', 'rationalist' or 'mentalist' answer, which holds that children are born with an innate ability to acquire languages of a specific type and that they go about such acquisition using principles that are unique to language learning. According to Noam Chomsky, children are born equipped with 'knowledge' of the general form that all languages must take and all that any child must do is figure out which particular variation of that form he or she is being exposed to. In this view the ability to acquire language is innate in the species and a child is born with a kind of 'blueprint' for language just waiting to be filled in.

The simplest behaviourist account of language learning is one that suggests that children acquire the language of the community into which they are born by simply 'imitating' what they hear around them. So language learning becomes a kind of imitative behaviour with its speed regulated by individual capabilities and opportunities. However, the evidence for the importance of imitation in language learning is quite unconvincing.

While we do know that children imitate some of the utterances of persons around them they do not imitate them indiscriminately. For example, even babies do not attempt to imitate all sounds in their environment but only human sounds, and they may actually be 'predisposed' toward human sounds. The prelinguistic vocalizations of deaf infants are also apparently quite indistinguishable from those of normal infants. A close analysis (Weir, 1962) of one very young child's pre-sleep monologues revealed numerous examples of repetitions and imitations of utterances encountered during the day, but also many original variations on those utterances. Congenital speech defects can also prevent speech activity but children with such defects can nevertheless learn to respond quite normally in other ways to the spoken language around them (Lenneberg, 1962).

If perfect reproduction is required for imitation to be successful, then children are very poor imitators. When children repeat parental utterances, they often reduce them so that *Daddy's briefcase* becomes *Daddy briefcase*, *Fraser will be unhappy* becomes *Fraser unhappy* and *I am drawing a dog* becomes *Draw dog*. Children offer 'telegraphic' versions of parental utterances and eliminate inflections, function words and non-salient elements. In situations when they do appear to be attempting to mimic adult behaviour they actually produce just the same kinds of utterances they are producing concurrently in spontaneous speech. If they are asked to imitate kinds of utterances they are not already using of their own accord, they fail badly, e.g. reproducing *The boy the book hit was crying* as *Boy the book was crying*, or they change what they hear to what they can say, e.g. saying *I saw the man and he got wet* for *The man who I saw yesterday got wet.*

Children's imitations do not seem to be grammatically progressive, i.e., children appear to imitate only in order to practise what they already know and not to try out new forms. Even deliberate and apparently simple requests made to children to imitate certain linguistic forms are likely to be unsuccessful. One child (see McNeill, 1966) asked ten times in succession to repeat *Nobody likes me* could finally do no better than to say *Nobody don't likes me*; another child asked repeatedly to say *She held them* instead of *She holded them* could not do so. In neither case did parental repetition effect any significant change in the child's language behaviour.

Children do imitate their parents and older children to some extent, but parents and older children also imitate young children. Conversations sometimes resemble exchanges of telegrams between two parties with each party trying to figure out exactly what the other meant by a particular message. But the older party often expands the utterances of the younger party. A child's *Baby highchair* leads an older child or adult to say *Baby is in the highchair* and *Eve lunch* brings *Eve is having lunch*. The child's words and structures are imitated and expanded and the expanded utterance serves as a kind of check on what the child said ('Is that what you meant?'). It may also act as a fully formed model for the child to use on some subsequent occasion, but one that, as we have seen, we cannot be at all sure the child will use.

Adults often do try to simplify their speech to children. They can be observed to use short uncomplicated sentences, repetitions, slow and careful articulation and exaggerated intonation. Older children can also be observed using some of these same characteristics in their speech to younger children and even quite young children will adopt such speech when playing with baby dolls. This kind of speech is sometimes called 'motherese' (Snow and Ferguson, 1977). However, it is not at all clear (Gleitman *et al.* 1984) that it produces the effects intended. Parents are usually unable to provide good accounts of just what kinds of language abilities their children have. Motherese itself tends to be random in both its consequences for language simplification and modification and in its actual application to adult–child interchanges. So while it seems in some ways to help children and to be 'natural', investigations into its use show that its effects on actual language acquisition are doubtful. What motherese obviously does do is allow for a form of language 'bonding' between language users and this bonding may be very important. Children could undoubtedly get just as much language exposure – perhaps even more – by just simply watching television, but it appears to be the case that children do not learn a language if their only exposure to it comes through television. They need real people to interact with.

There is plenty of evidence that middle-class mothers engage in a considerable amount of verbal interaction with their children. For example, they 'expand' about thirty per cent of the utterances of their young children. One study (Cazden, 1972) tested the hypothesis that expansion of children's utterances actually encourages language development in contrast to merely commenting on those utterances and that either activity would produce better results than using neither expansions nor comments. Twelve two-year-olds were divided into three groups. The first group of children received intensive and deliberate expansion of their utterances so that an utterance like *Doggie bite* was expanded to *Yes, the dog's biting*. The second group received an equal exposure to well-formed sentences that were comments on their utterances but not expansions, so that the same utterance might be commented on with something like *Yes, he's mad at the kitten*. The third group received no special treatment at all. The experiment, which lasted 12 weeks, did not show quite the expected differences because commenting not expanding proved to be the most effective treatment. That is, semantically-enriched responses of different syntactic form were more effective in encouraging language development than syntactically-enriched responses, even ones that closely followed the children's own language.

Two further studies (Brown and Hanlon, 1970; Brown *et al.* 1967) examined how adults responded to syntactic deviance in their children. One, based on an analysis of conversations between mothers and very young children, found that the syntactic correctness or incorrectness of a child's speech does not control the mother's approval or disapproval. Rather, the truth or falsity of the utterance does. Consequently, a child's *There's the animal farmhouse* was corrected because the subject was a light-house not a farmhouse. Parents also tend to reward true statements (*That's right, Very good, Yes*) and punish false ones (*That's wrong, No*); however, the result is that children eventually produce syntactically correct sentences but, paradoxically, not always truthful ones. The second study confirmed these findings.

In general it seems then that parents pay little or no attention to deviant utterances from young children. The truth value of utterances concerns them more than does their syntactic correctness. A parent may even repeat a child's *What you was having on your nose?* as *What I was having on my nose?* before answering it with *Nothing, I was rubbing my eyes*. The corrections that do occur are corrections of occasional mispronunciations, of irregular word forms such as *goed* for *went*, and of the use of socially disapproved words and expressions. On the other hand, deviant utterances like *Why not can you go?* seem to pass unnoticed on most occasions.

Children do imitate, parents do expand, some words and expressions are more frequent than others, analogies are made and generalizations are tested. There is therefore some evidence to support a few of the claims made in simple behaviouristic accounts of language learning. However, no one disputes the fact that data are important, that children must have access to the actual language they are to learn and that adults and older children provide help in that learning. The basic issue is whether what must be learned in language learning can be learned entirely through behaviouristic principles.

As we have seen, one serious difficulty with relying exclusively on such principles in order to explain all or even any important part of language acquisition is the fact that much of the speech to which children are exposed is fragmentary in nature and what children must do, and very quickly succeed in doing, is respond to and produce entirely novel utterances, not repeat fixed examples. Indeed, not a few examples to which they are exposed they must discard entirely because of their intrinsic deficiencies as models. This ability to reject poor examples is as difficult to explain as the ability to select good examples.

There is good reason too (Shipley *et al.* 1969) to believe that children actually prefer to be told *Throw me the ball* rather than *Throw ball* or just *Ball*, or *Bring me the book* rather than *Bring book*, even when they themselves can produce only the shorter utterances and are unable to repeat the longer ones. Imitation cannot account for such a preference. Children soon use forms and expressions that they have never heard, e.g. *goed* instead of *went, they sleeps* instead of *they sleep*, and utterances such as *Allgone shoe, Allgone lettuce, Allgone milk* and *Why not can you go?* No appeal to imitation, analogical creation or generalization can explain this creative aspect of language use. Any such appeal skirts the central issue of language acquisition: how does a very young child presented with such a small body of linguistic data, largely unorganized and patently deficient in many respects, come so soon to acquire mastery of a language whose rules are still not at all clear to us even though many hundreds, perhaps even thousands, of scholar-years have been spent trying to specify those rules?

The best-known exponent of the behaviourist position was the psychologist B. F. Skinner, because of his attempt to apply his theory of learning to the learning of language. Skinner's principal interest was the prediction and control of functional units of behaviour. He argued that language is of special interest because language behaviour is behaviour that only human beings 'reinforce', and language behaviour also reinforces the behaviour of others through the effects it produces on them. In his book *Verbal Behavior* (1957), Skinner attempted to specify the functional stimuli for utterance types, the functional response classes and the various kinds of reinforcements that relate the two.

The book describes two important categories of verbal behaviour, what Skinner calls 'mands' (from *commands* and *demands*) and 'tacts' (from *contacts*). Mands are words or groups of words which bring reinforcement in the form of rewards which satisfy needs that a speaker has, e.g. *Please pass the sugar, Stop, Got a moment?*, etc. On the other hand, tacts are comments about the world, e.g. *It's raining, I'm tired, I saw her yesterday*, etc. They receive no direct reinforcement but, according to Skinner, through a process of 'generalized reinforcement', e.g. a listener's smile, nod, praise or attention, a speaker is encouraged to keep on speaking. Minor categories of verbal behaviour, according to Skinner, include 'echoic responses' (imitations), 'textual responses' (responses involved in reading), 'intraverbal responses' (knowledge of word associations) and 'autoclitics' (verbal behaviour about one's own verbal behaviour, as in the use of expressions like *I think* or *I guess*).

In Skinner's view the reinforcement of selected responses is the key to our understanding language development: gradually, by a process of successive approximation, children learn the linguistic norms of the community. In this view a language is a sophisticated response system that humans acquire through processes of conditioning. For example, parents reinforce only certain sounds out of the vast array of sounds which children use in their babbling. Such reinforcement causes children's sounds to 'drift' toward those of their parents. In syntactic development the process involves making generalizations from one situation to another and children find that particular linguistic patterns are reinforced and others are ignored. Discriminations and generalizations that get results are therefore encouraged; on the other hand, those that fail are not reinforced and are eventually extinguished. Each child is to all intents and purposes a *tabula rasa* at the beginning of the process of language acquisition. What is universal are the principles of learning that all children apply to the raw data of their experiences. Society rewards them for evidence of linguistic conformity and either ignores or punishes their aberrations.

If we examine some of the previously cited data in the light of such a proposal, we can understand how it might be possible to claim that syntactic development occurs through a process of contextual generalization with two-word utterances of the pivot-open variety being the building blocks. According to such a claim, children observe that certain sets of items occur in certain positions in utterances and then proceed to make generalizations about the abstract characteristics of those items and positions. Initially, the positions may be linear, but they soon become hierarchical because three-word and four-word utterances must have a 'depth' to them as well as a 'length'. According to Skinner, such a generalization process can also account for the learning of extremely complex syntactic relationships.

Noam Chomsky (1959) was severely critical of Skinner's use of a principle like 'generalization' to account in this way for what happens in language learning. He argued that its use effectively eliminates from consideration just about everything that is of real interest in such learning. He also criticized Skinner's use of reinforcement as being the key to understanding how languages are learned. While acknowledging that reinforcement, casual observation of data, natural inquisitiveness, an ability to generalize and hypothesis-formation all have their place in language acquisition, Chomsky claimed that neither any one separately nor all together can account for what actually happens. Children cannot possibly generalize from word-order patterns because no dominant patterns of word order exist for them to generalize from, even in a language like English. As I have noted too, they also apparently produce similar fixed patterns even when the language they are learning has a very free word order, so neither reinforcement nor generalization can account for what happens in those cases. Chomsky's counter-claim is that children must acquire very abstract linguistic structures for which no overt patterns exist in the data to which they are exposed; consequently, language acquisition must involve some other principle or principles than those that interested Skinner.

## Further investigation

1 Find some examples of when 'reinforcement' does apply as an appropriate explanation for a child's learning some aspect of language.
2 Television is said to be a considerable influence on children's lives. What is its influence on their language?
3 Why is it that children behave more like their peers than their parents in their use of language?
4 In what ways are learning to speak and learning to read different?

## 7.3 Is the 'mind' in control?

The Swiss psychologist Jean Piaget and investigators like Dan Slobin and Roger Brown are associated with still another approach to trying to understand what happens when children acquire a language. They offer a 'cognitive' account, which holds that language development is just one aspect of total mental development. In this view children gradually come to terms with the world as their cognitive abilities develop and it is these cognitive abilities we must try to understand if we are ever to make sense of how children develop their language abilities.

Slobin (1979), for example, says that children are born possessing a set of procedures and inference rules that enable them to process linguistic data. The language acquisition process itself is an active process controlled at each stage by the various abilities of children, particularly the cognitive ability to make sense of the world and the mental ability to retain items in short-term memory, to store items in long-term memory and to process information increasingly effectively with age. It is the development of these abilities that controls the pace of language acquisition.

Other abilities are also important, e.g. the ability to segment utterances into component sounds and meanings and then to combine and recombine these segments, the ability to isolate meaning units and the ability to make wide generalizations before attempting to accommodate exceptions. However, according to Slobin, general cognitive and mental development is the critical determinant of language acquisition. Children are born 'knowing' something about both the structure and function of language and must actively seek to develop means for expressing what they know within their limitations and capacities. Slobin also maintains that language acquisition itself may well be completed by the age of three or so, and that what we view as language development after that age may be no more than further lifting of 'performance' restrictions and evidence of general cognitive growth.

Roger Brown (1973) used children's two-word and three-word utterances to show how their language develops so as to allow them to express more and more complicated meanings and relationships that go well beyond simply naming, referring or questioning. Two-word utterances in a variety of languages including English, German, Russian, Finnish, Turkish, Samoan and Luo, a language of Kenya, show that the combinations express many different semantic relationships if one gives the data a 'rich' interpretation. Such an interpretation seeks to establish the intent of an utterance in addition to describing its form. However, the intent of any utterance may not be at all clear and nowhere is this lack of clarity likely to be more apparent than with very young children. For example, what does a child who says *Daddy* in the absence of the child's father intend? However, if certain linguistic forms appear consistently in certain social contexts, we may be able to speak with considerable assurance about the intent of those forms. This, at least, is the assumption behind the classifications that follow.

In two-word utterances the most frequently expressed relationships, accounting for about seventy per cent of the utterances, are 'agent–action' (*Mummy push, Daddy throw*) and 'action–object' (*Bite finger, Throw ball*). However, 'object–location' (*Cow there, Teddy chair*), 'possessor–possession' (*Dolly hat, My shoe*), and 'attribute–object' (*Big bed, Big teddy*) also occur. Later in development come 'agent–object' (*Mummy cup, Daddy ball*), 'action–location' (*Sit chair*) and 'demonstrative–object' (*That book*). Simple 'negatives' (*Not Daddy*) and 'questions' (*Where Daddy?*) also occur, as well as minor patterns such as 'identification' (*Mummy lady*) and 'conjunction' (*Dog cat*). The order of the parts is often reversible without any change in meaning, e.g. *Finger bite* as well as *Bite finger* and *Chair sit* as well as *Sit chair*. These are examples from the English data but the other languages produce similar patterns and do so regardless of whether or not the language itself uses fixed word order to show such relationships. It would appear that all children use word order, initially at least, as a principle to organize the linguistic data they meet and it does not matter if that principle actually turns out to be rather unimportant in the language.

Children build up three-word utterances by omitting the redundant item in two two-word utterances that share a common item, so that *Mummy sit* and *Sit chair* can become *Mummy sit chair*, and *Eat lunch* and *Eve lunch* can become *Eve eat lunch.* But apparently for a while *Mummy drink coffee* and *Drink hot coffee* cannot be combined to form *Mummy drink hot coffee*. Children do not yet have the cognitive capacity to create such complex utterances. If at this stage children want to express a complicated idea, they must string together a long sequence of short utterances. As Lois Bloom, another investigator, has pointed out, young children say things like *Raisin there / Buy more grocery store / Raisins / Buy more grocery store / Raisin at grocery store*, instead of a single sentence about buying more raisins at the grocery store.

Bloom (1970, 1973) has also investigated the kinds of negation children use in their two-word utterances. She found that an utterance such as *No truck* can have various meanings and that these meanings showed a definite order in their emergence, e.g. 'non-existence' ('There's no truck here') precedes 'rejection' ('I don't want a truck'), which in turn precedes 'denial' ('It's not a truck; it's something else'). She concludes that children's underlying semantic competence is much more differentiated than the surface forms of their utterances might indicate. Children are aware of more types of meaning relationships than they are able to reveal through the linguistic forms that are available to them. They must necessarily use the forms they have acquired to express any new or complex meaning relationships that they want to express.

Both Slobin and Brown have been interested in the connection between 'linguistic forms' and 'language functions'. Slobin has observed that new linguistic forms in children's repertoires first express old language functions and that new language functions are first expressed by old linguistic forms. Brown examined how three children came to use verb inflections. Before they use any inflections at all the children used uninflected verbs like *break, come, drink* and *fall* to express one of four possible functions. These functions were indicating something of a temporary duration, referring to the immediate past, stating a wish or intention and commanding. Then inflections emerged to provide new forms for these functions: the *-ing* inflection for 'duration'; the *-ed* inflection for 'past'; the verb forms *hafta, gonna* and *wanna* for 'wish' or 'intention'; and the word *please* to serve as a clear indicator of a 'command' because the command form of a verb is itself uninflected. The development of a system of negatives would be a further example of new forms being acquired to express the various functions of the negative that Bloom discusses. Similarly, the *'s* genitive eventually comes to serve as a clear marker of 'possession', *Dolly's hat* coming to replace *Dolly hat*. Slobin also cites evidence of new functions being served by old forms. For example, children first attach words such as *now* and *yet* to statements about the past to indicate the 'perfective aspect', saying *Now I closed it* and *I didn't make the bed yet* before *I've closed it* and *I haven't made the bed*.

In this view the new forms and the new functions themselves both result from the increase in cognitive ability that accompanies increase in age. For example, as children get older they can increasingly free themselves from the immediate situation and the actual order of events in the world, they can imagine themselves to be at other points in both time and space and they can view events from other perspectives. This increase in cognitive ability enables children to express new meanings; they therefore acquire the grammatical forms that allow them to express these new meanings after they try for a while to get by with the forms that they have used to that point. The new forms were actually always available because there is nothing particularly rare or complicated about many of them, e.g. English uses past tenses frequently. However, cognitive limitations, which are gradually set aside, lead to particular forms and combinations of these forms being overlooked or neglected until children are ready for them.

So far as the acquisition of linguistic forms is concerned, Slobin has suggested that the order of emergence of various syntactic categories depends in general on their relative 'semantic' complexity rather than on their grammatical complexity. The first grammatical distinctions to appear are those like the 'singular–plural' distinction, which make direct reference to readily observable situations in the outside world. Later to emerge are the 'diminutive' suffixes of nouns, 'imperatives' in verbs and grammatical categories based on 'relational' criteria, such as markings for 'case', 'tense' and 'person'. 'Conditional' forms of the *if-then* variety are not learned until the end of the third year, when they are used to express abstract relationships. Still other abstract categories of quality and action continue to be added until the age of seven. Slobin points out that Russian children find 'gender' to be one of the most difficult categories of all to acquire because it has almost no semantic correlates. No easily discoverable principles exist to help Russian children in their learning and as a consequence they spend considerable time learning the correct gender assignments of words.

According to Slobin (1973, 1982), an analysis of what children actually do in language learning suggests that they come to the task with a set of principles that they apply to the data they meet. He says that these principles can be characterized somewhat as follows. Pay attention to the ends of words, a principle suggested by the fact that children learn 'suffixes' and 'postpositions' more easily than 'prefixes' and 'prepositions'. Phonological forms may be modified, a principle that allows children to accommodate to the often deliberately introduced distortions of adult speech, e.g. *bow-wow* and *doggie*. Word order is important and semantic relationships should be clearly marked, principles we have observed in many of the examples previously cited. Avoid interrupting syntactic units, a principle which is revealed in children's use of 'intonation' questions before '*yes–no*' questions, which involve syntactic inversion. Avoid exceptions, a principle which explains why irregularities are learned late or sometimes must be relearned. Finally, grammatical markers should make semantic sense, a principle which accounts for the difficulty encountered in learning gender.

Because of their cognitive limitations, young children do not attend to and perceive linguistic stimuli in the same way as adults. They also attend to language in different ways and adopt different processing strategies at different times. For example, children between 18 and 30 months pay more attention to utterances like their own than they do to the expanded utterances of older children and adults. We recognize this intuitively when we 'telegraph' our own speech in talking to very young children. But children must have the fuller adult utterances available to them if they are to learn to speak properly. Children also for a time try to relate words that occur closely together in terms of specific patterns with which they are familiar. They are likely therefore to interpret a passive sentence such as *The car is pushed by the truck* as though it were active (*The car pushed the truck*). Since most sentences are 'active' rather than 'passive', a strategy that seeks to interpret noun-verb-noun sequences as agent-action-object sequences usually 'pays off' in that it usually provides the correct interpretation without delay. It may be too that it is children's adoption of particular strategies that causes them the kind of difficulty that Carol Chomsky noted they experience for a while in understanding the verbs *tell, promise* and *ask* in sentences such as *I told John to go, I promised John to go* and *I asked John where to go.*

One consequence of adopting this cognitive view of language acquisition is that the evidence from investigations of different languages should indicate that semantic ability develops in a fairly consistent way across those languages, and that the same kinds of cognitive limitations appear in the expression of concepts. Such appears to be the case. Children everywhere seem to be actively pursuing the expression of more and more complicated meanings. In doing so, they appear to rely on certain innate abilities to guide them in knowing what to look for and how to go about the looking. There appears to be a universality about the process, just as there appear to be universal patterns of general human development.

Jean Piaget (Piaget, 1950; see also Evans, 1973; Flavell, 1963; Gardner, 1973) was long interested in universal patterns of growth and development in children. Trained as a biologist – his doctoral thesis was on molluscs – and experienced as a researcher on human intelligence in the laboratory of Théodore Simon, Piaget turned his attention while still a young man to studying how children experience the world and come eventually to fit into it. Piaget liked to refer to himself as a 'genetic epistemologist', rather than as a child psychologist, because of his overriding interest in the 'big issue' of how we come as children to 'know' the world around us. In his writings he postulates that the child is an active organism innately structured to develop according to a fixed pattern. Nature and nurture interact with each other in a principled way during the course of that development and Piaget set out to explain the principles of such interaction.

Piaget's early work was far ranging. In a series of books published between 1924 and 1937 he laid out many of his basic ideas in a way that he never intended to be definitive; hence his use of small samples, his sketchy reporting of research procedures and the individualistic, sometimes even opaque, style he adopted for the presentation of his ideas. Those ideas did become fashionable though, particularly as 'structuralism' itself gained intellectual ascendancy. Taking a 'whole' view of children was also seen as being necessary in trying to understand how they develop.

So far as cognitive development is concerned, Piaget postulated in his writings the existence of three separate, sequentially arranged and qualitatively different stages through which all normal children proceed. The first stage is a 'sensorimotor' stage lasting from birth to 18 months, the second stage one of 'concrete operations' lasting from 18 months to 11 years and the last stage one of 'formal operations' lasting from 11 to about 15. In each stage children explore their world and discover inconsistencies between their beliefs about that world and how it actually works. In each stage children are forced to make the adjustments that are necessary to deal with the inconsistencies so as to achieve the 'homeostasis' necessary to continued existence. The stages are successive and there is no clear linkage between them, and Piaget does not explain how one stage leads to the next.

During the sensorimotor stage children learn that objects in the environment have a permanent existence. Children learn that objects do not cease to exist when they stop looking at them, but that they appear and reappear because they have an independent existence of their own. At this time children also acquire the basic notions of 'space', 'time' and 'causality'. Sensorimotor intelligence itself is limited to the very simple operations which affect this small, concrete world.

The stage of concrete operations may be subdivided into a stage of 'preoperational thought' lasting until about the age of seven and one of 'concrete operational thought' lasting until 11. In the first of these substages children are able to manipulate symbols and signs but only in a very limited way in operations that are concrete, immediate and irreversible. During this substage children are heavily involved in what they are doing and they can see things only from their own perspective because of a pervasive 'egocentricity'. In the second substage children are able to manage classes and relationships of a much more complicated kind. For example, they can reverse operations, make compensatory adjustments, grasp the principle of 'conservation', and adopt another's perspective. The final stage of formal operations is the stage of deduction, of the manipulation of discrete variables, of hypothesis testing, of seeing implications and of handling many different kinds of abstractions and systems of abstraction.

If we look at the kinds of language that children use during the course of their linguistic development and the kinds of meanings they express in that language, we can see how both can appear to be limited by the particular Piaget-type stage in which children find themselves. In the sensorimotor stage, for example, children learn names for things and events and learn that the names can be used both in the presence and absence of whatever is named. In the first substage of concrete operations they learn to analyse events, e.g. into agents, actions and objects, or into objects and locations, or into existence versus non-existence, as in negation. At first children do not have the capacity to express more than two aspects of any event, but later develop this capacity and are then able to mention three or more aspects. The result of this cognitive limitation is, of course, 'telegraphic' speech, if we consider only the syntactic form of the resulting utterances.

Piaget (1980) believed that cognitive development controls language development and pointed to a specific test (Sinclair, 1971; Sinclair-de Zwart, 1969, 1973) of this hypothesis as proof. A number of children were divided into three groups on the basis of how well they made judgements about the sameness or difference of quantities in different circumstances. Children who understand the principle of conservation realize that when a quantity of liquid is poured from a glass of one shape into a glass of another shape, the quantity of the liquid does not change even though it may appear to do so. In Piaget's test, children who could not do the conservation task were almost always unable to describe two objects, e.g. a short thick pencil and a long thin one, using comparatives. They were able to comprehend an instruction to find a pencil that was longer and thinner than another, but they could not say *This pencil is longer and thinner* or *That pencil is shorter and fatter*. Instead, they used pairs of sentences such as *This pencil is long* and *That pencil is short*, i.e., independent sentences without comparatives. It also proved to be very difficult to teach the non-conservers the terms that the conservers used for comparison. Specific linguistic training resulted in only ten per cent of the non-conservers exhibiting a grasp of conservation when the initial conservation task was repeated. The results led Piaget to conclude that cognitive development precedes linguistic development, not vice versa. If such a conclusion is valid then language training designed to encourage cognitive growth may prove to be quite ineffective.

## Further investigation

1   Like 'language', 'intelligence' is a difficult concept to come to grips with. Put the two together and you compound the difficulty. Try to sort out what you understand by 'intelligence'

and what, if any, is its relationship to what you understand by 'language' and the 'ability to use language'.

2  Do animals lack language because they lack intelligence or lack intelligence because they lack language? Or is this just an insoluble riddle?

3  If language ability depends on cognitive growth and the human species continues to develop its cognitive capacity, we might expect our language capacity to grow too. But what could that last phrase, 'language capacity', mean?

## 7.4  Is language ability 'innate'?

We have been looking for a theory that best explains how a child learns language and how that learning relates to the learning of just about everything else a child must learn. We have assumed that we can find such an explanation. However, we must also consider that we have been asking entirely the wrong questions and addressing the wrong issues. Let us therefore look at some parallels between talking and walking and ask whether or not learning to talk might be like learning to walk. If it is, then we should possibly rethink not only what we mean by using a word like *learning* to describe what happens in language acquisition, but also the entire process of acquisition itself.

In what ways then is talking like walking so far as acquisition is concerned? Both abilities are acquired universally, effortlessly and without instruction. There is nothing that needs to be triggered, prompted or really encouraged at all in either activity and any help or encouragement we offer is of little consequence to what happens in either case. Both talking and walking 'happen' when children are 'ready' and, when they happen, both proceed in regular and predictable ways. Children learn to walk everywhere in the world and to talk everywhere in the world and they have always walked and talked everywhere in the world. There is also absolutely no reason to believe that either type of acquisition has changed over the millennia or that practice, instruction or training of any kind has produced any other than a few local and quite insignificant variations in either activity.

Talking is even like walking in that children do not really need either to talk or to walk, because usually almost every 'need' they have is met fairly promptly; however, they just seem compelled by some inner force to both talk and walk, as though there is something in the human organism itself that prompts both activities. And children talk and walk whether they are 'bright' or 'dull', so the two activities are completely unrelated to 'intelligence', whatever that is.

If we look specifically at the structure of human languages, it would appear that only if children were born 'preprogrammed' to acquire language would they have any chance at all of mastering the details of the specific language that confronts them. The data that do confront them from the specific language they encounter are also somewhat fragmentary, random in nature and sometimes rather deficient. As we have seen too, what deliberate 'teaching' they encounter is likely to be well-motivated to be sure but haphazard and usually poorly informed by fact. The very kind of instruction that might be helpful, e.g. instruction about ambiguity, paraphrase possibilities, grammaticality, etc., is entirely lacking. But then, fortunately, it does not seem to be necessary.

It does not seem necessary because in this view each child comes to the task of language acquisition with a set of 'innate' principles which enable that child to acquire the language of the surrounding community. In this view, just as learning to walk is an innate, biologically-determined activity, so is learning to talk. What is really remarkable is that many of us somehow persist in believing that we actually 'teach' children to talk but never claim that we teach them to walk.

In this view children 'know' the principles they are to apply to the raw data of language as they confront these data during the acquisition process. All they must do is set various 'parameters' (Lightfoot, 1991) to these principles, i.e., make certain decisions about the limits of application of each principle. But this parameter-setting too is an automatic process. What is not automatic is learning the actual sounds that the particular language employs, its specific vocabulary and its social conventions for language use. Conventional learning applies there.

This view of language acquisition is strongly favoured in much language-acquisition research today (see Goodluck, 1991). Those holding such a view believe that the correct way to investigate language acquisition is to test a theory of language and its predictions (see Pinker, 1984, 1989; Radford, 1990). The usual theory tested is one or other version of Chomsky's 'universal grammar'. For example, in the 'government and binding' version of universal grammar investigators might be concerned with how children learn to work out who does what in sentences like *Cookie Monster tells Grover to jump over the fence, Cookie Monster touches Grover after jumping over the fence, Cookie Monster stands near Grover after jumping over the fence, Grover touches Bert before he jumps over the fence* and *Grover told Bert that he would jump over the fence* (McDaniel and Cairns, 1990).

Investigators who have looked closely at what children appear to 'know' in the above sense of this word claim that there is considerable evidence that even very young children who cannot yet use phrases and clauses are aware that these are real units in language (Hirsh-Pasek *et al.* 1987). Very young children also show a preference for human speech over non-human speech (Fernald, 1984; Fernald and Simon, 1984; Jusczyk, 1986; Mehler *et al.* 1978). Children also do not produce sentences like *I know where he's* with a contracted *he's* for *he is*, and you can explain this phenomenon only by assuming that there is come underlying ability at work, because there appears to be no other way of accounting for such a non-occurrence. (That ability is the 'knowledge' that you can contract *he is* to *he's* only when it is part of a larger phrase, as in *where he's going.*) Similarly, children learning English quickly come to know the possibilities of reference of *she* in sentences such as *She took it when she left, She took it when Jane left* and *Jane took it when she left,* i.e., that *she* and *Jane* must refer to different people in the second of these sentences, but that the other *she*s are ambiguous. However, no explanation from 'learning theory' can account for the acquisition of knowledge of this kind.

In addition to Noam Chomsky himself, for whom the 'innateness' of language is a cornerstone of his linguistic theory, there are several other well-known exponents of this nativist view of language acquisition. One of them was the psycholinguist Eric Lenneberg (1967), who relied heavily on biological evidence of various kinds in developing his ideas on this subject. Lenneberg stressed the importance of human cognition in the acquisition of language, but maintained that cognition itself is in turn based on the specific combination of 'biological' characteristics that defines the human species. He emphasized the development of the various capacities of the human organism and demonstrated in his work how these mature according to what he considered to be a fixed biological schedule. According to Lenneberg, language emerges in children during the course of this maturational process when anatomical, physiological, motor, neural and, above all, cognitive developments allow it to emerge.

At about six months children can usually sit up alone and stand upright without support; these developments coincide with the onset of babbling and discernible sounds like *ma, mu, da* and *di*. At about one year children can usually walk if held by one hand, and they can understand and speak a few words, e.g. *mama* and *dada*. When they can creep downstairs backwards and become quite mobile at about the age of 18 months, they are ready to begin the really rapid development of language. At this stage they easily respond to requests such as *Show me your eyes*, have a vocabulary of 50 or more words, control a variety of intonation patterns and readily understand much more than they are capable of producing.

The ability to walk up and down stairs at about two correlates with the ability to use utterances of two or three words in length. Tricycle riding at three is accompanied by still more grammatical complexity and the ability to talk intelligibly to strangers. At the age of four, when children can readily catch a ball, or jump over a rope, or hop on one foot, they also exhibit considerable language competency.

All children must learn the specific details of the languages of the communities in which they find themselves, but language-learning ability itself is innate and part of the human organism's biological endowment. It is a species-specific ability which enables humans to learn languages of a certain type. The learning mechanisms, such as certain modes of perception, abilities in categorization and capacities for transformation, are biologically given. According to Lenneberg, children 'resonate' to the language of their environment during the acquisition process, i.e., they react automatically to the various kinds of language stimuli that surround them.

Since Lenneberg was interested in the biological bases of language he had little to say about the learning of specific grammatical details, and he actually allowed that statistical probability and imitation might have a place in learning. His basic claim, however, is that language activity is a 'natural' activity, much as learning to walk is a natural activity. Both activities occur universally unless a pathological condition exists. Both exhibit a regular development sequence, are relatively unaffected by the environment, are not particularly useful when they first occur and are initially quite clumsy but do not lose that clumsiness through practice alone. 'Learning', as learning psychologists traditionally define it, is not involved at all in either process. Lenneberg therefore carefully locked language development into the general biological development of the human organism. A necessary corollary is that no other species is capable of learning a human language because of the extreme specificity of language in the human species.

Another major exponent of this nativist, or rationalist, view is the psychologist David McNeill (1970), who in his work has attempted to explore some of the implications of Chomsky's theory for language acquisition. McNeill agrees with Chomsky in maintaining that investigators who claim to be seriously interested in the problem of language acquisition must first of all address the issue of what it is that is actually being acquired, i.e., such investigators must know something – in fact quite a lot – about language. (Unfortunately, many observations about child language and many claims about the learning of languages come from people who know little or nothing about language and who, much too often, may not even consider such knowledge to be necessary to that task.) McNeill agrees with Chomsky that children must acquire a grammar of a certain kind and that in order to acquire a grammar of this kind they must possess certain kinds of knowledge even before they begin the task of acquisition. If they did not, we could not possibly explain how children convert the random, finite, sometimes degenerate, linguistic input they are exposed to into the kinds of linguistic competency they rapidly display.

According to McNeill, one kind of innate knowledge that children have is the concept of 'sentence'. McNeill argues that children 'know' what sentences are from the very beginning of their experience with language. Another kind of knowledge is an awareness that only a certain kind of linguistic system is poossible and that other kinds are not. Therefore, children need entertain only a very limited set of hypotheses about how to organize the data that confront them. Like Chomsky, McNeill claims that children are born with an innate knowledge of linguistic universals, i.e., knowledge of the organizing principles underlying all languages. McNeill himself distinguishes between 'weak' linguistic universals, i.e., reflections in language of universal cognitive or perceptual abilities, and 'strong' linguistic universals, i.e., reflections in language of specific linguistic abilities. He is interested in the latter and actually quite sceptical of the existence of the former.

According to McNeill, one innate ability that all children have is the ability to distinguish speech sounds from other sounds in the environment; children are, as it were, 'pretuned' to human language. A second ability allows them to organize linguistic events into various categories that they can later refine. This ability also permits the development of both the phonological and syntactic systems out of these categories. Still another ability leads children to engage in continual evaluation of the developing linguistic system in order to construct the simplest possible overall system out of the linguistic data they encounter. They have a built-in evaluation system for language that pushes them in just the direction they need to go during the acquisition process.

McNeill, like Chomsky, maintains that behaviourist views of language acquisition are quite misguided. He claims that behaviourists actually must redefine language to make data fit their theories. He insists strongly on the abstractness of linguistic knowledge and the necessity of postulating an innate structure in humans which determines both what they can learn and how that learning occurs.

The behaviourist and nativist views of language acquisition are almost diametrically opposed. Behaviourists have been accused of making data fit their theories, of defining language to suit these theories and using processes such as 'association', 'generalization' and 'reinforcement' to 'explain' the unexplainable. Behaviourists assume that children make no active contribution to the total process of language learning: they learn language in much the same way as they learn anything else. They also come to the task of such learning in complete ignorance of what awaits them. It is the principles of learning that are important in whatever happens, not certain intrinsic characteristics of either learners or language. There is, however, in such a view a healthy insistence that the environment in which the learning occurs is important.

Nativists, on the other hand, tend to commit themselves to a particular linguistic theory and then use that theory to probe issues in language acquisition. Giving a linguistic theory like universal grammar a central place in investigations of language acquisition requires the postulation of innate predispositions toward the acquisition of very specific linguistic abilities, in fact just those abilities important to the theory. In this view, therefore, investigators must assume that children 'know' a considerable amount about language before they begin any 'learning'.

Such a view also tends to minimize the importance of environmental factors. Some language must be present in the child's environment but little seems to be necessary in the environment beyond that. The child inevitably acquires a language and the particular environment in which the acquisition of that language occurs leads to the learning of certain trivial matters. For example, one child learns *truck* and another *lorry*, one learns *duck* and another *snake*, one learns *I haven't any*, another *I don't have any* and a third *I ain't got none*. Eventually, dialect differences, stylistic differences and cognitive styles do emerge, but these are socially determined and are not really part of the acquisition process at all.

## Further investigation

1  Does the 'innateness' hypothesis find any kind of support from the example of people born blind, dumb and deaf, e.g. people like Helen Keller?

2  The idea that there is a 'critical period' for language learning has been much discussed, as have the reasons for its existence (if it does exist). How important is it to be sure about something like this?

3  We know that in learning a language, children get 'positive evidence' to go on, i.e., they hear grammatical utterances. Some get 'negative evidence', i.e., they are 'corrected' when they make mistakes, although we have seen that they often either misunderstand or ignore such corrections. They also get

'indirect positive evidence' in that people accept without comment their utterances. Some linguists argue that children also provide us with what they call 'indirect negative evidence' in that they do not use utterances we could reasonably have expected them to use. They hear and use *He gave the book to John* and *He gave John the book*. They also hear *He donated the books to the library* but they do not say things like *He donated the library the books*. This is a very interesting linguistic argument. What, in general, can you say though about something that you do not observe to exist? But, again, are absences in certain patterns not themselves significant?

## 7.5   What we do 'learn'

Children must not only acquire a language but they must also learn how to use that language appropriately. Jean Piaget, for example, was not concerned merely with relating language development to cognitive development, but was also concerned with trying to discover how children use language to relate to the world and to others within the world. This is an issue that has interested many investigators and it is a profoundly important one, since language is such a crucial mediator between individuals and everything that surrounds them.

Piaget's (1950) observations of the speech of kindergarten children led him to conclude that they exhibited two very different kinds of speech, what he called 'egocentric speech' and 'socialized speech'. Piaget defined egocentric speech as speech that lacked what he referred to as 'communicative intent'. It can occur either in solitude or in the presence of others, but in the latter case shows no concern for possible listeners. Egocentric speech is speech entirely bound up in the activity of the present moment. Children assume too that any listeners who are present are similarly bound up in that immediate activity and view it exactly as they do when they use such speech. It is therefore a kind of thinking out loud, with any listeners made party to whatever 'thoughts' are occurring. Children are unable to move outside themselves, as it were, in order to adopt another's perspective. They find themselves at the very centre of their own universes, and no one, especially the children themselves, can do anything about that fact.

According to Piaget, there are actually three different types of egocentric speech. There is 'repetition' or 'echolalia', in which children merely repeat themselves or others. There is 'monologue', in which children talk to themselves in a kind of thinking out loud. Finally, there is what he calls 'collective monologue', in which individuals within groups talk aloud in turn but do so without any real communicative intent. On the other hand, socialized speech does try to take listeners into account. It also leads to criticizing, commanding, stating and questioning, and ensures a real exchange of information. Socialized speech therefore has a clear communicative intent.

His various investigations led Piaget to claim that nearly half of kindergarten speech is egocentric in nature. In one study involving kindergarten children, young children were given information to relate to other children. The study showed that they did not communicate material very clearly to one another because they failed to consider the needs of listeners. However, the children believed that they had been understood. The children also did not even understand very well what they had been told, even though they almost always believed that they had understood. They were quite unaware that their gestures, their pronouns without clear reference and their abbreviated utterances were failing to communicate and did not realize that the intended communication was not the one that their listeners actually received.

Piaget's investigations convinced him that such egocentric behaviour is a pervasive characteristic of cognition in very young children. According to Piaget, socialized speech gradually replaces this egocentric speech as children grow older and develop both cognitively and socially. Egocentric speech gradually atrophies from growing disuse and eventually disappears altogether.

The Russian psychologist Lev Vygotsky disagreed considerably with Piaget's views of the relationship between language and thought and of the functions of language in childhood. Vygotsky's (1962) major concern was with the development and function of what he called 'inner speech'. By inner speech he did not mean either 'verbal memory', i.e., the storage of words and concepts, or 'subvocal speech', i.e., covert motor activities in the speech organs themselves, or even the mental processes underlying 'ideation', i.e., the formation of ideas. Inner speech is also not just talking to yourself. Vygotsky defined inner speech as speech for yourself alone and opposed it to 'external speech', which is speech for others. Inner speech, being speech for yourself alone, turns inward to thought; external speech, being speech for others, turns thought into words. External speech is therefore social speech.

According to Vygotsky, inner speech, because of its function, is highly abbreviated and dominated by predicates, which are often unmodified verbs and objects, when it employs language at all. Topics are already known and need not be stated because people know what they are thinking about. In social speech, on the other hand, topics must be stated and comments made about topics because predicates alone are not enough.

Vygotsky differed with Piaget on the nature of egocentric speech. He regarded egocentric speech as a phenomenon that marked the transition from the social and collective activity of children to more individualized activity. According to Vygotsky, individual speech really has its origin in collective speech. Egocentric speech, like inner speech, does not merely accompany activity but also helps to produce conscious understanding and is closely connected with the development of thought. Egocentric speech develops and becomes inner speech; it does not just simply atrophy. All speech is therefore social in origin and part of it becomes inner speech.

Vygotsky argued that at the age of three there is no difference between egocentric and social speech; however, at the age of seven the two are quite different. It is this differentiation that accounts for the lack of vocalization and the structural peculiarities of egocentric speech, and gives the latter the appearance of dying out. But, according to Vygotsky, saying that it has died out is like saying that children stop counting when they cease to count on their fingers and use their heads only. What has happened is that egocentric speech has developed into inner speech. External speech continues as before in order to support communication. Vygotsky, therefore, regarded all speech as social in origin but subject to a bifurcation, moving in one direction toward inner speech and thought and continuing in the other direction to serve the needs of social communication.

Vygotsky attempted to demonstrate the essential social basis of speech, particularly of egocentric speech, in a series of experiments. In one set of experiments he tried to destroy any illusion that children might have of being understood. Investigators first of all measured the amount of egocentric speech that the children used in situations similar to those that Piaget had used. The children were then placed in new situations, either with deaf-mute children or with children speaking a foreign language. In the majority of cases the amount of egocentric speech that the children used in the new situations declined to zero. Vygotsky concluded that in order to speak children need to feel that they are being understood.

The second set of experiments examined collective monologues and egocentric speech. Children's use of egocentric speech was measured in a situation that permitted collective monologues. Then each child was either placed in a group of strange children or required to sit or work completely alone. Once again the quantity of egocentric speech declined in the new situations to about one sixth of the original quantity. The decline was not as large as in the first set of experiments but it was still a considerable decline. However, if Piaget's theory is correct, the new situation should have led to an increase rather than to such a large decrease. The third set of experiments examined the vocal nature of egocentric speech. Either an orchestra played extremely loudly outside the laboratory where the children were gathered or the children were allowed to speak only in whispers. Once again the amount of egocentric speech declined to about twenty per cent of the original amount.

The various experiments eliminated one or more of the characteristics of egocentric speech which make it like social speech, particularly the characteristic that someone apparently understands what the child is saying. With each elimination the amount of egocentric speech declined. Vygotsky concluded that egocentric speech must be a form of speech that develops out of social speech. His experiments indicated that it was not yet separated from social speech in its manifestation, even though it was already distinct in its function and structure. It had not yet gone 'underground'.

We may well hesitate before accepting Vygotsky's conclusions. None of the experimental conditions was particularly conducive to any kind of speech activity and it has not been possible for other investigators to replicate the experiments, since Vygotsky provided only a few of the details necessary for replication. It would also be particularly difficult to test many of Vygotsky's assertions, provocative though some of them are, e.g. that inner speech is to a large extent thinking in pure meanings, or that the processes of thought and speech are not identical, or that thought, unlike speech, does not consist of separate units, individual thoughts being wholes which must be developed successively in speech, or that thoughts must first pass through meanings and then through words, or that some thoughts may actually be completely inexpressible.

The inexpressibility of certain thoughts and the ways in which certain thoughts originate have interested philosophers and artists from time immemorial, but little systematic evidence exists on the topic however much speculation there may be. It is not possible to proceed very far in accounting for how thought originates in the mind, even from reports by such reputable, yet in their way very different, persons as the poet Coleridge in his well-known account of the genesis of *Kubla Khan* under the influence of drugs, and Albert Einstein in his discussion of scientific creativity (see Ghiselin, 1955). Vygotsky's views on this subject must really be placed in the same speculative category.

One of the major problems we confront when we try to describe children's use of language for social purposes is that we know much less than we would like to know about *how* children actually use language. We know much more about *what* language they use, i.e., details about their control of sounds and grammar. Studies of the language use of young children have usually focused on how parents and older children use language in the presence of young children, e.g. 'motherese', and how children respond to that language. As we have seen, parents and older children both imitate the 'telegraphic' speech they hear from children and expand what they hear in a rather unsystematic manner. However, this kind of expansion of children's utterances produces no significant effects on children's consequent utterances. Evidently too (Shipley *et al.* 1969), children prefer that parents do not use telegraphic speech to them – they seem to recognize it as deviant in some way – even though they find it quite functional for their own purposes in the contexts in which they use it.

One interesting fact about telegraphic speech is that even though children find it works quite adequately in the majority of cases, they very soon abandon it for more complicated systems requiring the mastery of articles, inflections and involved syntactic patterns. One possible explanation is that either the innate language faculty of children or their developing cognitive capacities require them to construct increasingly detailed and inclusive systems for linguistic data; another is that the social pressures to communicate require increasingly explicit sentences and that children can make such sentences only by acquiring the appropriate linguistic devices.

So far as children's use of different kinds of 'speech acts' is concerned, again we have less evidence than we would like. Children do state things, ask questions, make requests and give commands. They also learn to react to the variety of subtle ways in which we use language to exercise social control. Their behaviour in play provides ample evidence that such learning is occurring as they manipulate each other and act out their versions of events and their roles within them, with toys and dolls for example. But just how such learning occurs is not at all clear.

As we saw in an earlier chapter, language is used for a variety of purposes, e.g. for self-control, controlling others, imaginative purposes, etc. But we have neither a complete inventory of usage types nor an overriding theory of language use, i.e., a theory of pragmatics. And we most certainly do not have any theory about how children acquire such a theory of use. Consequently, it is not surprising that we know much less about how children learn to use questions and answers, to make requests, to employ performative utterances, to state hypotheses and so on, than we do about adult use in each case. We do know (Fletcher, 1985) that by the age of three children are able to converse quite well with adults. They readily participate in conversation and continue to develop their social uses of language in order to manipulate others in a wide variety of ways. Social interaction (see Bruner, 1983) is a very important factor in the continued development of children's language.

Evidence from several sources suggests, however, that the cumulative effect of being in certain kinds of environment does influence children's use of language for thinking and self-expression. Telegraphic speech, for example, arises from speakers assuming that listeners are somehow privy to what speakers know. It contains much less that the usual amount of redundancy, and speakers assume that listeners share the same reference points in space and time and possibly even the same attitude toward the subject matter. The British sociologist Basil Bernstein has argued (Bernstein, 1971–5; see also Atkinson, 1985) that many children seem to retain many of these assumptions about language use long after the telegraphic stage of speech.

Bernstein claims that we can find two different kinds of language code in use in British life, 'restricted code' and 'elaborated code'. Restricted code is characterized by short, simple, often unfinished utterances, the simple and repetitive use of conjunctions such as *so*, *then* and *because*, little use of subordination, the dislocated presentation of information, a rigid and limited use of modifiers, a preference for using categorical statements that often confuse cause and effect and a large reliance on physical context, e.g. in pronoun use, or in calling on the sympathy of the listener in order to get a particular message across. On the other hand, elaborated code is characterized by accurate and full syntactic usage, grammatical complexity, the frequent and extensive use of subordination and modification and the qualification of statements. Restricted code is used by familiars in each other's presence and helps promote solidarity; however, it is necessarily severely limited in its functions. In contrast, elaborated code does not have these same restrictions.

According to Bernstein, it is possible to correlate the use of these codes to social class in Britain, with many members of the working class having access only to restricted code, but members of the middle class having access to both kinds and the ability to move at will between the two. (Bernstein uses 'working class' and 'middle class' somewhat differently from many other sociologists and gives much more weight to women's roles in determining class than others do. He particularly stresses the mother's role in the formative years of childhood.)

Bernstein regards the conditions that prevail in working-class life as responsible for the use of restricted code there, e.g. strong communal bonds, monotonous work, the lack of opportunities for decision making, a feeling of collective rather than individual responsibility, a preponderance of physical rather than mental work, overcrowded authoritarian home life and little intellectual stimulation for children. Restricted code reflects, therefore, the communal rather than the individual, the concrete rather than the abstract, substance rather than process, the immediate and the real rather than the hypothetical, action rather than motive and authority rather than persuasion.

Bernstein's ideas have been very widely debated and sometimes harshly challenged. The ideas are interesting if for no other reason than they are a serious attempt to explain how certain kinds of behaviour – in this case language behaviour – are continued across the generations. Sometimes Bernstein's ideas are rejected out of hand on the grounds that 'all languages and dialects are equal'. As objects of study such may well be the case, just as to biologists all animals may appear to be equally worthy of study. But to say that they are 'equal' in *every* respect is to make a human being as interesting, or as uninteresting, as a laboratory rat – which, of course, has also happened!

That parents behave differently in the ways in which they use language with their children surely is not in dispute. And that some of these ways produce advantages for children that others do not can hardly be denied either. Some parents encourage questions, enjoy discussion, indulge in a wide variety of verbal play and value tentativeness in the formulation of ideas and conclusions. They deliberately try to encourage the development of their children's intellects and personalities. They are 'person-oriented'. Other parents have little interest in such matters and tend to regard children as objects to be controlled, even to be seen not heard. They are 'position-oriented'.

Studies of mother–child interaction (Hess and Shipman, 1967; Robinson, 1971, 1972) in a variety of settings, e.g. while sorting blocks, working together on a sketching task or waiting in a physician's waiting room, show that parents of the first kind mentioned above are likely to try to answer questions prefaced with *why* with real reasons, whereas parents of the second kind are more likely to assert their authority and respond with an answer like *Because I said so*. The first group of parents is likely to be concerned that children understand what they are to do and why they are to do it, and with seeking verbal responses from children and providing verbal reinforcement. The second group is likely to rely more on actions than words and, in the use of words, provide negative verbal reinforcement. This parental behaviour is said to produce two very different 'cognitive styles' in children: in the first case a somewhat tentative person-oriented style and in the second case a somewhat authoritarian position-oriented style.

One crucially important function that all children must eventually become familiar with is the function of the written form of language. There is ample evidence, however, that many children experience a great deal of difficulty in developing a useful control of the written language. Whereas children acquire the spoken language gradually and the process of language acquisition has no conscious beginning or end, for many children learning to read and write has a sudden onset. There is also no reason to assume that humans are in any way 'prewired' to learn to read and write. Whereas talking is like walking, reading and writing seem to be more like swimming. Not everyone learns to swim; the opportunity has to be there, and there is no reason to assume that anyone who has not learned to swim has had some kind of biological need left unmet.

The level of anxiety that accompanies initial instruction in reading and writing may be quite high. Little such anxiety is present during the process of acquiring language, witness the pleasure of hearing a baby's 'first word'. There is also often a concomitant assignment of blame for any failure that occurs in the acquisition of the skills of reading and writing. Children are not blamed when they fail to acquire language; rather they are given special help. However, such failures are really quite rare. Instruction in reading and writing also tends to be very formal and deliberate. In marked contrast, children acquire the spoken language informally and unconsciously from a wide range of stimuli and no deliberate instruction is necessary. It is not learned from carefully arranged stimuli, from making conscious distinctions among such stimuli, from learning about language and from learning to apply a wide variety of analytic and synthetic procedures (many of which are in reality of quite dubious merit). Learning to speak, of course, is self-reinforcing, but the usual reinforcements that adults experience through being able to read are irrelevant to most children; to many young children the benefits of literacy are quite abstract, distant and meaningless, and the efforts to be expended for such a remote end may seem to be quite wasteful and unpleasant.

Learning to read and write and learning to listen and speak are also different in still other ways. Reading and writing depend on the visual modality. The kinds of redundancies found in the spoken language are different from those found in the written language. The two codes are used to convey different kinds of content. Writing is not just simply speech written down. Writing is usually more abstract than speech in its content; it tends to employ carefully edited and controlled language for purposes different from speech; and it functions differently in the lives of the recipients of the message.

Vygotsky (1962) pointed out that writing involves a very high level of abstraction. It is speech without a well-defined listener. The recipient exercises little or no control over what is said in writing, so there may be little motivation either to write or to read what someone else has written. Reading and writing are abstract, intellectual and remote in their motivation and lack the immediate relevance of speech. They also require deliberate, analytic responses. In speaking, children are not at all conscious of the sounds and mental operations they use. In writing, however, they must become aware of the structure of each word, and be able to dissect and reproduce it according to conventions that they must learn. Numerous investigators (Downing, 1970; Reid, 1966) have pointed out that many children do not really understand what reading and writing are all about, what they are supposed to be doing when they read and write and even what the terms mean that are used in the instructional process, terms like *sound, syllable, word* and *sentence*.

With these last remarks our wheel has really come full circle. We do not always know what we are doing when we involve ourselves in issues having to do with language. In fact, in retrospect, we can see that much we do may be quite misguided because we have failed to identify genuine issues, or have asked quite inappropriate questions, or have been unable to recognize the relevant facts. Only when we understand what language is like and what a unique place it has in our lives will we have any real hope of solving pressing issues having to do with language. Language is a unique phenomenon in the world and our best hope for success in handling issues that have to do with it lies in our acknowledging just how special it is and finding interesting questions to ask about it.

## *Further investigation*

1   When a teacher of a young child says of that child 'John is having trouble learning to read because he doesn't know his sounds', what do we learn about the teacher's understanding of language?

2   Why do so many people readily admit that although they were 'taught their grammar' in school, they no longer 'know' it? Why is it that some of the same people feel inadequate as a result, others aggressive and still others indifferent so far as language is concerned? And why among those who 'learned' what they were taught are there a few who become 'missionaries', always seeking to tell others how to use the language 'properly'?

3   Many 'teaching methods' have names with strong 'language' associations, e.g. 'whole word' or 'phonics' methods in teaching reading, the 'language experience' approach in teaching the language arts, the 'grammar–translation' method of teaching foreign languages and so on. What kinds of understanding (and possibly misunderstanding) of language are behind each of these?

4   What can we actually teach about language?

# 8

# *Describing language*

A fundamental goal of linguistics is to account for the knowledge that we have of language, usually of a specific language. For example, if we are speakers of English, we know that *A very big dog chased the cat from the room* is a 'good' English sentence whereas there is something 'bad' about each of *\*A very big dog the cat chased from the room*, *\*A very big dog chased cat from the room*, *\*A dog very big chased the cat from room* and *\*A big very dog chase the cat the room from*. Instead of saying that these sentences are 'good' and 'bad' let us say that they are 'grammatical' and 'ungrammatical'. (The ungrammatical sentences above are preceded by the symbol\*; linguists use this symbol to indicate that something is ungrammatical or violates the rules and principles of a particular language.) One part of our goal is to specify just what conditions a particular sentence must meet so that we can say that it is a grammatical sentence in the language with which we are concerned.

An initial assumption, of course, is that a language is a set of grammatical sentences (or utterances, if we think, as most linguists do, that language is primarily speech). Moreover, it is an infinite set of such sentences because it is always possible to create sentences that have never been produced before, e.g. through using joining devices like co-ordination (*and, but*), subordination (*because, although*), relativization (*who, which*), complementation (*that*), etc. (These last two sentences – and this one too – are sentences that are entirely novel to both of us, the writer and the reader, yet our knowledge of English grammar allows one of us to write these sentences and the other to read and comprehend them. We must assume, therefore, that they have been drawn from the infinite set of sentences that is available to us.)

Returning to our original grammatical sentence *A very big dog chased the cat from the room*, we find that our first task is one of trying to specify what its 'syntax' is, i.e., what its various constituent parts are, how these relate to one another and how the whole arrangement of parts is to be interpreted. Sentences are only superficially made up of words. What is really important about words is how they act as either constituents or as parts of constituents in larger patterns within a sentence. For example, in the sentence above the initial *a*, a determiner, is a quite insignificant constituent standing on its own, but in construction with *very big dog*, the whole of *a very big dog* is an important noun-phrase constituent, which serves as the subject of the sentence. Similarly *from* is by itself only a preposition, but in construction with the noun phrase *the room*, it forms a prepositional phrase *from the room*, which functions as a grammatical unit within the total predicate *chased the cat from the room*.

'Constituency' is an important property of all languages. In the sentence we are using, we find a variety of constituents. There are noun phrases like *a very big dog, the cat* and *the room*; there is a prepositional phrase *from the room*; there is an adjective phrase *very big*; and there is a verb phrase *chased the cat from the room*. In this view there may also be phrases within phrases, i.e., there is a noun phrase *the room* within the prepositional phrase *from the room*.

Now it is possible to show in diagrammatic form how the sentence is actually a hierarchy of constituents, as in Figure 1. All sentences can be described in similar terms as hierarchies of constituents; moreover, as hierarchies in which every part can be labelled in a manner similar to that used in Figure 1.

The phrasal constituents have their own principles of organization. *A very big dog* is a possible noun phrase in English, but *\*a dog very big* is not, nor is *\*dog* by itself. In the first case an adjective phrase must precede a noun rather than follow it, and in the second case the singular *dog* used by itself requires some kind of determiner in most circumstances. *From the room* is a possible prepositional phrase but *\*the room from* is not, nor is *\*from room*. Again, a preposition precedes a noun phrase rather than follows it, and *room* in this case requires a determiner. Whereas *chased the cat from the room* is a possible verb phrase, *\*the cat chased from the room* is not because a direct object in English

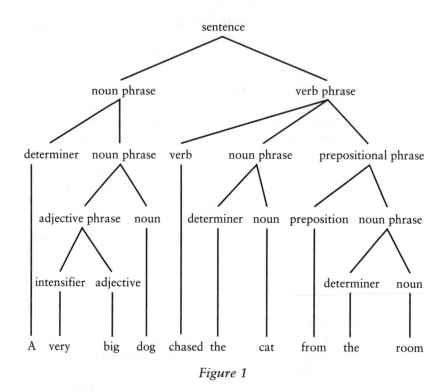

*Figure 1*

follows rather than precedes the verb. Finally, *big very* is not a possible adjective phrase because intensifiers precede adjectives; they do not follow them. It is for such reasons that we must reject some of our original sentences as being ungrammatical.

We can describe many English sentences in just such terms, particularly with a few additional grammatical devices. For example, conjunctions such as *and* and *but* usually join 'equal' constituents, as in *The cat and the dog like each other*, where *and* joins noun phrases. *And* also joins noun phrases in *The person who did it and you are both responsible* because both *the person who did it* and *you* are also noun phrases, whatever else they might be too. Subordinating conjunctions can also join sentences, as does *although* in *He left although he was reluctant to go*, where *although* joins *he was reluctant to go* to *he left*.

In this view English sentences may be described as being composed of a basic pattern of noun phrase plus verb phrase in that order. The resulting sentences may then be combined into larger patterns through various processes of joining. For example, *A very big dog chased the cat from the room* is such a pattern. In this case the verb phrase has as its head *chase*, which is a particular kind of verb that requires a following noun phrase as its object. Other verbs do not take objects, e.g. *sleep* and *go*. Still others typically take two objects, e.g. *give* and *tell*, and still others take complements, e.g. *be* and *seem*. Consequently, it is also possible to consider how the various noun phrases in a sentence function in relation to the particular verb that is present, as not only subjects but also as various kinds of objects and complements. We can see this principle at work quite clearly in the sentences *The dog smelled the cat* and *The dog smelled*. In the first of these sentences, in which there is a noun-phrase object *the cat* after the verb, the dog is actually performing the act of smelling and has detected the cat. However, in the second, the dog may well be asleep – or even dead – and it is someone else who is doing the smelling. One part of our grammatical knowledge then is our ability to interpret the particular arrangements of constituents that we find in sentences.

Finally, there is a principle in English that the verb in the predicate verb phrase of a sentence 'agrees' with the subject noun phrase. This principle explains why *dog* followed by *chased* is 'good' where it occurs in our original sentences, but *dog* followed by *chase* is 'bad'. With this last observation we have said most of the important things that we can say about the original sentences. Speakers of English must be assumed to 'know' all of this; the task of the linguist is to account for this knowledge.

However, speakers of English know more than just these facts about the language. They know, for example, that the sentence *The cat was chased from the room by a very big dog* is the 'passive' counterpart of the original 'active' sentence. They also know that *A very big dog didn't chase the cat from the room* is the 'negative' counterpart of the original 'affirmative' sentence, and that *Did a very big dog chase the cat from the room?* is a 'question' clearly related to the original 'statement'. What has particularly intrigued linguists over the years is the task of trying to account for this kind of knowledge too. The problem, however, goes even further. A question like *What chased the cat from the room?* also seems to be related to the original sentence, as does the clause that begins with *which* in *He caught the very big dog which chased the cat from the room*.

In the 'transformational–generative' account of such knowledge, it is assumed that all sentences have abstract 'deep structures' which are transformed into 'surface structures'. In this view a sentence like *Did a very big dog chase the cat from the room?* has as its deep structure the statement, *A very big dog chased the cat from the room*, together with an indicator of some kind that there is also a 'question' constituent present in that deep structure. The presence of this 'question' constituent requires two important transformations of that deep structure: one is the inversion of part of the verb phrase with the subject (since all questions of this kind – *yes–no* questions – require such inversion) and the other involves the addition of the verb *do* that we find in the actual question that results.

This same general principle would apply to all the other sentences too. A negative sentence would have a 'negative' constituent in its deep structure, a passive sentence a 'passive' constituent and so on. A sentence like *Wasn't the cat chased from the room by a very big dog?* would, of course, have the three constituents of 'question', 'passive' and 'negative' present in its deep structure, and that deep structure would undergo a series of transformations in order to account for the actual surface structure we find.

It is also possible to deal with relative clauses in this way, for we can assume that in the sentence we used above (*He caught the very big dog which chased the cat from the room*) we really have in deep structure *He caught the very big dog [the very big dog chased the cat from the room]* in which the clause given in brackets is attached to the noun phrase just outside the brackets. Because the noun phrase within the bracketed (or embedded) sentence repeats the preceding noun phrase, it must be 'relativized' by the 'relative transformation' and appear in the surface structure as *which*.

This system can be extended in various ways to explain how very complex sentences may be considered to be built up from simpler ones through certain basic transformational processes which apply time and time again in the language. For example, *He wants to go* can be said to originate from *He wants [he to go]*; because the two *he*s are identical, the second must be deleted transformationally. On the other hand, in *He wants him to go*, we also have *He wants [he to go]*, but in this case there is no such identity of the *he*s and the second *he* cannot be deleted. Moreover, although this *he* is the subject of *to go*, it actually must appear marked as the object of *wants*, i.e., as *him*.

It is just such considerations as these that lead linguists to look at sentences like *John is eager to please, John is easy to please* and *John is certain to please*, in order to give them different deep structures to account for their very different interpretations: *John is eager [John to please someone], Something is easy [someone to please John]* and *Something is certain [John to please someone]*. In each case it is necessary to postulate the existence of an abstract 'deep structure' underlying the actual 'surface structure'. In these cases the surface structures of the three sentences appear to be identical; however, the deep structures are not. It is the different deep structures that account for the very different interpretations that we give to these sentences.

The theory is called transformational–generative because it postulates that our ability to produce sentences can be explained by our possession of a grammar that contains two essential components. One of these components is a 'generative' component that accounts for our ability to produce an infinite set of deep structures. Each deep structure provides an account of all the information that is contained in a particular sentence in the language. The other component, the 'transformational' component, processes the deep structures so that they emerge as the actual sentences we produce and comprehend.

The 'government-and-binding' approach also recognizes that each sentence in the language has two types of structure, a 'd structure' and an 's structure'. The 's structure' is the structure that we actually observe. The 'd structure' is an abstract structure that provides a base for our understanding of the sentence. For example, the 'd structure' for *The cat was chased from the room by a very big dog* would be something like —— *was chased the cat from the room by a very big dog*. The principal difference between the sentence's 'd structure' and its 's structure' in this case is that *the cat* is moved from its object position in the 'd structure' to become the subject of *was chased* in the 's structure'. In a question like *What did a very big dog chase from the room?* the 'd structure' would be something like *A very big dog chased what from the room.* To get the 's structure' there must be inversion of the subject noun phrase and the tense of the verb, the verb *do* must be supplied to carry that tense and *what* must be moved to the initial position in the sentence.

In this approach a sentence like *He wants to go* would have no second occurrence of *he*, as it did in the transformational–generative account. Instead, the grammar contains a set of principles for deciding what the subject of *to go* is; in this case these principles tell us that the subject of *to go* is the same as the subject of *wants.* On the other hand, in *He wants him to go* the same set of principles informs us that *he* and *him* must be interpreted as referring to different people. Still another principle accounts for the different forms of these two pronouns, *he* and *him* respectively. The examples with *eager, easy* and *certain* used above would also be resolved in much the same way; a set of interpretative principles in the grammar accounts for how *John* must be related (or must not be related) to the following adjectives and must be related to the following verbs.

This government-and-binding approach assumes that our knowledge of grammar is best expressed as a knowledge of the rules and principles that are operative in constructing and understanding sentences. It keeps the structural differences between 'd structure' and 's structure' to a minimum; for example, only certain kinds of very simple movements of constituents are allowed. It must, of course, compensate for this simplicity by requiring that special interpretative principles also be part of the grammar.

We can use the example of the passive sentence *The cat was chased from the room by a very big dog* to show some of the differences between the transformational–generative approach and that of government and binding. In the first approach the deep structure would be something like *A very big dog passive chased the cat from the room by noun phrase.* That is, the deep structure would include a constituent called *passive* together with a co-occurring prepositional phrase, the *by noun phrase.* This structure would bring the passive transformation into action. This transformation moves the deep subject, *a very big dog*, into the *noun phrase* position in the final *by* phrase. It then moves *the cat* into the now vacant subject position. In the transformational–generative account we know that *a very big dog* is the real subject of *chase* and *the cat* is the real object because that is where they are in the deep structure of the sentence. However, the actual movement rules required by the passive transformation seem quite unmotivated.

In the government-and-binding approach the 'd structure' of the sentence is —— *was chased the cat from the room by a very big dog*. This is a much simpler structure than the previous one. There is a rule that English sentences must have subjects and, since *the cat* is the only noun phrase that could be moved to subject position, it is so moved. However, the price of this solution is that we must have as part of the grammar some principle that tells us that *a very big dog*, which here appears in a prepositional phrase headed by *by*, is the real subject of the verb *chase*.

Both kinds of approach – and others too – can be found in the linguistics literature today. Although these approaches make different claims about what the syntax of a language is like, we must not forget that they also make many similar claims. They assume, for example, that sentences are built up from constituents in hierarchical arrangements. They also assume that every sentence has two levels of structure, the one that we actually observe and a more abstract one. They differ only on the nature of the abstract level and how that level relates to the observed level. There is also an acknowledgement that the kinds of organizing principles we find in the syntax are principles that are found in all languages. Furthermore, they are principles that we cannot 'learn' in the usual sense of that word. The principles, therefore, are considered to be innate, not just in languages themselves but in the minds of humans.

The sentences we have been using are also made up of words, and it is interesting to look at these too. There are different kinds of words in a language like English, and it is possible to study their 'morphology', i.e., their composition. Words like *very* and *the* are always the same, i.e., they do not vary according to where they are used in a construction. (*A* is really much the same too in that the *a–an* difference is a minor one that depends on whether the following word begins with a consonant sound or a vowel sound.) On the other hand, words like *cat, dog, chase* and *big* do vary. Nouns like *cat* and *dog* can take 'plural' and 'genitive' 'inflections', e.g. *cats* and *cat's*, a verb like *chase* has inflected forms like *chased, chases* and *chasing*, and *bigger* and *biggest* are inflected forms of the adjective *big*. In fact, we can argue that it is this possibility for taking certain kinds of inflectional endings that gives words their essential 'noun'-ness, 'verb'-ness and 'adjective'-ness.

Still another kind of affix, called a 'derivational' affix, is used in word formation. The *-th* ending, for example, turns adjectives into nouns, as in *width* and *strength*. The *-ize* ending turns adjectives into verbs, as in *finalize* and *legalize*. The *-er* ending turns verbs into nouns, as in *worker* and *baker*. However, unlike inflections, derivations may also occur as prefixes, as in *redevelop* and *disinherit*. There are many different derivational affixes in English, and we use them to create a wide variety of 'complex' words, i.e., words that have an important central component and one or more less important derivational components; for example, *reindustrialization* is built up on the central *industry* with suffixes *-al*, *-ize* and *-ation*, and a prefix *re-*. The word is also built up in a very definite order, i.e., it has its own arrangement of constituents: *industry, industrial, industrialize, reindustrialize, reindustrialization*.

Another kind of word formation involves 'compounding'. In this case two words are combined to form a third. For example, *phone* and *card* can be combined to form *phonecard* or *cardphone*. A phonecard is a kind of card and a cardphone is a kind of phone. Other such compounds are *ballroom, hounddog* and *catwalk*. Such compounds also have a distinctive pattern of stresses, with the vowel in the first part of the compound pronounced with greater intensity than the vowel in the second part.

We can actually carry our analysis of words further. The various meaningful parts of words like *cats, width* and *reindustrialization* are called 'morphemes'. That is, *cats* is composed of two morphemes: one of these is 'cat', which refers to an animal in the real world, and the other is 'plural', the affix *-s*. *Width* is composed of 'wide' and the *-th* affix, the meaning of which is hard to define except as being something like 'the state of being' whatever adjective it is attached to. However, it is clear that it does have some kind of meaning in the language. Words are, therefore, built out of these meaning units called morphemes.

Morphemes sometimes change their appearance. We can see that this is so if we examine the plural forms of *cat* and *dog*, which are *cats* and *dogs* respectively. The *-s* ending of *cats* actually sounds like the beginning of *sip*, whereas the *-s* ending of *dogs* sounds like the beginning of *zip*. The sounds are actually *s* and *z* respectively. So the 'plural' morpheme has two different realizations (or 'allomorphs') in these two words. We can see the same kind of phenomenon in the pair *wide* and *width*. When *wide* occurs before the affix *-th*, the vowel changes from that found in *bite* to that found in *bit*. Consequently, 'wide' has two allomorphs, *wide* and *wid-*.

Words have a variety of other properties that are of interest. For example, the class of words we have called verbs can be subdivided into a number of different categories. As indicated previously, some verbs take objects and are therefore said to be 'transitive', e.g. *buy* and *take*, and some do not and are therefore said to be 'intransitive', e.g. *go* and *die*. Some verbs only appear to be transitive, e.g. *have* and *cost*, because, although they take objects, they cannot be used in passive sentences. Other verbs like *be* and *appear* can take only complements. Nouns may be either 'countable' nouns, e.g. *cat* and *dog*, or 'mass' nouns, e.g. *water* and *hope*. Whereas *two cats* and *many dogs* are possible, *\*two waters* and *\*many hopes* would strike us as being very unusual uses. (We say *many dogs* and *much hope* rather that *\*much dog* and *\*many hopes*.) In the same vein some adjectives are 'gradable', i.e., they can be related to qualities differing in amount, e.g. *very big, cooler* and *more enthusiastic*, but others cannot be used in this way, so that *\*very principal* and *\*more unique* become problematic so far as acceptability is concerned.

Together the syntax and the morphology provide the information we need to give a 'semantic' interpretation to any sentence we use or hear. Semantics is the study of meaning. It is the semantic rules of English that tell us that *a dog* in the sentence *A dog is an animal* is to be understood as 'any dog' and that what we are hearing is a statement about all dogs, i.e., that all dogs are animals. In fact, *All dogs are animals* has the same meaning as *A dog is an animal*. It is semantics that tells us that *A very big dog didn't chase the cat from the room* is a denial of the proposition that *A very big dog chased the cat from the room*. It is also to semantics that we must turn to find the principle or principles that tell us how *a not unhappy man* with its two negatives is not equivalent to *a happy man* (in spite of a common belief that 'two negatives make a positive').

There are numerous semantic issues that we can consider. Some of these become 'pragmatic' issues as well, i.e., issues of language in relation to its context of use. For example, *It's cold in here* appears to be no more than a statement, but in the right circumstances the words can have the force of a 'command' to someone to do something about the situation, e.g. turn up the heat. In the right circumstances *I sentence you to five years in jail* is not just a grammatical sentence but is a jail sentence. We all know, too, that a letter that we begin with *Will you please send me a copy of your paper* is a request not a question; hence our possible hesitation over its final punctuation – whether it should be a full stop or a question mark.

We eventually must pronounce the sentences we produce. To do this we make use of only certain sounds. The study of the sounds of languages is called 'phonology'. Each language has its own unique phonological system. Speakers of that language draw on a small inventory of distinctive sounds, or 'phonemes', when they produce utterances in the language.

These phonemes are either 'consonants' or 'vowels'. Consonants are sounds which show some kind of noticeable constriction in the vocal apparatus as they are produced, whereas vowels lack that constriction. The word *cat*, for example, has a vowel between two consonants, the *a* symbolizing an unconstricted sound, and the *c* and the *t* symbolizing two constricted sounds, the first in the back of the mouth with the back of the tongue pressed against the roof of the mouth and the second in the front of the mouth with the tip of the tongue pressed against the upper gum ridge.

We can also find out how many phonemes a language has by looking for 'minimal pairs' of words, i.e., pairs of words in which the change of a single sound results in an entirely different word. *Cat* is a good example because we can see very easily that *sat, rat, mat, fat, pat* and so on are quite different meaningful words in English. Therefore, the sounds symbolized by *c, s, r, m, f* and *p* must be English consonant phonemes. If we proceed to change the vowels in *cat*, we can find some English vowel phonemes, as in *coat, cut, cot, caught, kite* and *Kate*. (In this case we may need to be reminded that we are talking about the sounds of the language, not the way these sounds are spelled: so far as sounds are concerned *cat* and *Kate* differ only in the vowels that occur between identical initial and final consonants.) If we use different minimal pairs in this way, we will find that English has 24 consonant phonemes and, depending on the dialect spoken, about 14 vowel phonemes.

We will also find that these phonemes can be arranged into various classes. For example, consonants may be voiceless (*tip, fat*) or voiced (*din, van*). Some are stops (*pat, cut, bag*), others fricatives (*shoe, safe, this*) and still others nasals (*man, sing*). Some are pronounced in the front of the mouth (*pad, bat*) and others in the back of the mouth (*cog*). Individual phonemes can be described by reference to these characteristics, e.g. *p* is a voiceless bilabial stop.

Still other classifications may be made. Such classifications are important if one is to gain a thorough understanding of just what kinds of processes are occurring in the language. For example, the 'plural' ending on nouns has several allomorphs. *Cats* and *dogs* illustrate two of these, the *s* and the *z* variants. If we ignore examples like *classes* and *bushes* (and completely irregular plural forms like *children* and *sheep*), we can state the principle that governs the occurrence of the *s* and *z* allomorphs of the English 'plural' in strictly phonological terms: the voiceless *s* allomorph occurs after morphemes that end in voiceless phonemes and the voiced *z* allomorph occurs after morphemes that end in voiced phonemes.

Vowels too can be classified in a variety of ways. There are 'front' vowels (*bit, bait, bat*) and 'back' vowels (*boot, good, bought*), and 'round' vowels (*boot, boat*) and 'unround' vowels (*bit, bet, bat*). There are 'high' vowels (*beat, bit, boot*) and 'low' vowels (*bat, hot*), and 'tense' vowels (*beat, bait, boot*) and 'lax' vowels (*bet, bat*). There is also a difference between 'simple' vowels (*bit, bait, bet, boot*) and 'diphthongs' (*night, bout, boy*). Individual vowel phonemes can be described by reference to these characteristics, e.g. the vowel in *bit* is a high, front, lax vowel. Once again such classifications are very important if one is to understand what is happening in the language. For example, in English, back vowels must be round and front vowels are not round.

Just as morphemes assume different shapes on different occasions, so do phonemes. The positional variants of phonemes are called 'allophones'. For example, when *p, t* and *k*, which are voiceless stops, appear initially in a word in English they are always followed by a little puff of air – they are 'aspirated' – as the closure is released to produce the following sound. However, there is no such aspirated release when these phonemes follow an initial *s*. Consequently we find that each of these phonemes has one allophone, an aspirated one, in words like *pin, tone* and *kin* and another allophone, an unaspirated one, in words like *spin, stone* and *skin*. Such allophonic differences may be very important. For example, North American English has a distinctive allophone of *t* in words like *butter* and *better* – it sounds almost like a *d* – but this allophone is not found in British pronunciations. (However, in some British dialects the same *t* is pronounced in this position as a glottal stop, a brief catch in the vocal cords, which is sometimes indicated in writing as *bu'er* or *be'er*.)

There are other phonological matters that are of interest. Consonants and vowels are produced in certain sequences in syllabic patterns, and we can see how the 'syllables' of a language are structured. English, for example, has both open and closed syllables, i.e., syllables that end in vowels and syllables that end in consonants. Some languages have only open syllables. English also permits several consonants to occur together, as at the beginning of *sprint* and at the end of *lurched*; other languages do not allow consonants to cluster in this way.

Syllables may be pronounced with different degrees of intensity, or 'stress': compare *the rebel* with *to rebel*. Or they may have different 'pitch' (or tone) levels, as in Chinese or Vietnamese. Some languages, e.g. French, seem to give each syllable an equal amount of time, whereas others, such as English, give some syllables much more time than others, e.g. *I shouldn't've done it.* (This phenomenon is sometimes referred to, pejoratively, as 'slurring', but it is a natural part of English pronunciation.) Stress and pitch may also work together over whole clauses and sentences to create patterns of 'intonation' as in *Hé went*, *He wént* and *He went?*

An account of a language must also recognize the 'variation' that is found in the language because all languages vary by regional and social grouping. In English one speaker's *lorry* will be equivalent to another's *truck*, and one person's *dog* to another's *dawg*. In one situation you may find a speaker using *singing*, but in another you may find the same speaker using *singin'*. There will also be variations like *I asked if he could do it* and *I asked could he do it*, and *He hasn't any, He hasn't got any* and *He ain't got none*. We must suppose that all such uses are produced by rules and principles that must be called grammatical. Some just happen to be different from those that have also been given social approval.

Our account should also be one that allows us to conceive of how a language might change over time. One interesting feature of all accounts of languages that linguists have offered is that they all have what Edward Sapir referred to as 'leaks', or what some other linguists have referred to as 'fuzziness'. That is, there are always bits and pieces of any language we care to investigate that do not behave quite as they would if that language were a fixed and frozen system. It is possible to conjecture that such leakage and fuzziness exist because languages are always changing, or because that is the nature of language or of humans, or of both. Consequently, linguists have come to expect that while they might like to work with absolutely 'categorical' rules and principles, i.e., rules and principles that show no exceptions, they must be content with some 'variability' in the actual rules and principles they find.

Finally, any account of one language must be given within a framework that can be generalized to all languages. If we take syntax as an example, we should be concerned with finding principles that allow us not only to describe a language like English, in which verbs come before objects and nouns are preceded by prepositions, but also to describe a language like Japanese, in which verbs follow objects and nouns come before postpositions. That is, we must look for general rules and principles that apply to all languages, so that each particular language becomes just a special case. We would not want to propose one system for English, another completely different one for Japanese and still others for other languages. A fundamental goal of linguistics is to find the properties that all languages share, properties often called 'universals'. Having found these, we must then try to explain why they exist at all.

# Glossary of language terms

**active sentence**  In English, a sentence with a subject, verb and object in that order, e.g. *The dog chased the cat*.

**age-grading**  The language appropriate to a particular age group, e.g. two-year-olds, teenagers, adults, etc.

**agglutinative language**  A language that creates words by using a wide variety of affixes, e.g. Kiswahili.

**allomorph**  A variant of a morpheme, e.g. the two different 'plural' endings in *cats* and *churches*.

**allophone**  A variant of a phoneme, e.g. the different pronunciations of p in *pin* and *spin*, the first with an accompanying puff of air and the second without.

**ambiguity**  The two or more possible meanings of an utterance, e.g. *Flying planes can be dangerous*.

**Ameslan**  American Sign Language, a sign system used by many deaf people in North America.

**animate**  Having the grammatically relevant characteristic of 'being alive'.

**antonym**  A word with a meaning opposite to that of another word, e.g. *black* is the antonym of *white*.

**aphasia**  Any loss of language ability brought about by brain trauma of some kind.

**back vowel**  A vowel produced in the back of the mouth, e.g. the vowels in *boot* and *boat*.

**Black English**  The variety of English said to be characteristic of many black Americans.

**case**  A grammatical change in a word brought about by its relationship to some other word, e.g. both *he* and *him* in *He told him*, because of their relationship to *told*.

**categorical rule**  A rule that always applies, e.g. English verbs agree with their subjects.

**clause**  A syntactic unit consisting of a subject and a verb, e.g. *John sings*, and *him to go* in *I want him to go*.

**collective monologue**  The kind of speech found among small children when they talk to themselves rather than to each other.

**comparative method**  A method used in historical linguistics for comparing two or more languages to find out whether or not they have a common ancestor.

**competence**  The knowledge that a person has of a language, e.g. knowledge that a particular sentence is or is not grammatical.

**complementizer**  A word that introduces a clause without being an integral part of that clause, e.g. *that* in *I said that he could do it*.

**compounding**  The combining of equal grammatical units to form a higher level unit of the same kind, e.g. *house* and *boat* to form *houseboat*, and *I went in* and *He left* to form *I went in and he left*.

**content word**  A word that makes clear reference to some property of the real world, usually a noun, verb or adjective, e.g. *man, sing, old*.

**creole**  A language that appears to owe much of its vocabulary to another language, e.g. Haitian Creole with its large French-based vocabulary.

**critical-age hypothesis**  The hypothesis that it is difficult, perhaps even impossible, to acquire native-like ability in a second language after a certain age, usually set at about puberty.

**deletion**  The grammatical principle that explains how in a sentence like *I want a big slice and John a small one,* we understand the second clause as *John wants a small one*.

**derivation**  A grammatical affix that changes the meaning and/or part of speech category of a word, e.g. *un-* in *unhappy* and *-ness* in *happiness*.

**descriptivism**  The principle of describing languages as you find them to be used.

**dialect**  A regional or social variety of a language, e.g. Yorkshire English or lower-class New York speech.

**diphthongization**  The process by which a single vowel becomes a diphthong, i.e., two vowels pronounced as one. *House* once had the vowel of *moose*, a single vowel; it now has a diphthong.

**duality** The fact that all languages make use of a system of sounds and a system of meanings (words and syntax). So *bit*, for example, is made up of three discrete sounds in one system and is a verb with a particular meaning and function in the other.

**echo question** A question made in statement form, often (in English) accompanied by an upward movement of voice pitch at the end, e.g. *He told John?* and *You asked for what?*
**egocentric speech** Speech for oneself.
**elaborated code** A variety of the language that is said to allow those who employ it to give complete expression to thoughts of tentativeness, possibility, etc.

**front vowel** A vowel produced in the front of the mouth, e.g. the vowels in *beet, bit, bet* and *bat*.

**gender** A grammatical principle of word classification by such characteristics as sex, animacy, etc. For example, English has 'natural' gender in that nouns like *man, woman* and *dog* are referred to as *he, she* and *it* respectively. On the other hand, French has 'grammatical' gender in that each noun must belong to either the *le* category or the *la* category.
**glottochronology** The attempt to date the time at which two languages separated by using **lexicostatistical** data.
**government and binding** A grammatical theory associated with Noam Chomsky which employs a set of rules and principles to explain how sentences are both structured and interpreted.
**grammar** The set of rules and principles that accounts for how sentences are constructed and pronounced in a language.
**grammatical** Conforming to the grammar of a language.
**grammatical word** A word that has a grammatical function in the language but little semantic content, e.g. *did, the* and *at* in *Did the girl sing at the end?*

**high vowel** A vowel produced in the top of the mouth, e.g. the vowels in *beet* and *boot*.
**holophrase** A single word that functions as a complete utterance, e.g. a very young child's *Milk*.

**homonym**　One of two or more words that sound alike but have quite different meanings, e.g. *beer* and *bier*.

**homophone**　A word that is pronounced like another word, e.g. *meet* and *meat*.

**illocution**　The intent of an utterance, e.g. *He left* is a statement and *Did he leave?* is a request for information.

**imperative**　A syntactic structure associated with commanding, e.g. *Sit down!*

**implicature**　The implications that a particular utterance carries that are not in the words of the utterance itself but are derived from the context in which it is used, e.g. if a question like *Are you driving home or is John?* brings the answer *He's been drinking steadily all night*, the implication would be that John is not going to drive.

**inflection**　A grammatical affix that attaches to a word to mark it as a particular part of speech, e.g. the *-s* in *cats* is the 'plural' inflection of a noun and the *-ed* in *begged* is the 'past tense' inflection of a verb.

**inflectional language**　A language that makes changes within words to realize grammatical distinctions, e.g. Latin.

**internal reconstruction**　A method used in historical linguistics that employs data from within a single language in an attempt to reconstruct an earlier historical stage of that language, e.g. current English words like *weep* and *wept* are used to hypothesize an earlier stage of the language when the two vowels were alike not different.

**intonation**　The particular pattern of pitch rises and falls associated with an utterance.

**isogloss**　A line drawn on a map that separates the area in which a certain linguistic feature is found from the area in which it is absent.

**isolating language**　A language that makes use almost entirely of monosyllabic words, e.g. Vietnamese.

**jargon**　The technical language of a particular group, e.g. linguists, bricklayers, stockbrokers, etc.

**language family**　A group of languages that have a clear genetic relationship to one another, e.g. Indo-European.

**language typology** The classification of languages by their structural characteristics, e.g. whether they take objects after verbs, as in English, or before them, as in Japanese.

**language universals** The characteristics said to be shared by all languages.

*langue* A historically earlier formulation of the idea of **competence**.

**lateralization** The association of a particular hemisphere of the brain, the left one, with language use.

**lexicostatistics** The hypothesis that languages replace their words at a fixed rate.

**linguistic determinism** The belief that the structure of a language determines how users of that language view the outside world. Also known as the **Whorfian hypothesis**.

**linguistic variable** A language item that reveals variable usage among speakers of a language often according to the occasion of use, e.g. *floor* pronounced with or without the final *r* in some varieties of English, or the use of *singin'* rather than *singing* on certain occasions.

**localization** The association of particular areas in the brain with specific language abilities.

**locution** An utterance of any kind, e.g. *He left.*

**low vowel** A vowel produced in the bottom of the mouth, e.g. the vowels in *cat* and *bought*.

**morpheme** The smallest grammatically relevant element in a language, e.g. the various parts of *cats* (*cat* and *-s*) and *unhappiness* (*un-*, *happy* and *-ness*).

**motherese** The kind of language many mothers (and others too) adopt in speaking to very young children.

**nasal** A sound produced partly through the nose, e.g. the sounds at the ends of *them*, *then* and *thing*.

**nasal vowel** A vowel pronounced through the nose as well as the mouth.

**neutralization** The loss of a distinction in certain circumstances, e.g. *p* is distinct from *b* in English, as in *pin* and *bin*, but after *s*, we find only *p*, as in *spin*.

**noun phrase** A phrase headed by a noun, e.g. *boy, the little boy, the little boy with red hair*, etc.

**orthography** The spelling system that a language employs.

**parameter setting** The hypothesis that children are born with certain kinds of language knowledge, but they must make choices, i.e., set parameters, on such knowledge according to the actual languages they find themselves having to learn. This ability to set parameters is also a natural ability that they have.

**paraphrase** A rephrasing of a particular structure, e.g. 'a boat that is used as a house' is a paraphrase of *houseboat.*

*parole* A historically earlier formulation of the idea of performance.

**parsing** The assigning of words, etc., to various grammatical categories, e.g. *cat* to a noun category, *the cat* to a noun-phrase category and *The cat ran away* to a clause category.

**parts of speech** The various categories into which we can fit the words of a language. English is sometimes said to have categories such as noun, pronoun, verb, adjective, adverb, conjunction, preposition, interjection and sometimes determiner (or article). This categorization has serious weaknesses.

**passive sentence** In English, a sentence which has a subject corresponding to the object of an active sentence. Consequently, *The cat was chased* or *The cat was chased by the dog* are passives corresponding to the active sentence (*The dog*) *chased the cat.*

**performance** The actual utterances that people who speak a language use, with all their variety, uncertainty, hesitations, slips, etc.

**performative** An utterance that also performs an act if properly executed, e.g. *I pronounce you husband and wife* by an official in appropriate circumstances performs the act of marriage.

**perlocution** The effect of an utterance, e.g. *He persuaded me to go* reports the effects of his words on me, saying that they were persuasive.

**person** A grammatical principle used in categories like pronoun and verb to differentiate among speakers (first person – *I, we*), listeners (second person – *you*) and others spoken about (third and sometimes even fourth persons – *he, she, it, they*).

**phatic communion** A type of language used to establish social bonds rather than to bring about a genuine exchange of information, e.g. greetings like *Hello* or *How do you do?* and many exchanges about the weather and of social trivia.

**phoneme**   The smallest element in the sound system of a language such that changing one for another will create a difference of meaning, e.g. *p* is a phoneme in *pit* because a change to *b* would result in *bit*, to *f* in *fit*, to *k* in *kit*, etc.

**phonetic feature**   The smallest phonetic detail one can note in any part of an utterance, e.g. the puff of air that follows the *p* in *pin*.

**phrase**   The smallest syntactic unit in language, often, though not necessarily, more than one word. *John, the boy* and *the young man* are all noun phrases in *John left, The boy left* and *The young man left*.

**pidgin**   A type of language used by speakers of different languages for mutual communication, e.g. Pidgin English.

**prepositional phrase**   A phrase headed by a preposition, e.g. *at the back, to the top*, etc.

**prescriptivism**   The principle of describing languages as you would like them to be used.

**presupposition**   A built-in claim that a sentence makes, e.g. *Have you just retired?* presupposes that you worked until very recently.

**primitive language**   A language used by humans that is said to be less than a full or advanced language. Such languages are not found to exist, except for the case of genuine pidgin languages.

**proto-language**   A hypothetical language from which two or more languages are said to be derived. Proto-Indo-European has 'descendants' such as English, Gaelic, Hindi, Albanian, etc.

**restricted code**   A variety of the language that is said to restrict those who have access only to it to a limited range of expressions, largely 'concrete' in nature.

**round vowel**   A vowel produced with associated rounding of the lips, e.g. the vowels in *boot* and *boat*.

**semantic**   Concerned with the meanings of words or utterances.

**substratum**   The residue in a language of a previous language, e.g. a Celtic residue in either English or French.

**synonym**   A word with a meaning similar to that of another word, e.g. English *begin* and *commence*.

**syntax**   The permissible grammatical arrangement of elements in a language, usually elements of meaning.

**telegraphic speech** A kind of speech in which grammatical words tend to be omitted, e.g. *Mummy go*.

**tense** The grammatical ability to refer to time, e.g. English has two tenses, marked by making changes in the forms of verbs, a present tense (*I sing, he sings*) and a past tense (*I sang, he sang*).

**transformation** Any discrete change that occurs between an abstract structure that a sentence might be postulated as having and its actual structure as pronounced, e.g. the two changes, therefore two transformations, involved in transforming *He is where?* into *Where is he? (He is where?, Is he where?, Where is he?)*.

**transformational–generative grammar** A grammatical theory associated with Noam Chomsky, in which one set of rules generates an abstract grammatical description for a sentence and another set of rules transforms that description into an actually occurring sentence.

**ungrammatical** Not conforming to the grammar of a language.

**universal grammar** The set of rules and principles that all languages are said to share, possibly because they are innate in humans.

**unround vowel** A vowel produced with associated spreading (i.e., non-rounding) of the lips, e.g. the vowels in *bit, bet* and *bat*.

**usage** The way in which a language is actually used by those who speak it.

**variable rule** A rule that has certain conditions built into it, e.g. the rule that describes how people say either *singing* or *singin'*, depending on the presence or absence of certain factors.

**verb phrase** A phrase headed by a verb, e.g. *goes, has gone, will be going, went to the cinema*, etc.

**vernacular style** The way a language is actually spoken by native speakers.

**vocal tract** The various parts of the throat, mouth and nose that are used in producing speech.

**voicing** The activity in the vocal cords that produces sounds with resonance, e.g. voiced sounds like English vowels, and consonants such as *b, g, v, m, n*, etc. Without such activity we have voiceless consonants such as *p, k* and *f*.

**vowel raising**   The process by which a vowel is pronounced in a higher position in the mouth. *Weep* was once pronounced with the vowel in *mate* before it was raised.

**Whorfian hypothesis**   *See* **linguistic determinism.**
**wh- word**   A word usually beginning with *wh-*, used to begin a certain type of information-seeking question, e.g. *Who did it?* and *Where are they?*

# Further reading

## Chapter 1

Useful discussions of usage and correctness can be found in Baron (1982), Crystal (1984) and Milroy and Milroy (1985). Lyons (1991) provides a very readable introduction to the ideas of Noam Chomsky, and Cook (1988), Cowper (1992) and Haegeman (1991) provide technical accounts of his most recent theory, government and binding. For language universals, see Comrie (1989) and Greenberg (1963). Huddleston (1988) provides a concise introduction to English grammar and Kreidler (1989) to English phonology.

## Chapter 2

The following books all deal, among other things, with the language capabilities of animals, mainly of the great apes: Bright (1984, 1990), Goodall (1986, 1990), Linden (1974), Premack (1986), Sebeok and Umiker-Sebeok (1980) and Snowden, Brown and Petersen (1982).

## Chapter 3

Two older but still basic sources of information are Lieberman (1967) and Miller (1951). Fry (1979) is a good treatment of the 'physics' of speech. Both Clark and Yallop (1990) and Rogers (1991) deal with a wide range of phonetic issues.

## Chapter 4

Most good introductory texts in psychology or psycholinguistics deal with matters treated here, e.g. Taylor (1990). Two books that deal specifically with how language relates to mind are Aitchison (1987) and Miller and Johnson-Laird (1976). Fromkin

(1980) provides an interesting account of slips of the tongue. Greene (1972) offers an account of the early work that investigated the 'psychological reality' of grammars; Singer (1990) reports on later work.

## Chapter 5
Trudgill (1983) and Wardhaugh (1992) are general introductory books on sociolinguistics. Davis (1983), Francis (1983) and Petyt (1980) provide good introductions to the study of dialects, and Labov (1972a, 1972b) to the study of social dialects. Historical linguistics is the concern of Aitchison (1991), Antilla (1972) and Hock (1986). Mallory (1989) and Renfrew (1987) differ greatly in their treatment of the early Indo-Europeans. For issues related to the origins of language, see Bickerton (1990), Brown (1990) and Lieberman (1984, 1991). Brown and Levinson (1987) deals with matters of 'politeness', and Fairclough (1989) and Lakoff (1990) with matters of 'power.'

## Chapter 6
Austin (1962) and Searle (1969) illustrate what is now a traditional philosophical approach to language. Davis (1991), Leech (1983) and Levinson (1983) are concerned with general issues in pragmatics. Saville-Troike (1989) provides an outline of ethnography. Conversation is the subject of McLaughlin (1984) and Wardhaugh (1985), and discourse that of Stubbs (1983).

## Chapter 7
Bruner (1983) and de Villiers and de Villiers (1979) discuss what young children do with language. For Piaget's ideas, see Evans (1973), Flavell (1963) and, of course, Piaget (1950). Work in the innateness tradition is exemplified in Goodluck (1991), Lightfoot (1991), Pinker (1984, 1989) and Radford (1990). Atkinson (1985) and Rosen (1972) look at Bernstein's ideas. For an insightful view of the consequences of learning a particular variety of language, see Hoggart (1970), and for a consideration of some effects of literacy, see Stubbs (1980).

## Chapter 8
Finegan and Besnier (1989) and O'Grady and Dobrovolsky (1992) are useful introductions to linguistics.

# References

Aitchison, J. 1987. *Words in the Mind: An Introduction to the Mental Lexicon.* Oxford: Basil Blackwell.

Aitchison, J. 1991. *Language Change: Progress or Decay?* (2nd edn). Cambridge: Cambridge University Press.

Antilla, R. 1972. *An Introduction to Historical and Comparative Linguistics.* New York: Macmillan.

Atkinson, P. 1985. *Language, Structure and Reproduction: An Introduction to the Sociology of Basil Bernstein.* London: Methuen.

Austin, J. L. 1962. *How to Do Things with Words.* Cambridge, Mass.: Harvard University Press.

Baron, D. 1982. *Grammar and Good Taste: Reforming the American Language.* New Haven: Yale University Press.

Baron, D. 1986. *Grammar and Gender.* New Haven: Yale University Press.

Bates, E., Masling, M., and Kintsch, W. 1978. Recognition memory for aspects of dialogue. *Journal of Experimental Psychology: Learning and Memory*, 4: 187–97.

Berlin, B., and Kay, P. 1969. *Basic Color Terms: Their Universality and Evolution.* Berkeley: University of California Press.

Bernstein, B. 1971–5. *Class, Codes and Control* (vols 1–3). London: Routledge and Kegan Paul.

Berwick, R. C., and Weinberg, A. S. 1984. *The Grammatical Basis of Linguistic Performance: Language Use and Acquisition.* Cambridge, Mass.: MIT Press.

Bever, T. G. 1970. The cognitive basis for linguistic structures. In Hayes, J. R. (ed.), *Cognition and Development of Language.* New York: Wiley.

Bickerton, D. 1990. *Language and Species.* Chicago. University of Chicago Press.

Bloom, L. 1970. *Language Development: Form and Function in Emerging Grammars.* Cambridge, Mass.: MIT Press.

Bloom, L. 1973. *One Word at a Time.* The Hague: Mouton.

Bloomfield, L. 1933. *Language.* New York: Holt.

Boomer, D. S., and Laver, J. D. M. 1968. Slips of the tongue. *British Journal of Disorders of Communication*, 3: 2–12.

Bransford, J. D., and Franks, J. J. 1971. The abstraction of linguistic ideas. *Cognitive Psychology*, 2: 331–50.

Bresnan, J. 1981. An approach to universal grammar and the mental representation of language. *Cognition*, 10: 39–52.

Bright, M. 1984. *Animal Language*. London: British Broadcasting Corporation.

Bright, M. 1990. *The Dolittle Obsession*. London: Robson Books.

Bright, W. (ed.), 1992. *International Encyclopedia of Linguistics*. London: Oxford University Press.

Brown, M. H. 1990. *The Search for Eve*. New York: Harper and Row.

Brown, P., and Levinson, S. C. 1987. *Politeness: Some Universals of Language Use*. Cambridge: Cambridge University Press.

Brown, R. 1973. *A First Language: The Early Stages*. Cambridge, Mass.: Harvard University Press.

Brown, R., and Bellugi, U. 1964. Three processes in the child's acquisition of syntax. *Harvard Educational Review*, 34(2): 131–51.

Brown, R., Cazden, C. B., and Bellugi, U. 1967. The child's grammar from I to III. In Hill, J. P. (ed.), *1967 Minnesota Symposium on Child Psychology*. Minneapolis: University of Minnesota Press.

Brown, R., and Hanlon, C. 1970. Derivational complexity and order of acquisition in child speech. In Hayes, J. R. (ed.), *Cognition and the Development of Language*. New York: Wiley.

Brown, R., and McNeill, D. 1966. The 'tip of the tongue' phenomenon. *Journal of Verbal Learning and Verbal Behavior*, 5: 325–37.

Brownell, H., Potter, H. H., Bihrle, A. M., and Gardner, H. 1986. Inference deficits in right brain-damaged patients. *Brain and Language*, 27: 310–22.

Bruner, J. 1983. *Child's Talk*. London: Oxford University Press.

Burchfield, R. W. 1985. *The English Language*. London: Oxford University Press.

Burling, R. 1973. *English in Black and White*. New York: Holt, Rinehart and Winston.

Button, G., and Lee, J. R. E. (eds). 1987. *Talk and Social Organisation*. Clevedon, England: Multilingual Matters.

Campbell, L., Kaufman, T., and Smith-Stark, T. C. 1986. Meso-America as a linguistic area. *Language*, 62: 530–70.

Carmichael, L., Hogan, H. P., and Walter, A. A. 1932. An experimental study on the effect of language on the reproduction of visually perceived forms. *Journal of Experimental Psychology*, 15: 73–86.

Carroll, J. B. (ed.). 1956. *Language, Thought, and Reality: Selected Writings of Benjamin Lee Whorf*. New York: Wiley.

Carroll, J. B., and Casagrande, J. B. 1958. The function of language classifications in behavior. In Maccoby, E. E., Newcomb, T. M., and Hartley, E. L. (eds), *Readings in Social Psychology* (3rd edn). New York: Holt, Rinehart and Winston.

Cazden, C. B. 1972. *Child Language and Education*. New York: Holt, Rinehart and Winston.

Chambers, J. K., and Trudgill, P. 1980. *Dialectology*. Cambridge: Cambridge University Press.

Chomsky, C. S. 1969. *The Acquisition of Syntax in Children from 5 to 10*. Cambridge, Mass.: MIT Press.

Chomsky, N. 1957. *Syntactic Structures*. The Hague: Mouton.

Chomsky, N. 1959. Review: B. F. Skinner's *Verbal Behavior*. *Language*, 35: 26–58.

Chomsky, N. 1965. *Aspects of the Theory of Syntax*. Cambridge, Mass.: MIT Press.

Chomsky, N. 1967. The general properties of language. In Darley, F. L. (ed.), *Brain Mechanisms Underlying Speech and Language*. New York: Grune and Stratton.

Chomsky, N. 1976. *Reflections on Language*. London: Temple Smith.

Chomsky, N. 1981. *Lectures on Government and Binding*. Dordrecht: Foris.

Chomsky, N. 1986. *Knowledge of Language: Its Nature, Origin and Use*. New York: Praeger.

Clark, J., and Yallop, C. 1990. *Phonetics and Phonology*. Oxford: Basil Blackwell.

Clifton, C., Kurcz, I., and Jenkins, J. J. 1965. Grammatical relations as determinants of sentence similarity. *Journal of Verbal Learning and Verbal Behavior*, 4: 112–17.

Coates, J. 1986. *Women, Men and Language: A Sociolinguistic Account of Sex Differences in Language*. London: Longman.

Collinge, N. E. 1985. *The Laws of Indo-European*. Amsterdam: John Benjamins.

Comrie, B. 1989. *Language Universals and Linguistic Typology: Syntax and Morphology*. (2nd edn). Oxford: Basil Blackwell.

Cook, V. J. 1988. *Chomsky's Universal Grammar: An Introduction*. Oxford: Basil Blackwell.

Coulthard, M. 1977. *An Introduction to Discourse Analysis*. London: Longman.

Cowper, E. A. 1992. *A Concise Introduction to Syntactic Theory: The Government–Binding Approach*. Chicago: University of Chicago Press.

Crystal, D. 1984. *Who Cares about English Usage?* Harmondsworth, England: Penguin.

Crystal, D. 1987. *The Cambridge Encyclopedia of Language*. Cambridge: Cambridge University Press.

Curtiss, S. 1977. *Genie: A Psycholinguistic Study of a Modern-Day 'Wild Child.'* New York: Academic Press.

Davis, L. M. 1983. *English Dialectology: An Introduction*. University, Alabama: University of Alabama Press.

Davis, S. (ed.). 1991. *Pragmatics: A Reader*. London: Oxford University Press.

Denes, P. B., and Pinson, E. N. 1963. *The Speech Chain: The Physics and Biology of Spoken Language*. New York: Holt, Rinehart and Winston.

Diebold, A. R., Jr. 1987. Linguistic ways to prehistory. In Skomol, S. N., and Polomé, E. C. (eds), *Proto-Indo-European: The Archaeology of a Linguistic Problem*. Washington, D.C.: Institute for the Study of Man.

Diehl, R. L. 1981. Feature detectors for speech: a critical reappraisal. *Psychological Bulletin*, 89: 1–18.

Dillard, J. L. 1972. *Black English: Its History and Usage in the United States*. New York: Random House.

Downing, J. 1970. Children's concepts of language in learning to read. *Educational Research*, 12: 106–12.

Dowty, D. R., Kartunnen, L., and Zwicky, A. M. 1985. *Natural Language Parsing*. Cambridge: Cambridge University Press.

Dyen, I. 1975. *Linguistic Subgrouping and Lexicostatistics*. The Hague: Mouton.

Eifermann, R. R. 1961. Negation: a linguistic variable. *Acta Psychologica*, 23: 258–73.

Entus, A. K. 1977. Hemispheric asymmetry in processing of dichotically presented speech and non-speech stimuli by infants. In Segalowitz, S. J., and Gruber, F. A. (eds), *Language Development and Neurological Theory*. New York: Academic Press.

Epstein, W. 1969. Recall of word lists following learning of sentences and anomalous and random strings. *Journal of Verbal Learning and Verbal Behavior*, 8: 20–5.

Evans, R. I. 1973. *Jean Piaget: The Man and His Ideas*. New York: E. P. Dutton.

Evans, W. E., and Bastian, J. 1969. Marine mammal communication: social and ecological factors. In Andersen, H. T. (ed.), *The Biology of Marine Mammals*. New York: Academic Press.

Fairclough, N. 1989. *Language and Power*. London: Longman.

Fernald, A. 1984. The perceptual and affective salience of mothers' speech to infants. In Feagans, L., Garvey, C., and Golinkoff, R. (eds), *The Origins and Growth of Communication*. Norwood, N.J.: Ablex.

Fernald, A., and Simon, T. 1984. Expanded intonation contours in mothers' speech to newborns. *Developmental Psychology*, 20: 104–13.

Finegan, E., and Besnier, N. 1989. *Language: Its Structure and Use*. New York: Harcourt-Brace Jovanovich.

Flavell, J. H. 1963. *The Developmental Psychology of Jean Piaget*. Princeton: Van Nostrand.

Fletcher, P. 1985. *A Child's Learning of English*. Oxford: Basil Blackwell.

Fodor, J. A. 1983. *The Modularity of Mind: An Essay on Faculty Psychology*. Cambridge, Mass.: Bradford.

Forster, K. 1979. Levels of processing and the structure of the language processor. In Cooper, W. E., and Walker, W. (eds), *Sentence Processing*. Hillsdale, N.J.: Lawrence Erlbaum.

Fouts, R. S., Fouts, D. H., and Schoenfeld, D. 1984. Sign language in conversational interaction between chimpanzees. *Sign Language Studies*, 42: 1–12.

Fouts, R. S., Hirsh, A. D., and Fouts, D. H., 1982. Cultural transmission of a human language in a chimpanzee mother–infant relationship. *Child Nurturance*, 3: 159–93.

Francis, W. N. 1983. *Dialectology: An Introduction*. London: Longman.

Frisch, K. von. 1950. *Bees: Their Vision, Chemical Senses, and Language*. Ithaca: Cornell University Press.

Frisch, K. von. 1953. *The Dancing Bees: An Account of the Life and Senses of the Honey Bee*. New York: Harcourt, Brace and World.

Frisch, K. von. 1962. Dialects in the language of the bees. *Scientific American*, 207: 78–87.

Frisch, K. von 1967. *The Dance Language and Orientation of Bees*. Cambridge, Mass.: Harvard University Press.

Fromkin, V. A. 1968. Speculations on performance models. *Journal of Linguistics*, 4: 47–68.

Fromkin, V. A. 1973. Slips of the tongue. *Scientific American*, 229: 110–17.

Fromkin, V. A. 1980. *Errors in Linguistic Performance: Slips of the Tongue, Ear, Pen and Hand*. London: Academic Press.

Fry, D. B. 1979. *The Physics of Speech*. Cambridge: Cambridge University Press.

Gamkrelidze, T. V., and Ivanov, V. V. 1990. The early history of Indo-European languages. *Scientific American*, 262: 3: 110–16.

Gardner, B. T., and Gardner R. A. 1971. Two-way communication with an infant chimpanzee. In Schrier, A., and Stollnitz, F. (eds), *Behavior in Nonhuman Primates*. New York: Academic Press.

Gardner, H., 1973. *The Quest for Mind: Piaget, Levi-Strauss, and the Structuralist Movement*. New York: Knopf.

Gardner, H., Brownell, J., Wapner, W., and Michelow, D. 1983. Missing the point: the role of the right hemisphere in the processing of complex linguistic materials. In Perecman, E. (ed.), *Cognitive Processes in the Right Hemisphere*. New York: Academic Press.

Gardner, R. A., and Gardner, B. T. 1969. Teaching sign language to a chimpanzee. *Science*, 165: 664–72.

Gardner, R. A., and Gardner, B. T. 1975. Evidence for sentence constituents in the early utterances of child and chimpanzee. *Journal of Experimental Psychology*, 104: 244–67.

Garrett, M., Bever, T., and Fodor, J. A. 1966. The active use of grammar in speech perception. *Perception and Psychophysics*, 2: 149–62.

Gazdar, G., Klein, E., Pullum, G., and Sag, I. 1985. *Generalised Phrase Structure Grammar*. Oxford: Basil Blackwell.

Geertz, C. 1960. *The Religion of Java*. Glencoe, Ill.: The Free Press.

Ghiselin, B. 1955. *The Creative Process*. New York: Mentor Books.

Gleitman, L. R. 1982. Maturational determinants in language growth. *Cognition*, 10: 103–14.

Gleitman, L. R., Newport, E. L., and Gleitman, H. 1984. The current status of the motherese hypothesis. *Journal of Child Language*, 11(1): 43–80.

Goodall, J. 1986. *The Chimpanzees of Gombe: Patterns of Behavior*. Cambridge, Mass.: Belknap Press.

Goodall, J. 1990. *Through a Window*. Boston: Houghton Mifflin.

Goodglass, H., and Kaplan, E. 1983. *The Assessment of Aphasia and Related Disorders*. Philadelphia: Lea and Febiger.

Goodluck, H. 1991. *Language Acquisition: A Linguistic Introduction*. Oxford: Basil Blackwell.

Gough, P. B., 1965. Grammatical transformations and speed of understanding. *Journal of Verbal Learning and Verbal Behavior*, 4: 107–11.

Greenberg, J. H. 1962. *The Languages of Africa*. Bloomington: Indiana University Press.

Greenberg, J. H. (ed.). 1963. *Universals of Language*. Cambridge, Mass.: MIT Press.

Greenberg, J. H. 1987. *Language in the Americas*. Stanford: Stanford University Press.

Greene, J. 1972. *Psycholinguistics: Chomsky and Psychology*. Harmondsworth, England: Penguin.

Grice, H. P. 1975. Logic and conversation. In Cole, P., and Morgan, J. L. (eds), *Syntax and Semantics, Vol. 3: Speech Acts*. New York: Academic Press.

Haegeman, L. 1991. *Introduction to Government and Binding Theory*. Oxford: Basil Blackwell.

Halliday, M. A. K. 1973. *Explorations in the Function of Language*. London: Edward Arnold.

Haugen, E. 1966. Dialect, language, nation. *American Anthropologist*, 68: 922–35.

Hayes, C. 1951. *The Ape in our House*. New York: Harper and Row.

Hayes, K. J., and Hayes, C. 1951. Intellectual development of a home-raised chimpanzee. *Proceedings of the American Philosophical Society*, 95: 105–9.

Hebb, D. O. 1949. *The Organization of Behavior: A Neurophysiological Theory*. New York: Wiley.

Hess, R. D., and Shipman, V. C. 1967. Cognitive elements in maternal behavior. In Hill, J. P. (ed.), *1967 Minnesota Symposium on Child Psychology*. Minneapolis: University of Minnesota Press.

Hewes, G. W. 1975. *Language Origins: A Bibliography* (2nd edn). The Hague: Mouton.

Hirsh-Pasek, K., Nelson, D. G. K., Jusczyk, P. W., Cassidy, K., Druss, B., and Kennedy, L. 1987. Clauses are perceptual units for young infants. *Cognition*, 26: 269–86.

Hock, H. H. 1986. *Principles of Historical Linguistics*. Berlin: Mouton de Gruyter.

Hockett, C. F. 1958. *A Course in Modern Linguistics*. New York: Macmillan.

Hockett, C. F. 1963. The Problem of universals in language. In Greenberg, J. H. (ed.), *Universals of Language*. Cambridge, Mass.: MIT Press.

Hockett, C. F., and Altmann, S. A. 1968. A note on design features. In Sebeok, T. A. (ed.), *Animal Communication: Techniques of Study and Results of Research*. Bloomington: University of Indiana Press.

Hoggart, R. 1970. *The Uses of Literacy: Aspects of Working-Class Life with Special Reference to Publications and Entertainments*. London: Oxford University Press.

Hubel, D. H. 1963. The visual cortex of the brain. *Scientific American*, 209: 54–62.

Hubel, D. H., and Wiesel, T. N. 1962. Receptive fields, binocular interaction and functional architecture in the cat's visual cortex. *Journal of Physiology* (London), 160: 106–54.

Huddleston, R. 1988. *English Grammar: An Outline*. Cambridge: Cambridge University Press.

Hudson, R. A. 1980. *Sociolinguistics*. Cambridge: Cambridge University Press.

Hymes, D. 1974. *Foundations in Sociolinguistics: An Ethnographic Approach*. Philadelphia: University of Pennsylvania Press.

Ingram, D. 1989. *First Language Acquisition: Method, Description, and Explanation*. Cambridge: Cambridge University Press.

Jakobson, R. 1960. Linguistics and poetics. In Sebeok, T. A. (ed.), *Style in Language*. Cambridge, Mass.: MIT Press.

Jakobson, R. 1968. *Child Language, Aphasia and Phonological Universals*. The Hague: Mouton.

Jakobson, R. 1971. The sound laws of child language and their place in general phonology. In Bar-Adon, A., and Leopold, W. F. (eds), *Child Language: A Book of Readings*. Englewood Cliffs, N.J.: Prentice-Hall.

Jamieson, J. W. 1988. The problem of Indo-European origins. *Mankind Quarterly*, 28: 4: 421–6.

Johnson-Laird, P. N. 1969a. On understanding logically complex sentences. *Quarterly Journal of Experimental Psychology*, 21: 1–13.

Johnson-Laird, P. N. 1969b. Reasoning with ambiguous sentences. *British Journal of Psychology*, 60: 17–23.

Joos, M. 1962. *The Five Clocks*. Bloomington: Publications of the Research Center in Anthropology, Folklore, and Linguistics, no. 22.

Jordan, J. 1971. Studies on the structure of the organ of voice and vocalization in the chimpanzees. *Folio Morphologica* (Warsaw), 30: 97–126, 222–48, 323–40.

Jusczyk, P. W. 1986. A review of speech perception. In Kaufman, L., Thomas, J., and Boff, K. (eds), *Handbook of Perception and Performance*. New York: Wiley.

Keenan, E. L. 1971. Two kinds of presupposition in natural language. In Fillmore, C. J., and Langendoen, D. T. (eds), *Studies in Linguistic Semantics*. New York: Holt, Rinehart and Winston.

Keenan, J. M., MacWhinney, B., and Mayhew, D. 1977. Pragmatics in memory: a study of natural conversation. *Journal of Verbal Learning and Verbal Behavior*, 16: 549–60.

Kellog, W. N. 1968. Communication and language in the home-raised chimpanzee. *Science*, 162: 423–7.

Kellog, W. N., and Kellog, L. A. 1933. *The Ape and the Child*. New York: McGraw-Hill.

Kimura, D. 1967. Functional asymmetry of the brain in dichotic listening. *Cortex*, 3: 163–78.

Klima, E. S., and Bellugi, U. 1966. Syntactic regularities in the speech of children. In Lyons, J., and Wales, R. J. (eds), *Psycholinguistic Papers: The Proceedings of the 1966 Edinburgh Conference*. Edinburgh: Edinburgh University Press.

Kreidler, C. W. 1989. *The Pronunciation of English*. Oxford: Basil Blackwell.

Labov, W. 1969. Contraction, deletion, and inherent variability of the English copula. *Language*, 45: 715–62.

Labov, W. 1972a. *Language in the Inner City: Studies in the Black Vernacular*. Philadelphia: University of Pennsylvania Press.

Labov, W. 1972b. *Sociolinguistic Patterns*. Philadelphia: University of Pennsylvania Press.

Labov, W., and Fanshel, D. 1977. *Therapeutic Discourse: Psychotherapy as Conversation*. New York: Academic Press.

Lakoff, R. 1975. *Language and Woman's Place.* London: Longman.

Lakoff, R. T. 1990. *Talking Power.* New York: Basic Books.

Lane, H. 1965. The motor theory of speech perception: a critical review. *Psychological Review*, 72: 275–309.

Leech, G. N. 1983. *Principles of Pragmatics.* London: Longman.

Lehiste, I. 1970. Temporal organization of spoken language. *Ohio State University Working Papers in Linguistics*, 4: 95–114.

Lehmann, W. P. 1990. The current thrust of Indo-European studies. *General Linguistics*, 30: 1–52.

Lenneberg, E. H. 1962. Understanding language without ability to speak: a case report. *Journal of Abnormal Social Psychology*, 65: 419–25.

Lenneberg, E. H. 1967. *Biological Foundations of Language.* New York: Wiley.

Lettvin, J. Y., Maturana, H. R., McCulloch, W. S., and Pitts, W. H. 1959. What the frog's eye tells the frog's brain. *Proceedings of the Institute of Radio Engineers*, 47: 1940–51.

Lettvin, J. Y., Maturana, H. R., McCulloch, W. S., and Pitts, W. H. 1961. Two remarks on the visual system of the frog. In Rosenblith, W. A. (ed.), *Sensory Communication.* Cambridge, Mass.: MIT Press.

Levinson, S. 1983. *Pragmatics* Cambridge: Cambridge University Press.

Liberman, A. M., Delattre, P., and Cooper, F. S. 1952. The role of selected stimulus-variables in the perception of the unvoiced stop consonants. *American Journal of Psychology*, 65: 497–516.

Lieberman, P. 1967. *Intonation, Perception, and Language.* Cambridge Mass.: MIT Press.

Lieberman. P. 1968. Primate vocalizations and human linguistic ability. *Journal of the Acoustical Society of America*, 44: 1574–84.

Lieberman, P. 1975. *On the Origins of Language: An Introduction to the Evolution of Human Speech.* New York: Macmillan.

Lieberman, P. 1984. *The Biology and Evolution of Language.* Cambridge, Mass.: Harvard University Press.

Lieberman, P. 1991. *Uniquely Human: The Evolution of Speech, Thought, and Selfless Behavior.* Cambridge, Mass.: Harvard University Press.

Lieberman, P., and Crelin, E. S. 1971. On the speech of Neanderthal Man. *Linguistic Inquiry*, 2: 203–22.

Lieberman, P., Crelin, E. S., and Klatt, D. H. 1972. Phonetic ability and related anatomy of the newborn and adult human, Neanderthal Man, and the chimpanzee. *American Anthropologist*, 74, 287–307.

Lightfoot, D. 1991. *How to Set Parameters.* Cambridge, Mass.: MIT Press.

Lilly, J.C. 1967. *The Mind of the Dolphin.* New York: Doubleday.

Lindauer, M. 1961. *Communication among Social Bees.* Cambridge, Mass.: Harvard University Press.

Linden, E. 1974. *Apes, Men, and Language.* New York: Saturday Review Press.

Lorenz, K. 1952. *King Solomon's Ring.* London: Methuen.

Lyons, J. 1991. *Chomsky* (3rd edn). London: Fontana Books.

McDaniel, D., and Cairns, H. M. 1990. The processing and acquisition of control structures by young children. In Frazier, L., and de Villiers, J. (eds), *Language Processing and Language Acquisition.* Dordrecht: Kluwer.

McLaughlin, M. L. 1984. *Conversation*. Beverly Hills, Calif.: Sage.

McNeill, D. 1966. Developmental psycholinguistics. In Smith, F., and Miller G. A. (eds), *The Genesis of Language: A Psycholinguistic Approach*. Cambridge, Mass.: MIT Press.

McNeill, D. 1970. *The Acquisition of Language: The Study of Developmental Psycholinguistics*. New York: Harper and Row.

Malinowski, B. 1923. The problem of meaning in primitive languages. In Ogden, C. K., and Richards, I. A. *The Meaning of Meaning*. London: Kegan Paul.

Mallory, J. P. 1989. *In Search of the Indo-Europeans: Language, Archaeology and Myth*. London: Thames and Hudson.

Martinet, A. 1964. *Elements of General Linguistics*. London: Faber and Faber.

Masica, C. P. 1978. *Defining a Linguistic Area*. Chicago: University of Chicago Press.

Mehler, J., Bertononcini, J., Barriere, M., and Jassik-Gerschenfeld, D. 1978. Infant recognition of mother's voice. *Perception*, 7: 491–7.

Miller, G. A. 1951. *Language and Communication*. New York: McGraw-Hill.

Miller, G. A. 1956. The magical number seven plus or minus two: some limits on our capacity for storing information. *Psychological Review*, 63: 81–97.

Miller, G. A., and Isard, S. 1963. Some perceptual consequences of linguistic rules. *Journal of Verbal Learning and Verbal Behavior*, 2: 217–28.

Miller, G. A., and Johnson-Laird, P. N. 1976. *Language and Perception*. Cambridge, Mass.: Harvard University Press.

Miller, G. A., and McKean, K. E. 1964. A chronometric study of some relations between sentences. *Quarterly Journal of Experimental Psychology*, 16: 297–308.

Milroy, J., and Milroy, L. 1985. *Authority in Language*. London: Routledge and Kegan Paul.

Milroy, L. 1987. *Observing and Analysing Natural Language*. Oxford: Basil Blackwell.

Montagu, A. 1974. *Man's Most Dangerous Myth: The Fallacy of Race*. Cleveland: World Publishing.

Montgomery, M. 1986. *An Introduction to Language and Society*. London: Methuen.

Mühlhausler, P. 1986. *Pidgin and Creole Linguistics*. Oxford: Basil Blackwell.

Newman, E. 1974. *Strictly Speaking: Will America be the Death of English?* Indianapolis: Bobbs-Merrill.

Newman, J. D. 1988. Primate hearing mechanisms. In Steklis, H. D., and Erwin, J. (eds), *Comparative Primate Biology, Vol. 4: Neurosciences*. New York: Alan R. Liss.

Newmeyer, F. J. 1987. *Linguistic Theory in America* (2nd edn). New York: Academic Press.

Newmeyer, F. J. (ed.). 1988. *Linguistics: The Cambridge Survey*. 4 vols. Cambridge: Cambridge University Press.

Nottebohm, F. 1970. Ontogeny of bird song. *Science*, 167: 950–6.

O'Grady, W., and Dobrovolsky, M. (eds) 1992. *Contemporary Linguistic Analysis* (2nd edn). Toronto: Copp Clark Pitman.

Opie, I., and Opie, P. 1959. *The Lore and Language of Schoolchildren*. Oxford: Clarendon Press.

Patterson, F. G. 1978. The gestures of a gorilla: language acquisition in another pongid. *Brain and Language*, 5: 72–97.

Patterson, F. G., and Linden, E. 1981. *The Education of Koko*. New York: Holt, Rinehart and Winston.

Penelope, J. 1990. *Speaking Freely*. Oxford: Pergamon Press.

Petyt, K. M. 1980. *The Study of Dialect: An Introduction to Dialectology*. London: André Deutsch.

Pfungst, O. 1911. *Clever Hans: The Horse of Mr. von Osten*. New York: Holt.

Piaget, J. 1950. *The Language and Thought of the Child*. London: Routledge and Kegan Paul.

Piaget, J. 1980. The psychogenesis of knowledge and its epistemological significance. In Piattelli-Palmarini, K. (ed.), *Language and Learning. The Debate between Jean Piaget and Noam Chomsky*. London: Routledge and Kegan Paul.

Pinker, S. 1984. *Language Learnability and Language Development*. Cambridge, Mass.: Harvard University Press.

Pinker, S. 1989. *Learnability and Cognition: The Acquisition of Argument Structure*. Cambridge, Mass.: MIT Press.

Poliakov, L. 1974. *The Aryan Myth: A History of Racist and Nationalist Ideas In Europe*. New York: Basic Books.

Pollack, I., and Pickett, J. 1964. The intelligibility of excerpts from conversations. *Language and Speech*, 6: 165–71.

Premack, A. J., and Premack, D. 1972. Teaching language to an ape. *Scientific American*, 227: 92–9.

Premack, D. 1970. A functional analysis of language. *Journal of the Experimental Analysis of Behavior*, 14: 107–25.

Premack, D. 1971 Language in chimpanzee? *Science*, 172: 808–22.

Premack, D. 1986. *'Gavagai!' or the Future History of the Animal Language Controversy*. Cambridge, Mass.: MIT Press.

Premack, D. and Premack, A. J. 1983. *The Mind of an Ape*. New York: W. W. Norton.

Pribram, K. 1969. The neurophysiology for remembering. *Scientific American*, 220: 73–86.

Radford, A. 1990. *Syntactic Theory and the Acquisition of English*. Oxford: Basil Blackwell.

Reid, J. F. 1966. Learning to think about reading. *Educational Research*, 9: 56–62.

Renfrew, C. 1987. *Archaeology and Language: The Puzzle of Indo-European Origins*. London: Jonathan Cape.

Robinson, W. P. 1971. Social factors and language development in primary school children. In Huxley, R., and Ingram, E. (eds), *Language Acquisition: Models and Methods*. New York: Academic Press.

Robinson, W. P. 1972. *Language and Social Behaviour*. Harmondsworth, England: Penguin.

Rogers, H. 1991. *Theoretical and Practical Phonetics*. Toronto: Copp Clark Pitman.

Romaine, S. 1988. *Pidgin and Creole Languages*. London: Longman.

Rosen, H. 1972. *Language and Class: A Critical Look at the Theories of Basil Bernstein*. Bristol: Falling Wall Press.

Ross, P. E. 1991. Hard words. *Scientific American*, 264: 4: 138–47.

Rumbaugh, D. M. (ed.). 1977. *Language Learning by a Chimpanzee: The LANA Project*. New York: Academic Press.

Russell, C., and Russell, W. M. S. 1971. Language and animal signals. In Minnis, N. (ed.), *Linguistics at Large*. New York: Viking.

Sachs, J. S. 1967. Recognition memory for syntactic and semantic aspects of connected discourse. *Perception and Psychophysics*, 2: 437–42.

Safire, W. 1980. *On Language*. New York: Times Books.

Safire, W. 1984. *I Stand Corrected: More on Language*. New York: Times Books.

Sapir, E. 1921. *Language: An Introduction to the Study of Speech*. New York: Harcourt, Brace and World.

Saussure, F. de. 1959. *Course in General Linguistics*. New York: Philosophical Library.

Savage-Rumbaugh, E. S. 1986. *Ape Language: From Conditioned Response to a Symbol*. New York: Columbia University Press.

Saville-Troike, M. 1989. *The Ethnography of Communication: An Introduction* (2nd edn). Oxford: Basil Blackwell.

Savin, H. B., and Perchonock, E. 1965. Grammatical structure and the immediate recall of English sentences. *Journal of Verbal Learning and Verbal Behavior*, 4: 348–53.

Scherer, K. R., and Giles, H. (eds). 1979. *Social Markers in Speech*. Cambridge: Cambridge University Press.

Schwartz, M. 1984. What the classical aphasic syndromes don't tell us, and why. *Brain and Language*, 21: 479–91.

Searle, J. R. 1969. *Speech Acts: An Essay in the Philosophy of Language*. Cambridge: Cambridge University Press.

Searle, J. R. 1972. What is a speech act? In Giglioli, P. P. (ed.), *Language and Social Context*. Harmondsworth, England: Penguin.

Sebeok, T. A., and Umiker-Sebeok, J. 1980. *Speaking of Apes*. New York: Plenum Press.

Shankweiler, D. 1971. An analysis of laterality effects in speech perception. In Horton, D. L., and Jenkins, J. J. (eds), *Perception of Language*. Columbus, Ohio: Charles E. Merrill.

Shevoroshkin, V. 1990. The mother tongue. *The Sciences*, 30: 3: 20–7.

Shipley, E. F., Smith, C. S., and Gleitman, L. R. 1969. A study of the acquisition of language: free responses to commands. *Language*, 45: 322–42.

Simon, J. 1980. *Paradigms Lost*. New York: Clarkson Potter.

Sinclair, H. 1971. Sensorimotor action patterns as a condition for the acquisition of syntax. In Huxley, R., and Ingram, E. (eds), *Language Acquisition: Models and Methods*. New York: Academic Press.

Sinclair-de Zwart, H. 1969. Developmental psycholinguistics. In Elkind, D., and

Flavell, J. H. (eds), *Studies in Cognitive Development: Essays in Honor of Jean Piaget*. New York: Oxford University Press.

Sinclair-de Zwart, H. 1973. Language acquisition and cognitive development. In Moore, T. E. (ed.), *Cognitive Development and the Acquisition of Language*. New York: Academic Press.

Sinclair, J. M., and Coulthard, R. M. 1975. *Towards an Analysis of Discourse: The English used by Teachers and Pupils*. London: Oxford University Press.

Singer, M. 1990. *Psychology of Language: An Introduction to Sentence and Discourse Processes*. Hillsdale, N.J.: Lawrence Erlbaum Associates.

Skinner, B. F. 1957. *Verbal Behavior*. New York: Appleton-Century-Crofts.

Sledd, J., and Ebbitt, W. R. (eds). 1962. *Dictionaries and THAT Dictionary*. Chicago: Scott, Foresman.

Slobin, D. I. 1966. Grammatical transformations in childhood and adulthood. *Journal of Verbal Learning and Verbal Behavior*, 5: 219–27.

Slobin, D. I. 1973. Cognitive prerequisites for the development of grammar. In Ferguson, C. A., and Slobin, D. I. (eds), *Studies of Child Language Development*. New York: Holt, Rinehart and Winston.

Slobin, D. I. 1979. *Psycholinguistics* (2nd edn). Glenview, Ill.: Scott, Foresman.

Slobin, D. I., 1982. Universal and particular in the acquisition of language. In Wanner, E., and Gleitman, L. R. (eds), *Language Acquisition: The State of the Art*. Cambridge: Cambridge University Press.

Smith, P. M. 1985. *Language, the Sexes and Society*. Oxford: Basil Blackwell.

Snow, C. E., and Ferguson, C. A. (eds). 1977. *Talking to Children: Language Input and Acquisition*. Cambridge: Cambridge University Press.

Snowden, C. T., Brown, C. H., and Petersen, M. P. 1982. *Primate Communication*. Cambridge: Cambridge University Press.

Spender, D. 1980. *Man Made Language*. London: Routledge and Kegan Paul.

Sperber, D., and Wilson, D., 1986. *Relevance: Communication and Cognition*. Oxford: Basil Blackwell.

Sperry, R. 1964. The great cerebral commissure. *Scientific American*, 210: 42–52.

Sperry, R., and Gazzaniga, M. S. 1967. Language following surgical disconnection of the hemispheres. In Darley, F. L. (ed.), *Brain Mechanisms Underlying Speech and Language*. New York: Grune and Stratton.

Stubbs, M. 1980. *Language and Literacy: The Sociolinguistics of Reading and Writing*. London: Routledge and Kegan Paul.

Stubbs, M. 1983. *Discourse Analysis: The Sociolinguistic Analysis of Natural Language*. Chicago: University of Chicago Press.

Studdert-Kennedy, M., Liberman, A. M., Harris, K. S., and Cooper, F. S. 1970. The motor theory of speech perception: a reply to Lane's critical review. *Psychological Review*, 77: 234–49.

Studdert-Kennedy, M., and Shankweiler, D. 1970. Hemispheric specialization for speech perception. *Journal of the Acoustical Society of America*, 48: 579–94.

Swadesh, M. 1971. *The Origin and Diversification of Language*. Chicago: Aldine-Atherton.

Taylor, I. 1990. *Psycholinguistics: Learning and Using Language*. Englewood Cliffs, N.J.: Prentice-Hall.

Terrace, H. 1984. 'Language' in apes. In Harré, R., and Reynolds, V. (eds), *The Meaning of Primate Signals*. Cambridge: Cambridge University Press.

Terrace, H. S., Petitto, L. A., Sanders, R. J., and Bever, T. G. 1979. Can an ape create a sentence? *Science*, 206: 891–902.

Thorne, J. P. 1966. On hearing sentences. In Lyons, J., and Wales, R. J. (eds), *Psycholinguistic Papers: The Proceedings of the 1966 Edinburgh Conference*. Edinburgh: Edinburgh University Press.

Trudgill, P. 1983. *Sociolinguistics: An Introduction to Language and Society* (rev. edn). Harmondsworth, England: Penguin.

Trudgill, P. 1990. *The Dialects of England*. Oxford: Basil Blackwell.

Villiers, P. A. de, and Villiers, J. G. de 1979. *Early Language*. Cambridge, Mass.: Harvard University Press.

Vygotsky, L. S. 1962. *Thought and Language*. Cambridge, Mass.: MIT Press.

Wang, W. S-Y. 1971. The basis of speech. In Reed, C. E. (ed.), *The Learning of Language*. New York: Appleton-Century-Crofts.

Wardhaugh, R. 1985. *How Conversation Works*. Oxford: Basil Blackwell.

Wardhaugh, R. 1992 *An Introduction to Sociolinguistics* (2nd edn). Oxford: Basil Blackwell.

Wason, P. C. 1961. Response to affirmative and negative binary statements. *British Journal of Psychology*, 52: 133–42.

Wason, P. C. 1965. The contexts of plausible denial. *Journal of Verbal Learning and Verbal Behavior*, 4: 7–11.

Weir, R. 1962. *Language in the Crib*. The Hague: Mouton.

West, C. 1984. *Routine Complications: Troubles with Talk between Doctors and Patients*. Bloomington: University of Indiana Press.

Wolfram, W., and Fasold, R. W. 1974. *The Study of Social Dialects in American English*. Englewood Cliffs, N.J.: Prentice-Hall.

Wright, R. 1991. Quest for the mother tongue. *The Atlantic*, 267: 4; 39–68.

# Index